DEVELOPING STRUCTURED SYSTEMS

DEVELOPING STRUCTURED SYSTEMS

A Methodology
Using Structured Techniques

by Brian Dickinson

Yourdon Press
1133 Avenue of the Americas
New York, New York 10036

Library of Congress Cataloging in Publication Data

Dickinson, Brian, 1948-
    Developing structured systems.

    Bibliography: p.
    Includes index.
    1. Electronic digital computers--Programming.
2. Structured programming. I. Title.
QA76.6.D52   001.64'2   80-54609
ISBN 0-917072-23-5 (pbk.)   AACR2
ISBN 0-917072-24-3

Developing Structured Systems is based on the methodology in the *Project Development Guidelines*. The *Project Development Guidelines* were developed under the sponsorship of Bank of America National Trust and Savings Association. In addition to Bank of America personnel, the organizations that made the primary contributions to this effort are Bender & Associates; The IBM Corporation, Data Processing Services; Structured Methods, Inc.; and YOURDON inc.

The organizations, other than Bank of America and IBM, involved in this effort may be contacted at the following addresses:

Bender & Associates	Structured Methods, Inc.	YOURDON inc.
P.O. Box 849	7 West 18th Street	1133 Avenue of the Americas
Larkspur, CA 94939	New York, NY 10011	New York, NY 10036
(415) 924-9196	(212) 741-7720	(212) 730-2670
	(800) 221-8274	

Printed in the United States of America

Library of Congress Catalog Number 80-54609

ISBN: 0-917072-24-3

This book was set in Times Roman by YOURDON Press, 1133 Avenue of the Americas, New York, N.Y., using a PDP-11/45 running under the UNIX[†] operating system.

Cover design and diagrams by Robert Ojas Hidalgo. Special thanks to Westform Industries for art support.

[†]UNIX is a registered trademark of Bell Laboratories.

To Mrs. D. and Ms. D.

CONTENTS

ACKNOWLEDGMENTS

A great deal of effort is involved in producing a book of a technical nature. Therefore, I would like to acknowledge the following people for their ideas, suggestions, support, reviews, and, occasionally, many long hours of discussion, which helped me to develop this book:

Richard Bender   Lou Mazzucchelli   III
Bob Block   Steve McMenamin   Jerry Walker
Matt Flavin   Ira Morrow   Shirley Wild
George Herzog   Meilir Page-Jones   Vince Vargas
Andrei Jezierski   John Palmer
Miguel Jimenez   Mary Rogers

I'd like to especially acknowledge Tom DeMarco for his structured analysis course, which I have had the opportunity to teach. I'd like to thank Ed Yourdon for providing me with the opportunity to write the book. Also, I owe thanks to my students, drawn from a variety of data processing and user environments, who made me think out my ideas for fear of being nailed to a seminar-room wall.

Special thanks to Debbie Holden, my fiancée, for her help and for putting up with my being a workaholic for many months. I also acknowledge the help of Barbara Kurek, my editor, during the arduous process of editing this book

PREFACE

In my consulting assignments with companies using the structured techniques,* one key question keeps arising: "How do these state-of-the-art techniques fit together?" Another typical question is "What are the managerial and quality assurance activities in a project using structured techniques and where do they fit in?" Such questions arise partly because some of the associations are not obvious, such as that of structured analysis with data modeling, but also because each of the structured techniques was developed separately. The methods have never been formally integrated to show how to develop a system.

Now, however, the time has come to formalize the techniques as an integrated approach: The main purpose of this book is to do just that. I have subtitled this book *A Methodology Using Structured Techniques.* Many people hear the word methodology and immediately think of standards. Unfortunately, standards have a bad name in many organizations. In environments in which systems were produced with no documentation and were developed in an idiosyncratic manner, maintenance became a nightmare and its cost became uncontrollable. So, the other extreme — rigid standards with masses of documentation — was applied to solve the problem.

This solution, of course, did not solve many problems but instead became a restriction and tended to inhibit creative thinking. I believe we need to strike a balance between these two extremes, and this balance is what I call a "guideline." Therefore, this book presents a practical guideline for system development, not a rigid standard to be used religiously. I use the word "guideline" to imply that you can tailor this development methodology to your particular project. However, such tailoring should be done only when it is absolutely necessary and only if the customizing is documented.

It should be noted that the book is meant to do more than merely tie all of the structured, state-of-the-art techniques into one complete guideline; it is intended as well to show a practical partitioning of the complete system development process and to present the guideline itself in a partitioned, readable manner.

Finally, I want this book to be a reference for system development and a document to be used to present the system development process to upper-level management, users, auditors — all those people who are involved in or affected by system development.

Utopian though it sounds, I believe we can reach the day when all computer systems are developed in a similar manner (using the same effective communication tools

---

*If you are not familiar with the structured techniques, or if you would like a refresher on their purpose and tools, refer to the introductory sections preceding the data flow diagrams, the data dictionary, and the process descriptions, as well as to the overview presented in Appendix A.

and techniques) with quality systems as the result. Then, I should not hear war stories from my students summarized by comments such as: "The user doesn't want the system anyway." "They kept changing the system requirement, so we froze the spec." "We're too busy keeping the old systems alive to do much new development." And, "This system's too big to handle." We have the tools and techniques available to us now to cure these common data processing ills and to bring us a great deal nearer to a utopian environment. Further, I think there is a need for a methodology to unite all of these tools and techniques and to show how to control them.

We are entering an age of true software engineering, which by definition involves having to adjust our emphasis in the development activities of a system. In other professions, a great deal of responsibility and effort is front-end loaded (for example, in building a home, the actual building of walls is a minor undertaking compared with the job of specifying the requirements and design of the home). So should it be in the development of a system: Analysis and design should be the main considerations. As you will see in this methodology, that's where my emphasis *is* placed — on analysis and design deliverables, or products.

This book, then, presents a system to develop systems. It is not my intention to show extreme detail. You will have to supply the details based on what technical and managerial approaches you use and on what kind of project — business or scientific — you are working. It is not my aim to restate or discuss the ideas of structured analysis, structured design, structured programming, or database modeling, or to convince you of their value. There are many excellent books already available on these subjects (see the Bibliography). However, I will present some of the basic ideas of these techniques in the process descriptions whenever a technique is required.

This book is not intended to be a panacea, especially for such problems as company politics, but I do believe that increased communication and better tools for communication, as presented in this methodology, will cure many data processing ills. Also, no matter how good a methodology is for a particular project, there can be no substitute for people with experience, good judgment, and motivation. If a project team has such qualities already, then this methodology should provide a perfect complement.

Although this book is a working guide for everyone involved in the system development effort, from user to programmer, it is really aimed at the managers of this effort, from project managers to upper-level managers. Depending on your managerial level, you could approach this methodology from various perspectives.

Upper-level management should know the major activities and deliverables needed to develop a structured system and to understand the amount of effort required before program coding can start. These senior managers most likely want an overview. Furthermore, once a project starts, managers typically get worried when there aren't lines of code to show for the first half of a structured development effort. In their ignorance, they may think the project is failing and may cancel it. Therefore, upper-level managers themselves need to understand the new development process. I am not saying they need to understand every detail, but they should know what is involved. So, a document is needed that allows them to see just an overview. Such a document is a high-level data flow diagram, which is a model of the entire system.

Middle-level managers probably don't want just an overview, but neither do they want to get involved in the details of system development in the way a designer or coder does. Because this methodology's set of data flow diagrams is in levels, middle-level managers can seek out the level of diagram appropriate to their area of concern.

Project managers — who guide the development of a system from initiation to installation and who produce the plans and schedules — have to see all of the activities and data necessary to produce a working system. Therefore, this entire methodology — data flow diagrams, process descriptions, data dictionary, and appendices — is aimed at them. This book should also be used by analysts, designers, and coders to identify their individual development activities and data and to get an overview of the other data and activities with which they interface.

It is also a good idea for users (owners of the final system) to have an overview of the development process, so they can be aware of the costs and time involved and the quality of development. Not only do users need to identify the effects of mid-stream changes to system requirements, they also need to see the resource commitments required from their area, for example, interview times and review points.

Because I have talked about projects, project teams, and project management, I should define "project": A project is the total activity of developing a system. It begins with a formal acknowledgment of business objectives and related problems and ends with a formal acknowledgment that the solution to these objectives and problems has been implemented. The total activity includes identifying user and data processing management approval points of resources for further development and major quality control points in the methodology. These approval points help the users gain knowledge of the system development at different stages as well as aid the communication process between system developers, users, and data processing management.

Further, let me give a couple of simple definitions of a methodology:

As an *object*, a methodology is a product that shows all tasks/activities (managerial and technical) needed to produce a working system, with their deliverables.

As a *process*, a methodology is the practical set of procedures (sequential, asynchronous, or iterative) that facilitates the development of a system.

In brief, a methodology identifies how to develop a system.

All systems, regardless of their size, complexity, or application, pass through similar development activities. These activities and the data they use can be linked to form a standard framework that can support several types of projects (new development, rewrites, maintenance and modification, or software package selection/installation) along with several technologies (centralized or decentralized, batch or on-line systems). Traditionally, data processing people tend to limit their view of systems to only an automated environment. Let me declare here — and have it apply for the rest of the book — that a system is not just a set of automated procedures but a set of manual and/or automated activities that produce a desired result. Encompassing both manual and automated activities, this methodology identifies a standard framework that shows

- integrated structured techniques for developing a complete system
- all major deliverables, intermediate deliverables, and data flows necessary to produce a system
- all technical activities at a working level that develop and transform the data
- major quality control points (walkthroughs/reviews)
- all managerial activities in which plans are produced
- user and data processing management approval points (feasibility approval or hardware/software approval)

If there is no established company method — that is, if there is no standard framework to guide system development — the project manager is probably guiding the development process by using a conglomeration of methods he or she has acquired over the years. This approach is sometimes called the Tinkertoy® method of developing systems.

On the other hand, having a methodology can help reduce the potential for system failure by avoiding haphazard system development and by achieving consistency between projects, for example, by establishing compatible interfaces and by efficiently reassigning people so that they don't need retraining. Companies should have some kind of standard interface between their different divisions. One of the advantages in using a methodology is that it provides such standardized development techniques. A methodology provides a prototype from which to fashion the appropriate set of activities and data for each development effort, thus aiding the system development process by identifying the partitioning, controlling complexity, allowing partitioning of effort, and forming a reference guide to activities, data, and people interfaces.

We need to partition the effort and cost of system development, if for no other reason than to be able to *monitor* that effort and cost. To achieve such monitoring, a methodology should be used to produce plans, schedules, and estimates. Since most projects fail because of problems in planning, monitoring, and controlling, they are probably the three most important reasons for having a methodology. As we all are aware, the cost of hardware in data processing is rapidly decreasing, while that of software — that is, the cost of personnel who develop software — is rising. At a Data Processing Management Association meeting in New York, one speaker stated that we can expect data processing salaries to double in the next five years, whereas the cost of machine power is expected to continue decreasing even more than it has in the past because of technological breakthroughs. Thus, we need to control software costs, as the following graph shows:

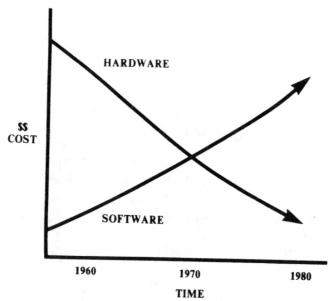

Figure 1. Hardware/software cost ratio.

We need, then, to make people more efficient. This does not mean that we must train a programmer to code two programs simultaneously with a terminal at each hand or that we must develop systems faster. What it does mean is that we must produce *quality* systems that have *cheaper lifetime costs,* including low maintenance costs. Using a methodology is a way to do so.

What this all boils down to is the need for good communication tools, that is, a means of documentation to aid both in development and maintenance efforts. In the past, documentation has consisted of narrative and reams of forms. I believe that in the future, documentation will consist of paper models, which will serve as replicas of a piece of the real world. Models facilitate conceptualization, communication, simulation, and refinement (iteration). These are exactly the reasons for having any tool used to develop, maintain, and modify any product, not just a computer system. Creating a model helps us to break down the complexity (size) of a problem to aid our thought processes by allowing us to see the problem in a picture. Because the left side of the brain deals with logic (words) and the right side of the brain deals with ideas (pictures), we gain "brain power" by using pictures, or models, in addition to words to understand and solve a problem. Using models, we may even avoid converting from ideas into logic and back again during the problem-solving process. For example, when somebody gives you directions for how to get to his or her house, isn't it always better when he or she gives you a hand-drawn map annotated with streets and landmarks?

I am not saying that we can completely get rid of narrative in system development and documentation but what we can delegate to a model, we should. (In fact, this methodology is presented as a model: a data flow diagram.)

There are methodology packages on the market that are intended to guide developers of systems, but unfortunately many of them turn out to be paper generators or paint-by-number methodologies. Many classical methodologies neatly divide development into phases, suggest some deliverables that might result from each, and then require a series of penciled-in checklists to serve as evidence of phase completion. They fail to logically define the content of the deliverables, and they give precious little guidance concerning the technical methods for creating them.

Using these methodologies, developers attempt to create systems by filling in standard forms; for example, analysis is declared finished when you have completed the analysis forms. Completed forms may satisfy upper management, but they do not help the actual development effort. Most classical methodologies do not encourage the creation of meaningful models of the system being developed. In fact, they tend to view system development as a linear process without any emphasis on either iteration or refinement. The system development activities are viewed merely as "process lumps," namely, analysis, design, programming, and installation.

This is development by flow of control, usually tracked by phases or milestones, which are bad tracking tools. Phases have too large deliverables, have long distances between start and finish times, and are not specific in their contents. The end of a phase is usually determined by the money running out or the calendar indicating the phase has finished.

Projects slip gradually and noticeably; that is, you do not suddenly wake up on the morning of the design phase review and realize you are three months late. When you notice a slippage occurring, then is the time to acknowledge and try to make up for it, not after many of them have cost weeks or perhaps months. Therefore, if we track an individual deliverable instead of, for example, a complete analysis specification to make up for time slippage, we can take steps such as reallocation of resources or scheduling overtime, or at least we'll be able to identify that the project will be late before panic sets in.

Here is a diagram to illustrate the problem of measuring by milestones:*

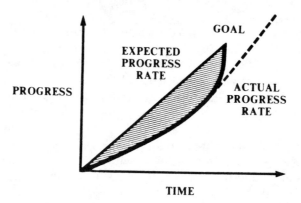

Figure 2. Measuring by milestones.

As I have mentioned, many classical methodologies concentrate on documentation such as standard forms, checklists, and so on. Such documentation is usually solution-oriented without sufficient emphasis on problem definition. Also, the documentation is usually not used for maintenance. Maintenance documentation is an after-the-fact issue consisting of a fresh set of forms to fill in when the system is completed. In addition to such negative aspects, classical methodologies usually also are

- shelf stuffers (seven volumes seems to be the standard number)
- excessively redundant (repetition occurs throughout the methodology because narrative is difficult to partition)
- excessively wordy (words are the main communication tool)
- excessively physical (they consist of many forms and a sequential method of developing systems)
- terribly tedious to read (they are wordy, too lengthy, and unpartitioned)

I am not saying that all existing methodologies are bad. Some seem to have made a genuine effort to aid the developer. However, they can sometimes give you a false sense of security, such as leading you to think that if you've completed the forms, you've completed the system.

In this methodology, system development is accomplished by identifying definable intermediate deliverables. Each deliverable is defined in advance by the statement of its content, and each is small enough that a reasonable estimate may be figured for its creation. These intermediate deliverables, which in total form the system, can be tracked. This type of development is development by tracking the flow of data instead of development by major phases, such as analysis and design milestones. In contrast to the measuring-by-milestones diagram in Fig. 2, the following diagram shows the advantages of tracking intermediate deliverables.

---

*Diagram originally presented by Bob Block at an internal YOURDON inc. staff seminar.

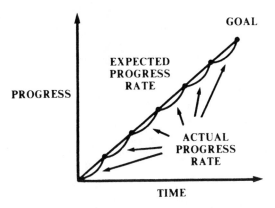

Figure 3. Measuring by inch-pebbles (intermediate deliverables).

As Fig. 3 illustrates, identifying and tracking intermediate deliverables helps you meet one large goal by meeting many smaller goals or at least by recognizing that a final goal cannot be met. Tracking smaller deliverables and correcting their possible slippage is also desirable in case a deliverable is not approved during a quality assurance review or walkthrough in a time-critical project, in which lack of time preempts correcting the slippage in a later activity. Therefore, the emphasis is on deliverables first, with activities as the way to produce these deliverables. For the production of these deliverables, iteration and refinement are explicitly shown in the methodology.

One of the main reasons for much of the documentation produced in classical methodologies is to protect you if you have to maintain a product or if you have to pick up and continue the development of somebody else's product. My view is that, as far as possible, documentation should be a natural by-product of the work and should be completed as soon as the comparable project stage is done, not after a complete development effort has been finished. Documentation should also be kept to a minimum. Structured techniques help do this, as the models used in development become the maintenance documentation.

This methodology also puts the necessary emphasis on problem definition, rather than mostly concentrating on the solution to poorly defined problems.

In summary, as a guideline for system development, this methodology is flexible. This flexible approach facilitates introduction of a new method of developing systems into traditional shops because it is not rigid or too detailed. As you become more familiar with these guidelines and structured techniques, you may want to apply them on a level more detailed than the one shown in this book.

This book, then, is for people who want a formal way of developing a system using structured techniques and tools, without wading through volumes of standards and forms. It is also for those who are discontent with existing, inflexible paint-by-numbers methodologies, which gather dust and fill up shelves.

INTRODUCTION

Tools used to present the methodology

The methodology is presented in the form of a structured specification, which contains a leveled set of data flow diagrams — the main tool of structured analysis — backed up with a data dictionary and process descriptions. I have used the data flow diagram, which models a system by tracking the flow of data through the system, as my modeling and communication device. Because the tools present a system in a top-down, partitioned manner that shows different levels of detail, they can be used for presentation to audiences with varying technical backgrounds.

In specifying the guidelines in this book, I have tried to be as un-physical (logical) as possible; that is, I do not require a particular format for a deliverable, but I declare the make-up of that deliverable and let you format it in any way your company may require. Data flow diagrams and the data dictionary are appropriate logical tools for this methodology, but I support them with process descriptions of activities, as the activities are not at the lowest level of detail (functional primitives), which is the real specification level.

The methodology's data flow diagrams present the logical data and functions necessary to produce a system, but I also indicate some sequence and the political and managerial go/no-go points. The latter make the diagrams somewhat physical and illustrate the flexibility and adaptability of data flow diagrams, which are essentially logical. In fact, I believe a "physicalized" model is the first model we should produce in a system development effort. We should attempt to accomplish as much logicalization as possible in this first model as long as we still produce a user-verifiable model. The extent to which we logicalize will depend on how well the user understands *what* is being accomplished in the system as opposed to *how* it is currently being accomplished.

This methodology's contents are partitioned into

- data flow diagrams, which compose a model that is mostly graphic and partly narrative and that declares the processes and data flowing through it

- a data dictionary, which defines, in one place, all data used in the methodology

- process descriptions of activities, which are concise specifications, in one place, of all activities

Before I present the actual methodology, one major concept needs explanation: the concept of explicit iteration, or cycling, of the analysis and design activities, which

1

is a means of handling the complexity of a system in partitionable levels of detail. The methodology consists of primary activities — initiate project, analyze and design, build system, and install system — with analysis and design cycled through three times at the preliminary, general, and detailed levels of decomposition. The major reason for cycling through analysis and design is to work down to the details after we understand the broad view. The process of cycling through levels of decomposition is called explicit iteration. The following diagram illustrates this:

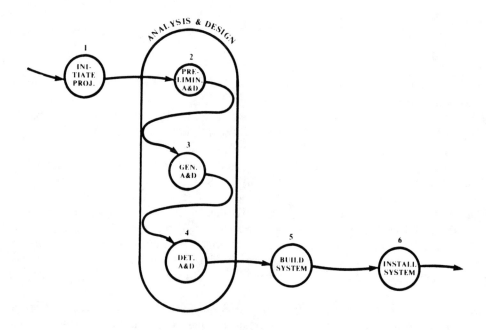

Figure 1. Cycling through the analysis and design activities.

It has always amazed me that, at the beginning of a project, we try to estimate the time or effort needed for system development before we know any details of the system. Even a feasibility study will give only a rough idea of what to expect. We are limited to giving an estimate based on the extent of our knowledge of a system, which is the Catch-22 of estimating: We can give the best estimate only after we have finished the system. So, I believe we should make an *incremental commitment* to the cost and effort of developing a system. An illustration of incremental commitment is presented in Fig. 2.

By the end of the preliminary study, we should have produced a feasibility report, with an estimate for the cost of the system, which could be off by as much as fifty percent. However, if the preliminary estimate is acceptable, then the general study can take place. At the end of this general study, we should have what I call an "initial proposal" and a more accurate estimate for the system, say, plus or minus twenty percent. If this estimate is acceptable, then the detailed study can proceed.

This third stage produces a final proposal and an updated estimate which should be accurate within five percent. Of course, by this time, you should have finished the majority of the structured development effort, and so you should be able to arrive at a precise estimate for the complete system.

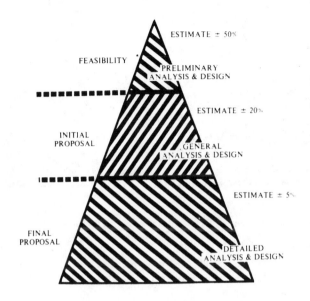

Figure 2. Cost and effort distribution through analysis and design.

Obviously, the usefulness of cycling to produce accurate estimates will only interest those of you who make use of estimates. Many companies develop systems based on an edict from the boss; or, as a more realistic example, a system has to be built because the government states you must add some functions to your payroll system by next April. Estimates in such cases may be regarded as "funny money."

Cycling through analysis and design, or explicit iteration, diverges from the process-lump idea and instead helps us to build a product by refinement. The human mind is not able to see all the ins and outs of a problem and then come up with the best solution instantaneously; but it is capable of criticizing and improving a bad solution. Thus, we need to iterate and return to a process to refine a product. In fact, refinement is one of the main reasons for cycling; producing good estimates for management and users is secondary.

This second reason forces us into a political approach to development, while cycling allows us to take the practical approach to development. On the next page are two diagrams representing these approaches.

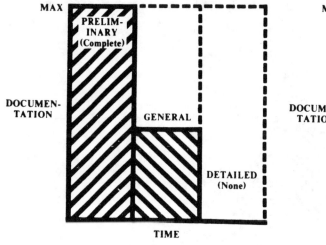

Figure 3a. Political approach.

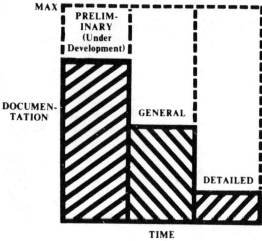

Figure 3b. Practical approach.

The diagram at the left indicates that we complete all of the preliminary documentation to produce an accurate estimate and once that is completed, go on to general development. Then we do the same procedure for detailed development.

The diagram at the right indicates that during preliminary study we will probably gather and develop general-level documentation and even some detailed information. This second approach suggests an extra iteration within the three-level, explicit iteration, which implies that the practical approach may be harder to plan and manage.

The percentages of effort to assign to each major development activity — excluding system installation, which can vary greatly — should follow this rough guide:

Initiate Project	up to 2%
Preliminary Analysis and Design	about 8%
General Analysis and Design	about 25%
Detailed Analysis and Design	about 40%
Build System	up to 25%

Temper these percentages with your knowledge of your system. For example, if you are developing a straight batch system with no frills, a twenty-five percent allocation of effort to build (and test) a system may be too large; but if you are producing a distributed on-line system using a new database management system, you may want to allocate a higher percentage.

Of course, this three-level decomposition cycle may not be suitable for projects of all sizes. If your system is very small, you will probably want to compress the preliminary, general, and detailed cycles into one. The other extreme may apply if you have a complex system and want to approach its development in more than three levels. (I have allowed for this customization activity in the methodology, in process reference number 1.2.1.)

The idea of cycling through part of the system development activity is not new. Various methodologies have attempted to show some type of iteration (for instance, of initial and final phases), usually limited to the design activity. Almost all projects have one kind of feasibility study or another, typically consisting of identification of a possible solution without real problem analysis.

Cycling through both analysis and design is important for the following reasons. I have previously stated that analysis consists of identifying the requirements of a system using such tools as data flow diagrams, and design involves developing a solution to those requirements using structure charts or similar documentation. "Model" is an appropriate word to use in describing the deliverables of these two activities, because both data flow diagrams and structure charts are paper models, and are therefore far easier to modify than complete programs.

A good analogy here would be with custom home-building, since in data processing we are most often concerned with custom system-building. The product of analysis and design would be similar to an architect's drawing and blueprints of the home. The equivalent of coding would be the construction of walls. It's obviously a lot easier to move pencil walls on an artist's drawing or blueprints than it is to move constructed walls. Most companies cannot afford the luxury of building programs (or walls) and then checking to see if they accomplish what the user wants. So we must have thoroughly specified the problem and have a solid solution before we code actual programs. This then is one reason for iterating through both analysis and design.

Another reason, as I have mentioned before, is achieving a more realistic estimate of a system's development time and cost. (In this methodology, such an estimate is represented successively by the feasibility report, initial proposal, and final proposal.) I do not believe we can give a realistic estimate or cost/benefit analysis after completing only analysis. Certainly, the cost/benefit analysis of a system will depend on the solution we propose in design. It's a poor manager or analyst who would produce a cost/benefit or feasibility study without strongly taking into account conversion, training, hardware and software installation, and system installation, all of which are governed by the design solution.

I have stated one technical reason (top-down decomposition) and one managerial reason (estimating) for cycling through analysis and design, but cycling is also advantageous from the point of view of the user or customer. Iteration during the development of a system increases the opportunities for communication and feedback from the user, minimizing the possibility of producing an unacceptable design; and building a system in cycles gives the customer a continuous sense of progress, rather than a long development period with no visible signs of progress followed abruptly by full implementation. Obviously, the goal of the system development effort is not to produce just estimates. In fact, estimates are produced by quantifying sufficiently detailed technical deliverables.

The methodology's deliverables

I identify two main types of deliverables: *specifications,* which describe a product (they identify what needs to be produced at each step of development); and *plans,* which identify how the development of a product is managed. There is a minimum set of addressable deliverables that applies to all projects regardless of their size, complexity, or type. The following list shows what I believe is the minimum set of addressable deliverables for a project.

Technical Deliverables	Managerial Deliverables
Project Charter	Customized Methodology
	Project Initiation Report
Current Physical Specification	Development Plans
Current Logical Specification	
New Logical Model	
Bounded New Logical Specification	
New Physical Specification	
Hardware/Software Specification	
Data Specification	
	Implementation Plans
Operations Manual	Feasibility Report
Procedures Manual	Initial Proposal
	Final Proposal
System Installation Specification	
Hardware/Software Installation	
Specification	
Conversion Specification	
Training Specification	
Test Specification	
Development Libraries	Implementation Reports
Production Libraries	Maintenance Plan
	Project Completion Report

These are defined in detail in the methodology: their composition, in the data diction-ary; their purpose, in the process description that produces the deliverable. Notice that these are *addressable* deliverables; all of them may not be produced for every project, but they all should at least be addressed, that is, referenced, for their applicability (for example, the "Hardware/Software Installation Specification" may be unaddressed, since an objective is to use only existing hardware/software). I have used the word "model" for a deliverable. This indicates an intermediate deliverable as opposed to the term "specification," which is a formal deliverable. However, the terms are basically synonymous.

If you are familiar with DeMarco's book on structured analysis, you will notice that I have partitioned the analysis deliverables in a similar manner. The obvious difference is what I call the "Bounded New Logical Specification" and DeMarco calls the "New Physical Data Flow Diagram."[*]

The order of the deliverables suggests the sequence in which they are produced. The block of technical deliverables from Current Physical Specification through Test Specification is cycled through in the methodology at preliminary, general, and detailed levels of decomposition. This means I have shown an explicit iteration in the develop-ment of these deliverables. (Note that there are only two, and not three, iterations per-formed on the operations and procedures manuals.) At the completion of all iterations, the system has been completely analyzed and designed.

To further clarify these analysis and design deliverables, here is a diagram that il-lustrates their progression in part of the system development process.

---

[*]T. DeMarco, *Structured Analysis and System Specification* (New York: YOURDON Press, 1979), p. 30.

CURRENT DESIGN	CURRENT ANALYSIS	NEW ANALYSIS	NEW DESIGN	
CURRENT PHYSICAL SPECIFICATION	CURRENT LOGICAL SPECIFICATION	NEW LOGICAL MODEL	BOUNDED NEW LOGICAL SPECIFICATION	NEW PHYSICAL SPECIFICATION
USER AND COMPUTER "HOW"	USER "WHAT"	USER "WHAT"	USER AND COMPUTER "HOW"	

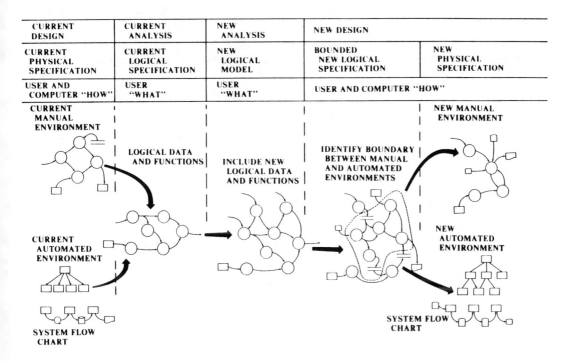

Figure 4. Progression of deliverables through analysis and design.

In Fig. 4, structure charts and data flow diagrams are used to represent the current physical through the new physical specifications. If we have to develop a new system consisting of manual and automated activities from an environment that is already part manual and part automated, then we should produce data flow diagrams for the current manual environment and design charts for the current automated environment. If we already have documentation that shows the flow of information through these manual and automated environments and we can verify that these are up to date, then we can probably use them to derive a current logical specification. In other words, we can abstract what the existing system is accomplishing from how it is being accomplished right now. I believe that most users can validate this logical view as it should be a model of the actual "business" environment. At worst, we may have to annotate this model with some extra physical characteristics to aid verification.

This current logical model then forms the foundation for incorporating any new functions or data to form a "New Logical Model." (Many of my clients find their most difficult problem to be identifying, confirming, and fitting future needs to an existing environment; yet once a readable logical model of the current environment has been developed, they are suddenly able to suggest a number of improvements.) With this New Logical Model, we can now identify how we should partition the whole model of the system into new manual and automated environments, without being influenced by the system's current partitioning. In fact, we should identify different options of manual/automated partitioning for the new system. While identifying this partitioning, we will probably also identify the media used for the data flowing between the manual and automated environments. The result of this process is a Bounded New Logical Specification, a logical model with the man/machine boundary indicated.

We are now able to concentrate on physicalizing the new manual area by filling in roles, data forms, and other physical details, and physicalizing the new automated area by identifying the control structure for new programs. This control structure will identify "worker" routines from the New Logical Specification, "manager" routines to control the worker routines, and additional routines to handle data access and storage. The control structure will be used to identify the partitioning of executable programs that will form the application development libraries and will also help form the system flowchart, which will become part of the operations manual. The physical specification of the new manual area will be used to help form the procedures manual. Finally, for us to be able to produce and track these deliverables, we must have a solid definition of their contents. This is the job of the data dictionary, which is one of the tools used to present the methodology.

The structure of the methodology

The set of data flow diagrams contained in this book represents a graphic model of the methodology or system life cycle at several levels of detail (see Fig. 5).

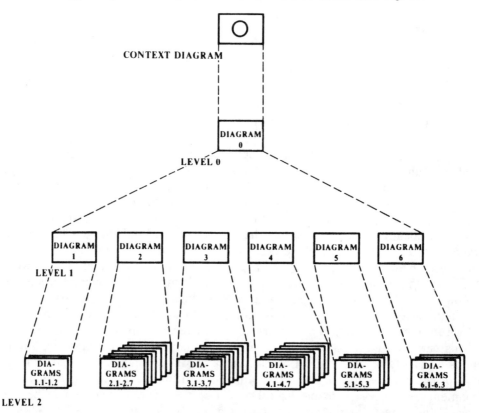

Figure 5. Leveled set of data flow diagrams.

Each complete level of detail forms a network-oriented representation of the system and forms a system model to use in developing systems. All the levels together form a hierarchical set. This system — leveled data flow diagram set backed up with a data dictionary and specifications for the detailed-level processes — stops at Level 2. Nothing is significant about Level 2 other than that it forms a good, general "guideline" for the methodology. Going into further detail would require specifying systems, such as classing a system "scientific" or "on-line," which is too narrow an approach for this methodology.

The number of levels in any data flow diagram will depend on the complexity of the partition being represented, how much detail is shown at each level, and to what degree an area needs to be studied and represented. In data flow diagram 1.1, I show the process "Classify the project by gross size and risk" in the bubble numbered 1.1.5, which corresponds to process reference number 1.1.5. This process is at the level of a functional primitive; that is, a process I would not want to further decompose. However, the process "Create detailed design model for the new automated environment," process reference number 4.4.3 in diagram 4.4, is obviously not at the functional primitive level; it requires further decomposition. Since the nature of the decomposition will depend on the design technique chosen, I have stopped at this level. This example also shows that functional primitives will be reached at different levels of decomposition.

The data flow diagrams in this methodology appear in the following order:

Context diagram — basically identifies the boundary of the methodology, that is, identifies the area to be studied by the project team as well as the net originators and terminators of data.

Level O diagram — is a one-diagram overview of the methodology.

Level 1 diagrams — are a high-level view of the methodology.

Level 2 diagrams — are a working-level view of the methodology.

The diagrams are followed by the data dictionary, which contains the definitions of the data flows, data stores, and data originators and terminators declared on the data flow diagrams. Then, finally, are the process descriptions that pertain to the Level 2 processes. A summary of the data dictionary and process descriptions can be used for presenting the less detailed levels, if more than the process names are required.

While reviewing all of these diagrams, observe the following:

☐ The project plan, which is only shown when accessed in managerial processes, guides all processes. I view the project plan as a form of agent that performs a process, and agents are not shown on a data flow diagram. Each process description identifies the portion of the project plan that guides the process. This plan contains the identification of the estimated resources (time, money, people, and materials) and should be updated with the resources actually used after each process. The actual resources can also be updated by product; for example, the current physical data dictionary took X amount of resources to produce. The project plan is only shown in the data flow diagrams of the methodology when its data is created or used, as when the estimated and actual data are used in a progress report. This estimated and actual data should be used by the project manager to constantly monitor the project for slippage in schedules and excessive use of resources.

☐ Although I recommend an informal walkthrough on each deliverable or major portion of a deliverable, only the reviews and the walkthroughs on a coded program module are shown. Of course, the number of reviews and walkthroughs (and the degree of formality) will depend on the cost-effectiveness of the system and therefore on the requirements placed on the reviews and walkthroughs themselves. For example, a project that develops a system to track the number of pencils in a company can probably get by with fewer quality control inspections than a project that develops an air-traffic control system.

☐ The Level 1 diagrams for Activities 2, 3, and 4 appear more cluttered than will diagrams for your systems. (Don't worry if your physical data flow diagrams are cluttered, only if your logical ones are.) Analysis and design have been deliberately joined at this level in order to emphasize, in graphic terms, the three-stage cycling.

☐ The activities in this methodology concentrate on the data for one system. The exceptions to this are the data modeling activities (Activities 2.4, 3.3, and 4.3) that review the system's data in relation to that of other systems (a data administration group might conduct the review); when reviewing these data modeling activities, you should take a more global view of the data.

☐ Whenever possible, I have separated what needs to be accomplished from how it gets accomplished: The conversion *specification* identifies the data conversion requirements, and the conversion *plan* identifies the strategy, schedule, and resources needed to accomplish these requirements. I have carried this separation one step further and differentiated between technical processes (what is required in the development of a system), which are represented by solid circles, and managerial processes (how we control the development of a system), which are represented by dashed-line circles.

☐ I have tried to starve processes of input data flows that are not necessary to produce the output. There will be a number of instances in which extra inputs will aid in a process, such as in a review, when all the data that was used to form the product under review would probably be of assistance in clarifying answers to questions. Of course, when using this methodology, you can use any additional applicable data to get the job done. On the other hand, there may be some input data flows shown that may not be available, such as a current operations manual. In this case, the data flow is allowed to be empty, and the processes can start without this data.

☐ I have deliberately identified very few roles, such as those of analyst, designer, or coder, in this methodology. I class such role identification as additional physical information that is determined by a particular environment. (For example, the process for ordering new hardware/software may be performed by a technical support group, a special purchasing agent, or individuals responsible for each area — the operations manager orders backup equipment, the database administrator orders the database management system, and so on.) These and other physical details — such as methodology forms, report layouts, special audit controls — should be identified for each environment or project.

As it is expressed by this methodology, my view of system development, presented as data and processes, with an explicit interaction between managerial and technical activities, is only one view. There are others. Depending on the nature of your environment, you may find different ways of applying this methodology that are more appropriate. Your selection or adaptation of these guidelines must be based on your environment and objectives.

INTRODUCTION TO
DATA FLOW DIAGRAMS

The four basic data flow diagram symbols

A directed line represents a flow of information or objects. The arrow indicates the direction of the data flow. The name of the data flow is written through or next to the line.

A circle represents a task or process. It identifies a transformation of input data flows into output data flows. A brief descriptive name and a reference number for the process is written inside the circle.

Two parallel lines represent a store of information or objects, irrespective of the storage medium. The store identifies a time delay for its contents. The name of the store is written between the lines.

A rectangle represents an area where data originates or terminates from the point of view of the system study. It identifies a boundary of the system study; the identification of the originator/terminator is written inside the box.

Other data flow diagram symbols

A data flow divergence indicates a distribution of the data flow with no actual transformation of data content or status. The data flow may be distributed in total or component data flows extracted from the main data flow.

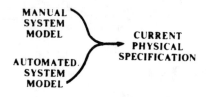

A data flow convergence indicates a collection of data flows that forms a single data flow with no actual transformation of data content or status.

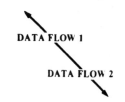

A two-way data flow indicates a two-way flow of data. The data flows are separate and should be viewed as two independent flows of data. This kind of data flow is usually used to indicate that data flowing in produces the data flowing out, but I have violated this rule to reduce the visual complexity of a diagram by using it for two unrelated data flows.

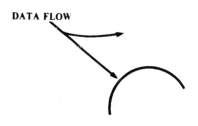

A dangling data flow indicates that a data flow is used in a subsequent process. Data flows "burn up" once they have reached their destination; that is, an item of data is no longer available in the flow once it reaches its destination. So, if it is used again in its present state and is not placed in a store, I have shown it proceeding with a dangling data flow.

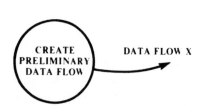

Within Activities 2, 3, and 4 (preliminary, general, and detailed cycles), I have not prefixed a data flow name with its level of detail except when it connects with another diagram, in which case I have included the level of detail in parentheses. The process that develops the data flow will contain its level of detail. (Entries in the data dictionary for such data flows are not qualified.)

A dashed circle indicates a management process. Because the agent performing a process is never shown on a data flow diagram, I use this to distinguish the processes that are totally managerial from the technical processes. The managerial processes make the diagrams most physical because they tend to be control/sequence oriented, as is the presentation of an activity report to indicate a go/no go system approval point.

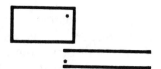

An asterisk indicates that the accompanying item is repeated elsewhere on the same diagram. Items are repeated to improve the readability of a diagram.

In this methodology's data flow diagrams, I have tried to show the actual flow of data. Therefore, where possible, I have avoided using stores because unnecessary data stores hide the true flow, and most stores are unnecessary. Therefore, the stores in the data flow diagrams are mainly used to represent multi-referenced data. For example, within a level of study, the test specification doesn't need to be shown as a store because the data is dynamic, not historical. However, showing the incremental building and use of this specification as a store aids readability.

Unlike most other authors of data flow diagrams, I use crossed data flow lines. My explanation for this is that the real world is three-dimensional, but I have only a two-dimensional medium with which to represent my model of the real world.

Process reference number notation

Each diagram and each process on a diagram has a reference number that can be used to navigate through the leveled data flow diagram set. The reference number of a process will point to the diagram that contains the next level of detail for that process; for example, to find the detail of process reference number 3, look at Diagram 3 (Activity 3). All processes on Diagram 3 will be prefixed with 3 — 3.1, 3.2, 3.3, and so on. The detailed processes of process reference number 3.2 will be numbered 3.2.1, 3.2.2, 3.2.3, and so on, until the functional primitive is reached.

How to read data flow diagrams*

One of the major problems newcomers have with data flow diagrams is that they try to read them as flowcharts, that is, by viewing each process on a diagram as a one-time execution involving a single lump of effort and time. Another problem occurs because novices attempt to apply control and timing to the processes shown on a DFD. These problems are conceptual and are leftover habits from many years of working with flow of control instead of flow of data.

The difficulty in adapting to the iterative way of thinking used for DFDs is that the practical way to perform any task, even outside of the data processing field, traditionally has been sequential: working until a finished product is obtained and only then going on to the next task. Change does not come easily, but if you persist in following the old way of thinking, you are liable to produce increasingly inefficient and costly systems. Analysts no longer can be reluctant to go back and rework; iteration must replace the single-lump approach.

In order for newcomers to master DFDs, they must understand how DFDs differ from flowcharts. For simplicity's sake, the distinction is that a data flow diagram is a model of a requirement or problem, whereas a flowchart is a model of how a requirement is accomplished. Obviously, the processes form the basic components of a system, but the way you determine and segregate (or partition) the processes is the important consideration of analysis.

DFDs show partitioning of a process from the point of view of the data, rather than from the point of view of control. Hence, just as a process can be partitioned, data itself can be partitioned and processed in packets, instead of all at one time. In other words, you can perform a partial process on partial input and produce partial output. For example, a person developing a payroll report that must be completed by a deadline can cycle through the processes, one by one, to arrive at the finished report piece by piece. Using this partitioning approach, the developer can process an item of payroll

---

*This section originally appeared as an article entitled "Iteration of Data Flow Diagrams" in *The YOURDON Report*, Vol. 5, No. 1 (January-February 1980), p. 6. Copyright © 1980 by YOURDON inc. Reprinted by permission.

data as he or she receives it, regardless of where in the report production process the data is received.

You can infer from this that DFDs have a built-in cycling mechanism. This inherent cycling resolves another problem that some newcomers have with DFDs — namely, how to show loops such as GET ANOTHER RECORD and how to show the reprocessing of a task if an error is found. You simply pick your finger up off the DFD, move it back to the process you want to reiterate, and put it back down: All control on a DFD is shown two inches above the diagram.

You can cycle through a DFD in this way until you have a completed product or have accomplished your goal. In fact, as in our example of a payroll report development, cycling is inherent in the business problem of which the DFD is a model.

The second problem mentioned above, that of trying to apply timing to a DFD, can also be addressed with this data approach. From a logical point of view, data should drive the processes; but from a physical point of view, events drive processes. This is best explained by an analogy, depicted in the figure below. Think of the DFD symbols as a real working environment. For example, a process is an individual's desk. The data flows are IN and OUT trays on the desk, and stores are file cabinets that an individual can access.

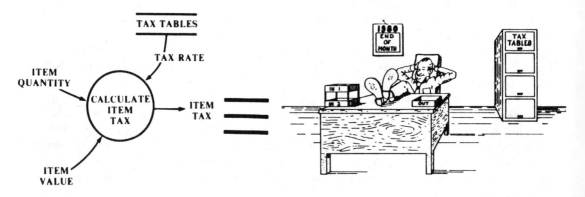

A person sits with feet up on the desk until a piece of data arrives at the IN tray. If a task can be accomplished on this piece of data by itself, then the person will perform it, place the transformed data in the OUT tray, and then put his or her feet (DFDs can be male or female) back on the desk.

It may be that two inputs are needed before a process can take place, as for a match routine, in which case the person remains inactive until both input trays each have at least one piece of data. To extend the analogy to the event- or policy-driven processes mentioned above, imagine that the individual puts data in a file cabinet for later use, rather than in an OUT tray; an event-driven process would produce, on request or monthly, a report on this stored data. In this case, the individual may not have an IN tray but just a policy statement requesting that a certain file cabinet be reorganized and reported on at a specific point in time.

To summarize, the most common difficulties experienced by newcomers to the DFD occur because of the change from an explicitly procedural way of thinking and diagramming to a time-independent one. Instead of imagining the analysis process and the processes within a system as sequential — necessarily linked by order in time — you should view data flow diagrams with a built-in cycling concept: using partial input and producing partial output until the final product is completed or until your goal is accomplished.

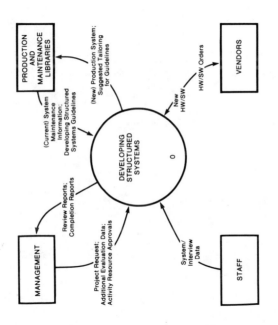

Context Diagram

PRODUCTION AND MAINTENANCE LIBRARIES

(New) Production System;
Suggested Tailoring
for Guidelines

(Current) System
Maintenance
Information;
Developing Structured
Systems Guidelines

DEVELOPING
STRUCTURED
SYSTEMS

0

New
HW/SW

HW/SW Orders

VENDORS

Review Reports;
Completion Reports

MANAGEMENT

Project Request;
Additional Evaluation Data;
Activity Resource Approvals

System/
Interview
Data

STAFF

DIAGRAM 0   17

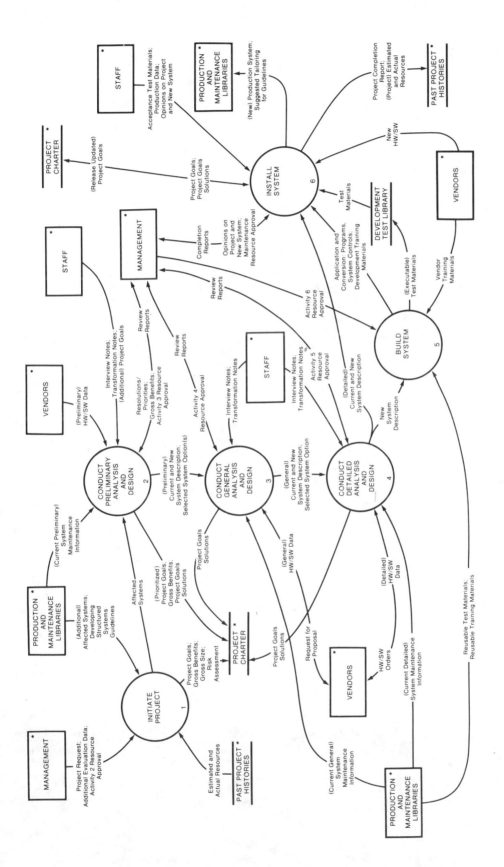

Diagram O   Developing Structured Systems

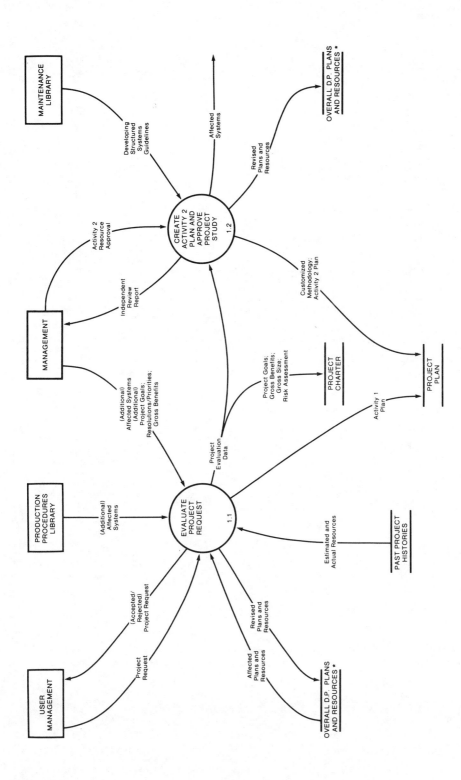

Activity 1 Initiate Project

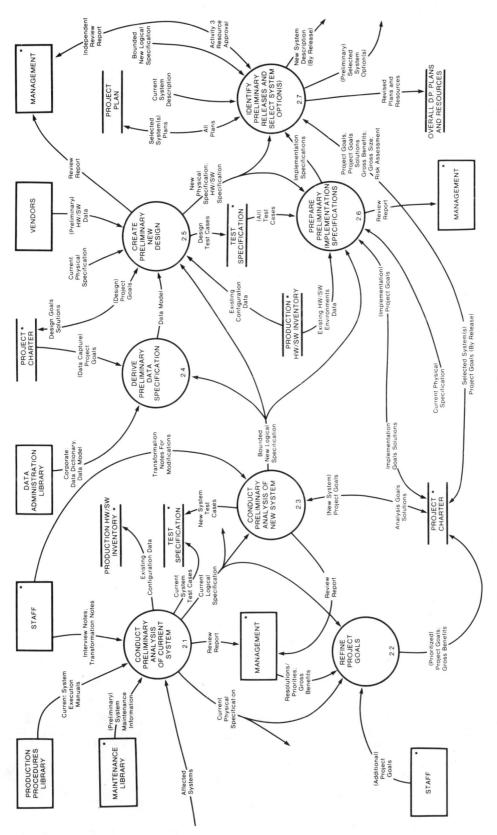

Activity 2   Conduct Preliminary Analysis and Design

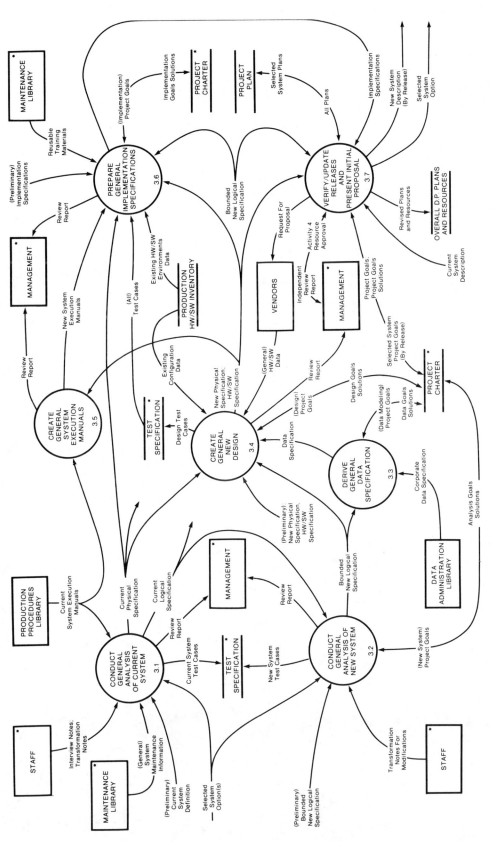

Activity 3   Conduct General Analysis and Design

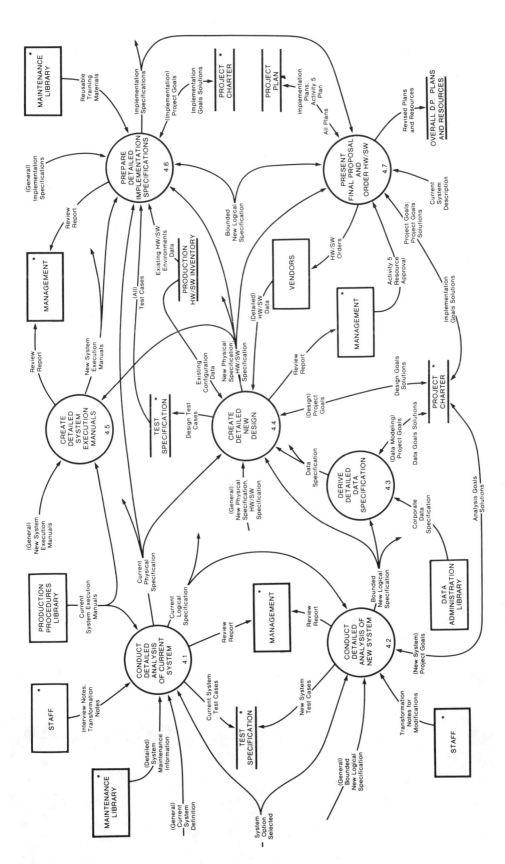

Activity 4   Conduct Detailed Analysis and Design

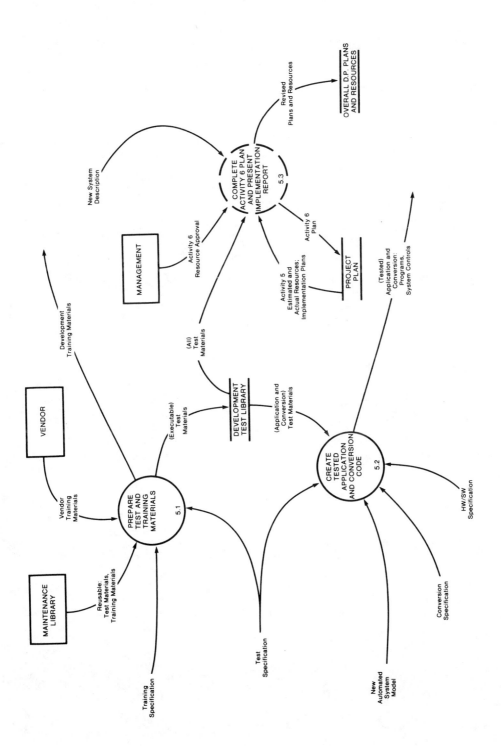

Activity 5   Build System

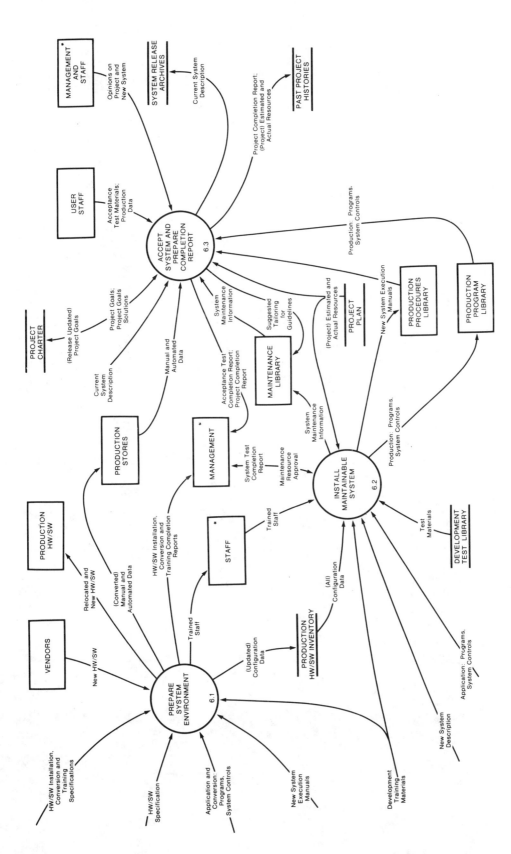

Activity 6   Install System

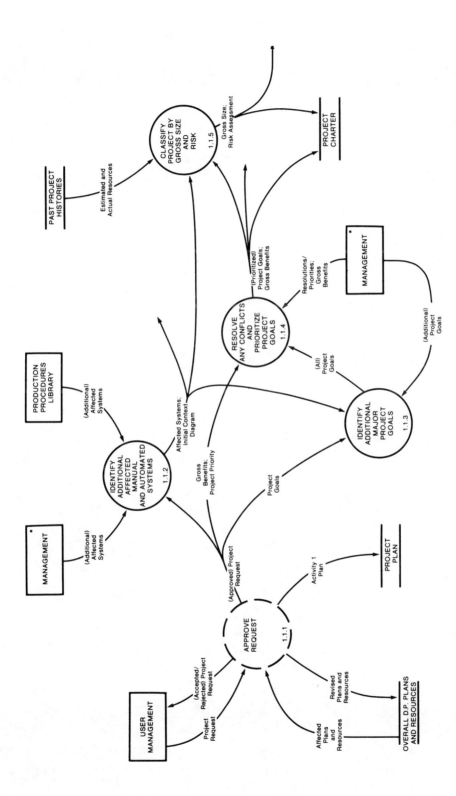

Activity 1.1   Evaluate Project Request

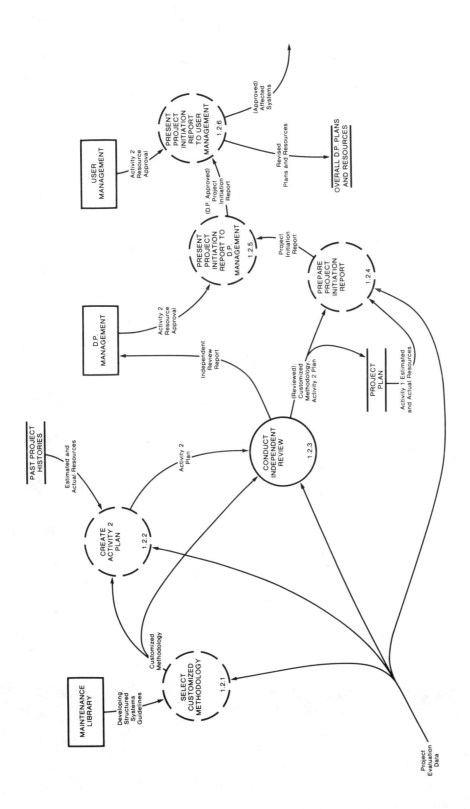

Activity 1.2 Create Activity 2 Plan and Approve Project Study

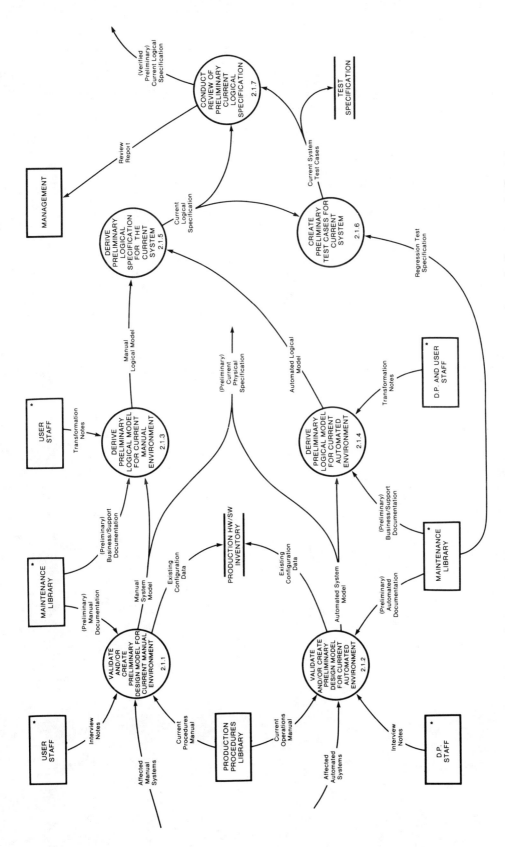

Activity 2.1 Conduct Preliminary Analysis of Current System

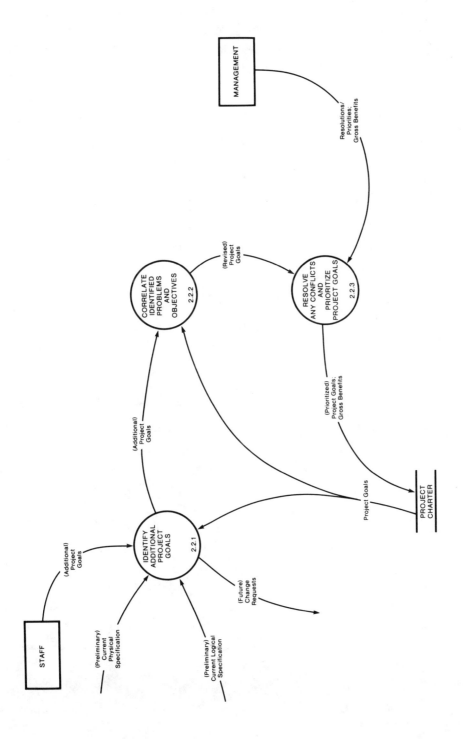

Activity 2.2   Refine Project Goals

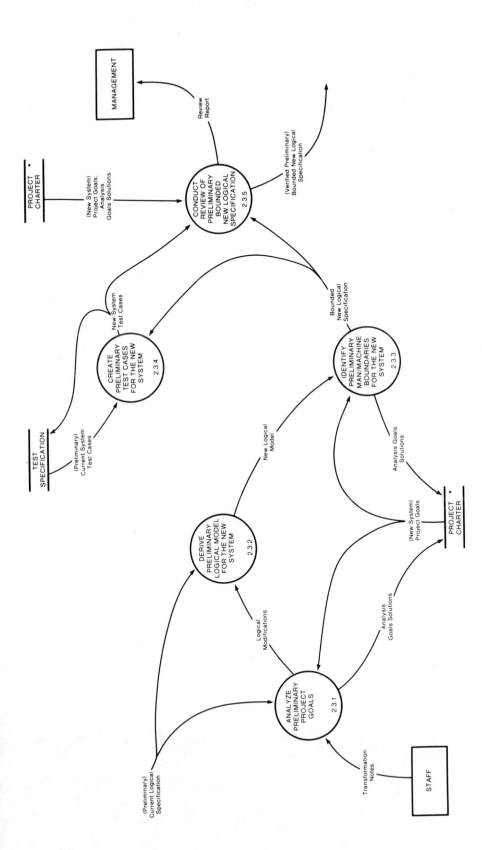

Activity 2.3   Conduct Preliminary Analysis of New System

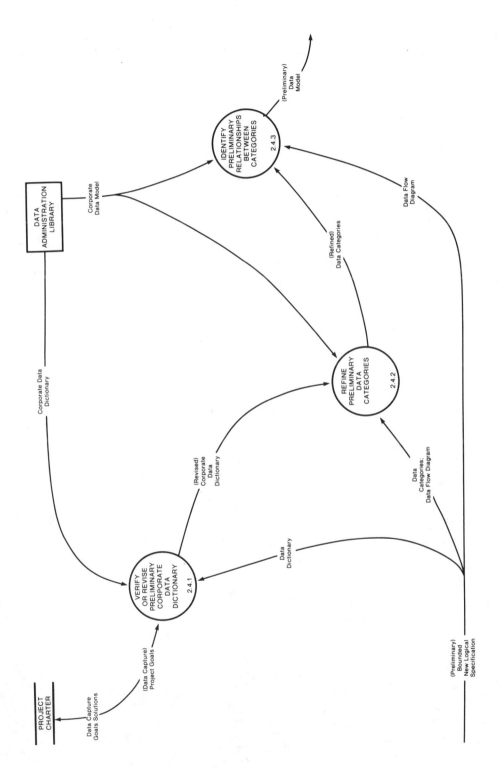

Activity 2.4 Derive Preliminary Data Specification

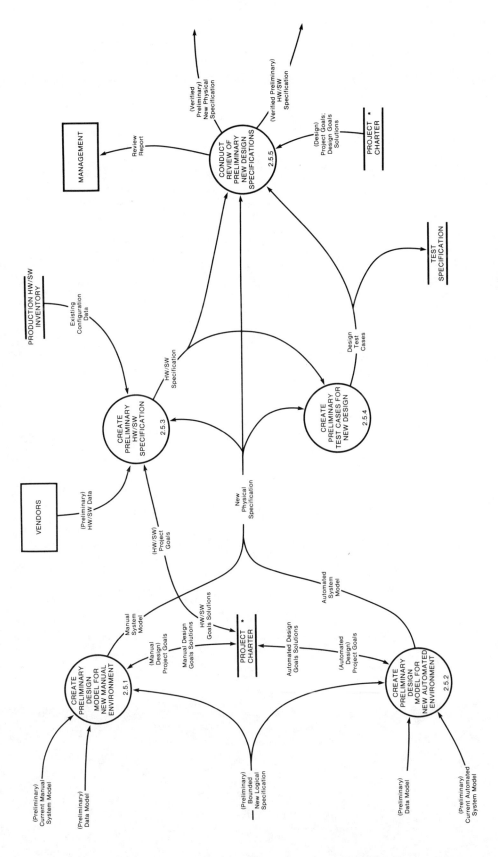

Activity 2.5   Create Preliminary New Design

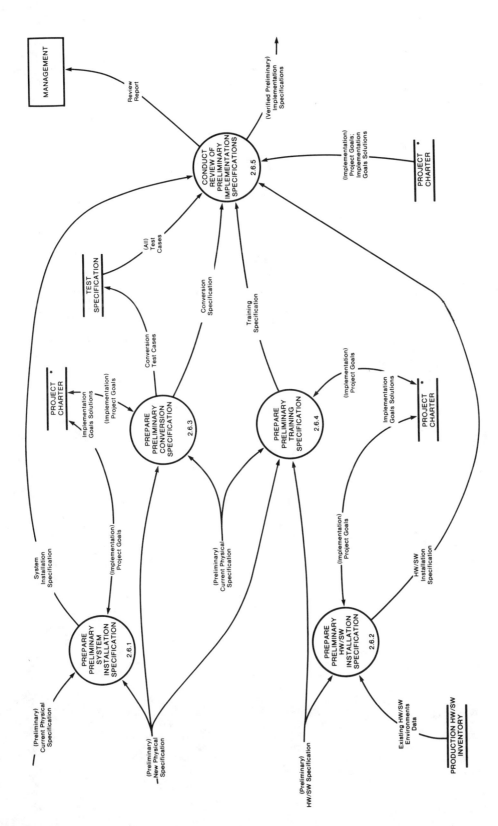

Activity 2.6 Prepare Preliminary Implementation Specifications

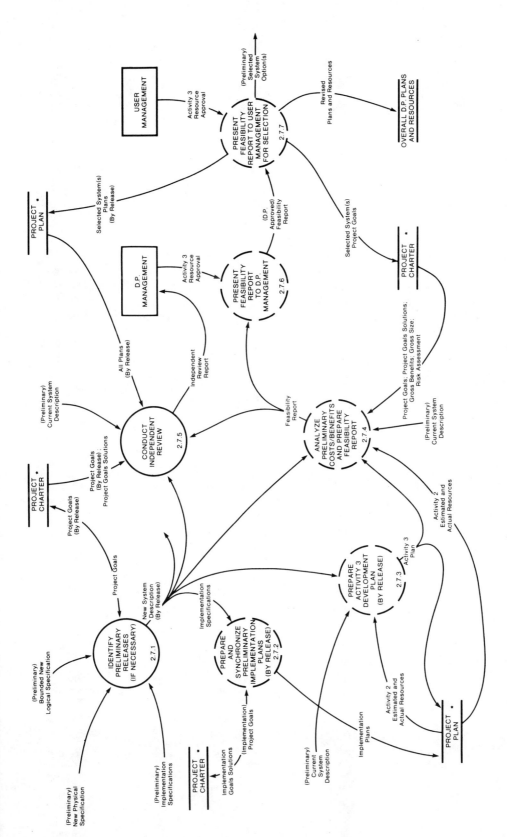

Activity 2.7   Identify Preliminary Releases and Select System Option(s)

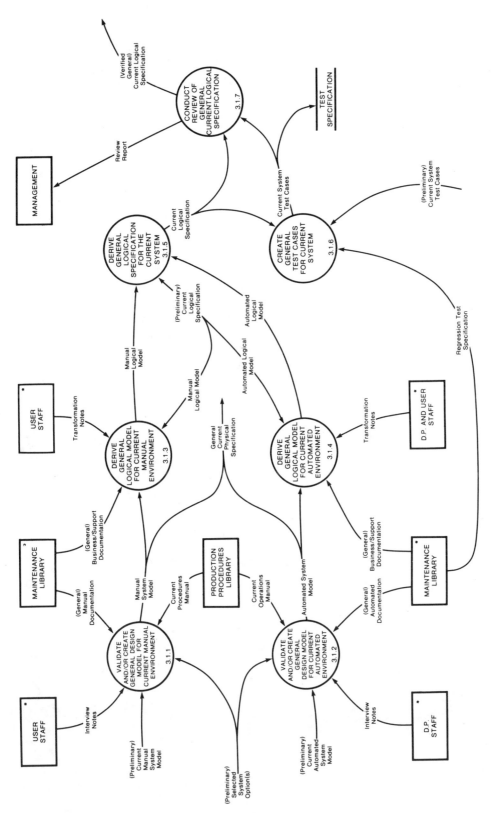

Activity 3.1   Conduct General Analysis of Current System

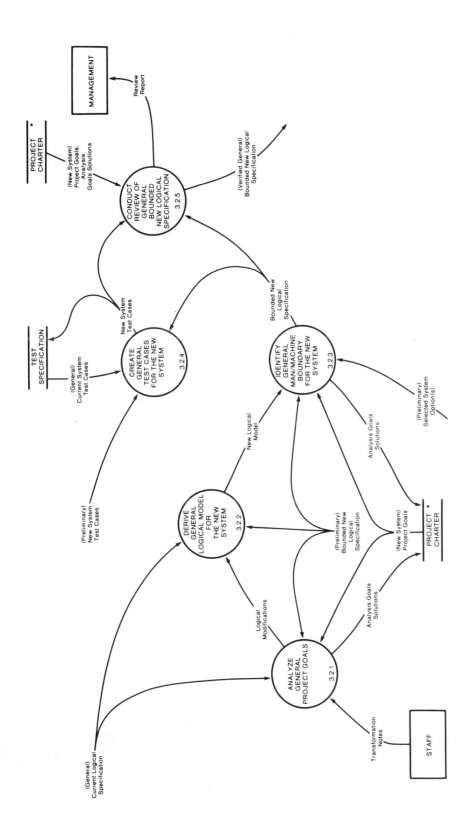

Activity 3.2   Conduct General Analysis of New System

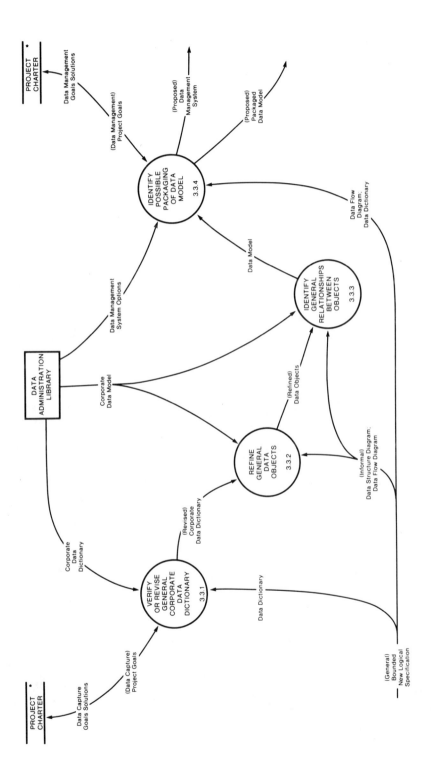

Activity 3.3   Derive General Data Specification

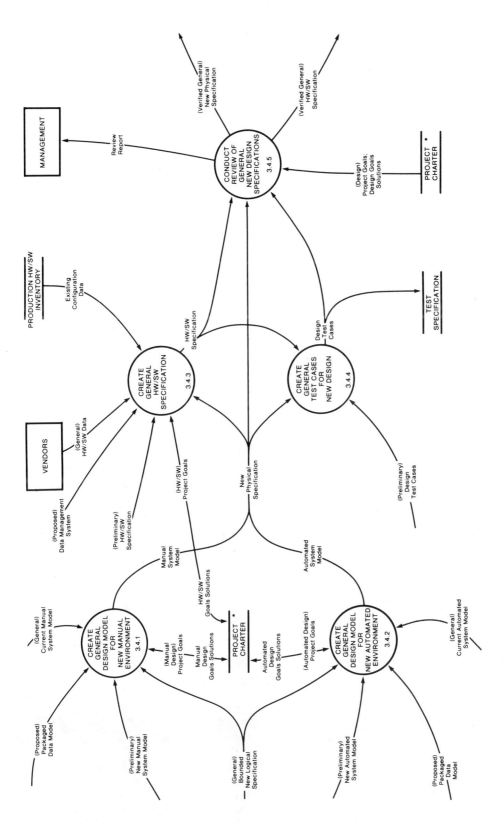

Activity 3.4 Create General New Design

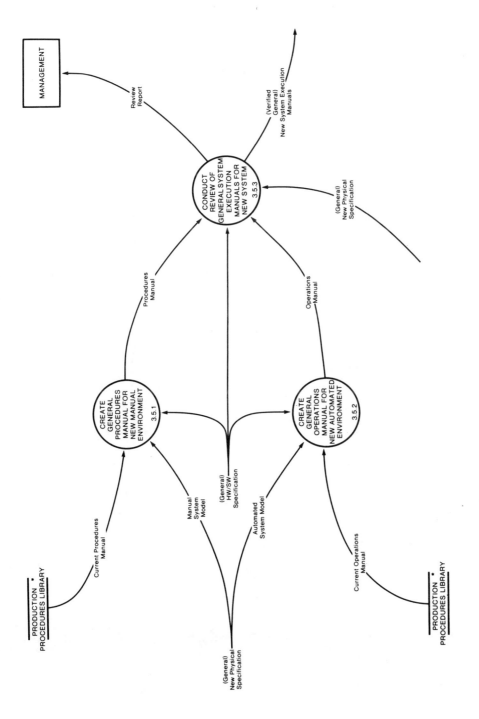

Activity 3.5   Create General System Execution Manuals

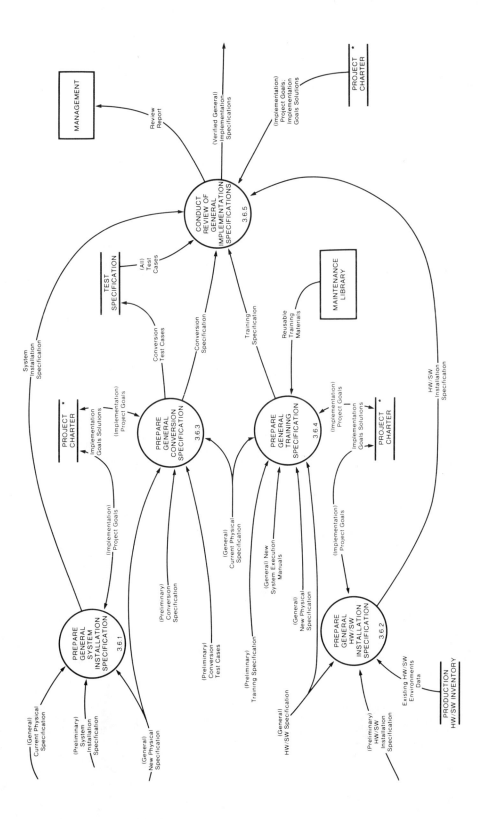

Activity 3.6 Prepare General Implementation Specifications

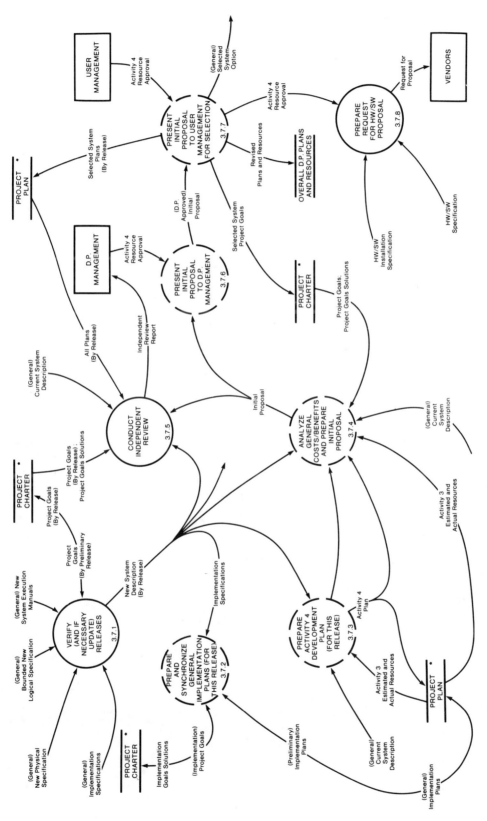

Activity 3.7 Verify/Update Releases and Present Initial Proposal

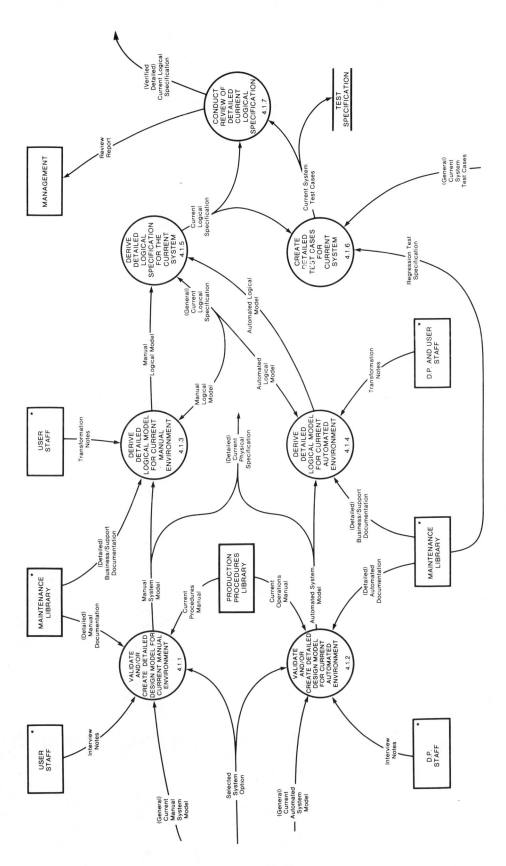

Activity 4.1   Conduct Detailed Analysis of Current System

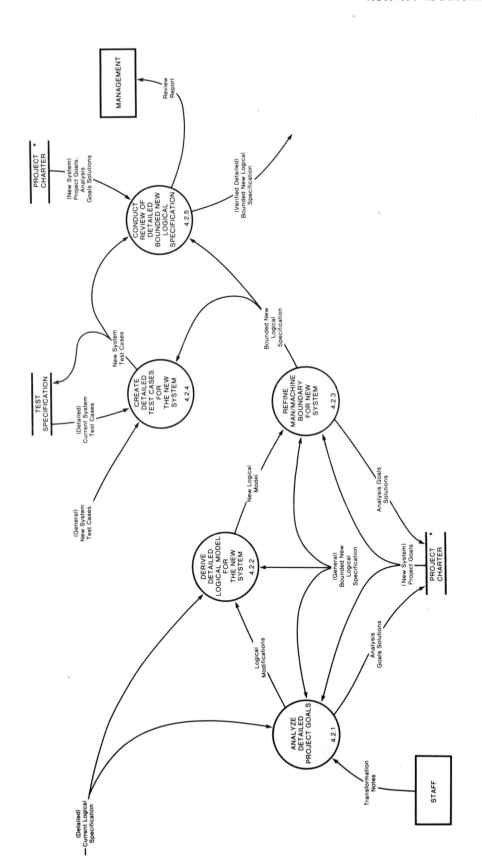

Activity 4.2   Conduct Detailed Analysis of New System

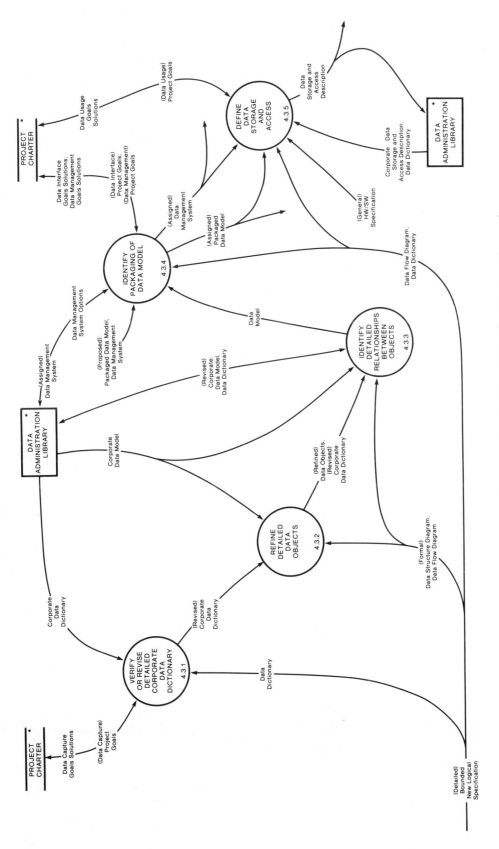

Activity 4.3   Derive Detailed Data Specification

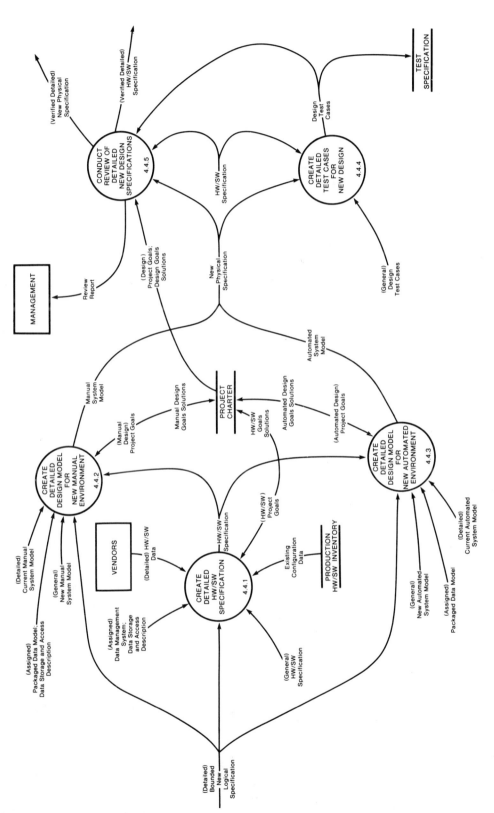

Activity 4.4 Create Detailed New Design

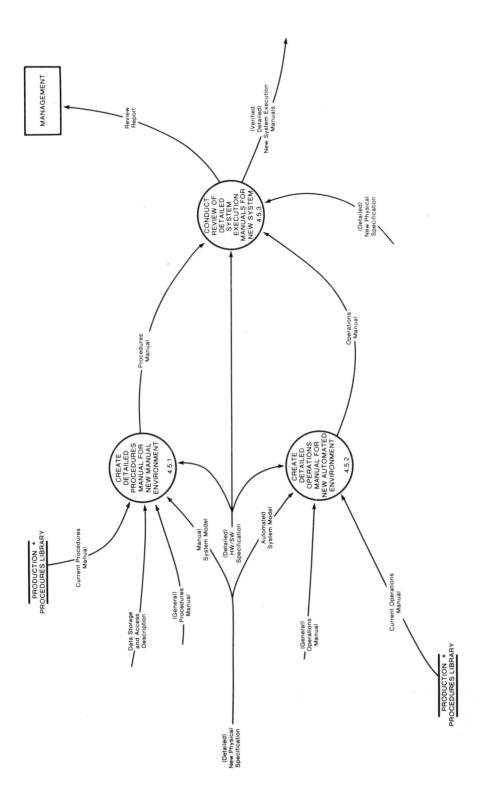

Activity 4.5   Create Detailed System Execution Manuals

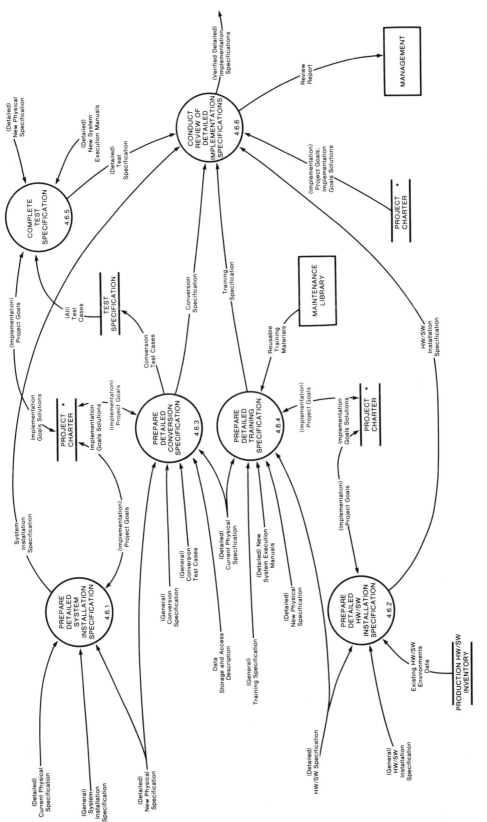

Activity 4.6 Prepare Detailed Implementation Specifications

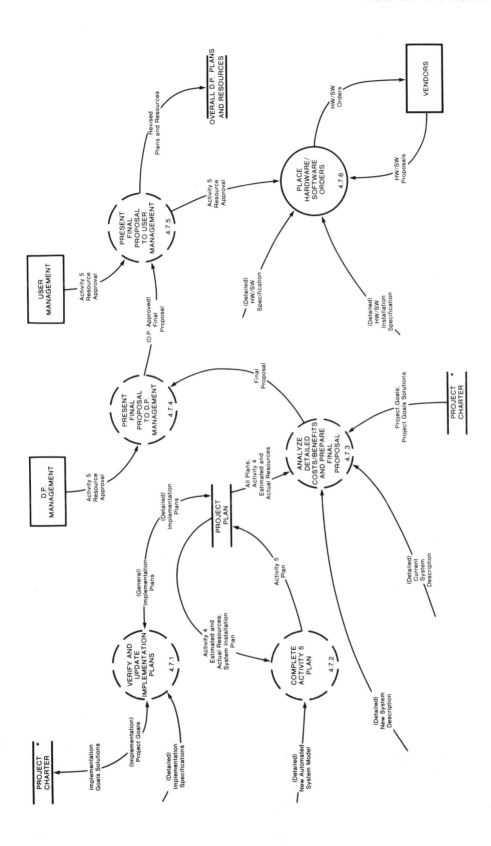

Activity 4.7   Present Final Proposal and Order HW/SW

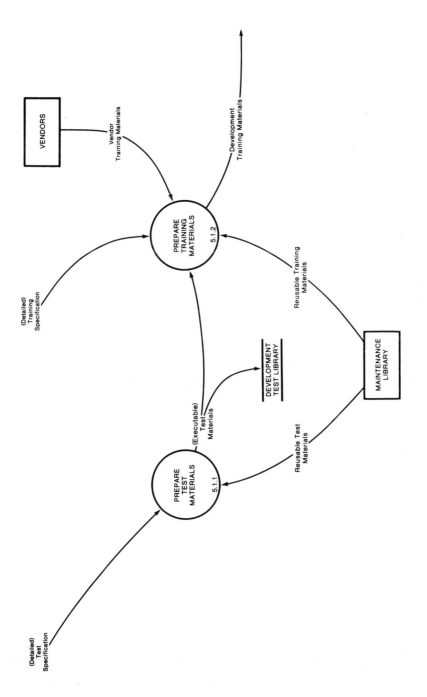

Activity 5.1   Prepare Test and Training Materials

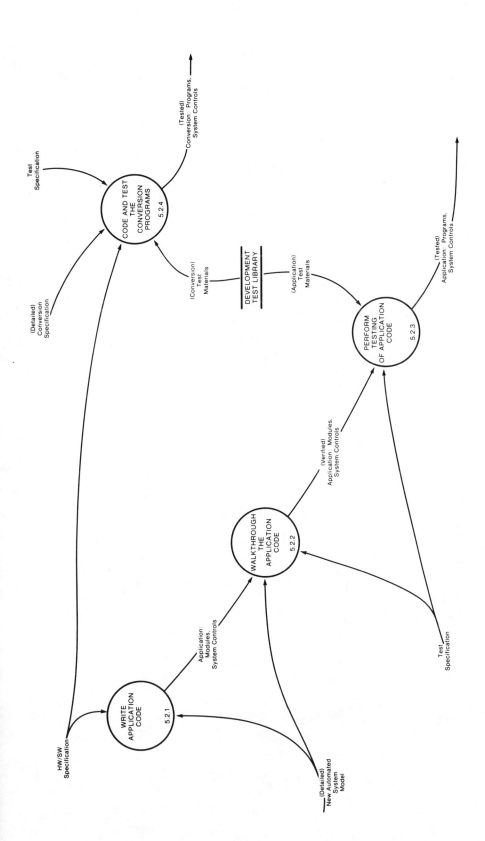

Activity 5.2   Create Tested Application and Conversion Code

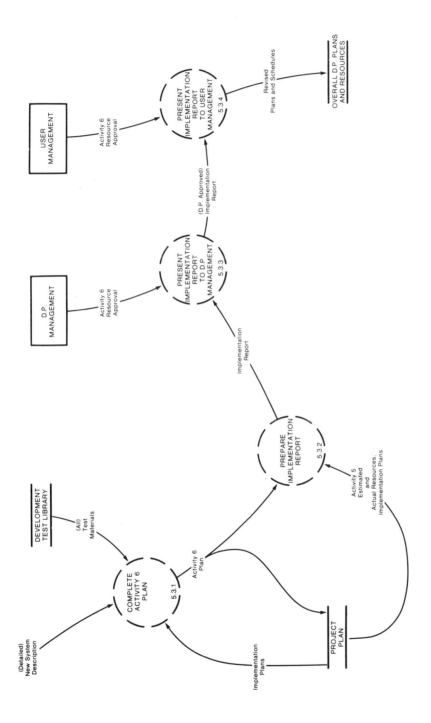

Activity 5.3   Complete Activity 6 Plan and Present Implementation Report

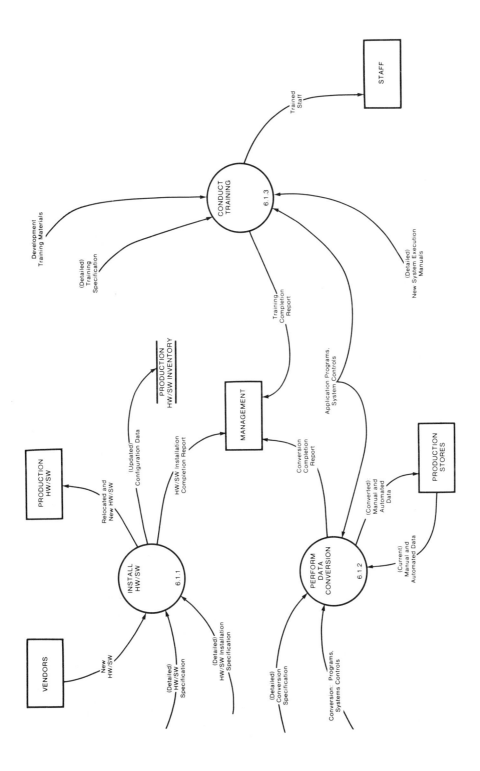

Activity 6.1 Prepare System Environment

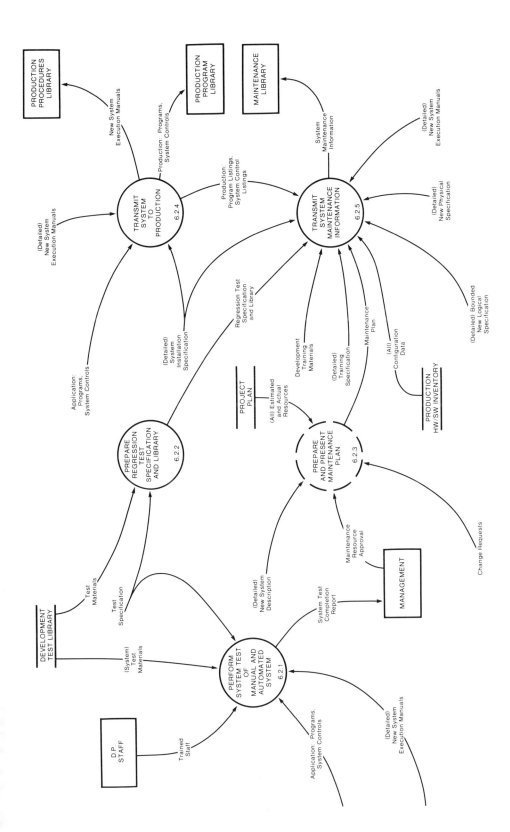

Activity 6.2 Install Maintainable System

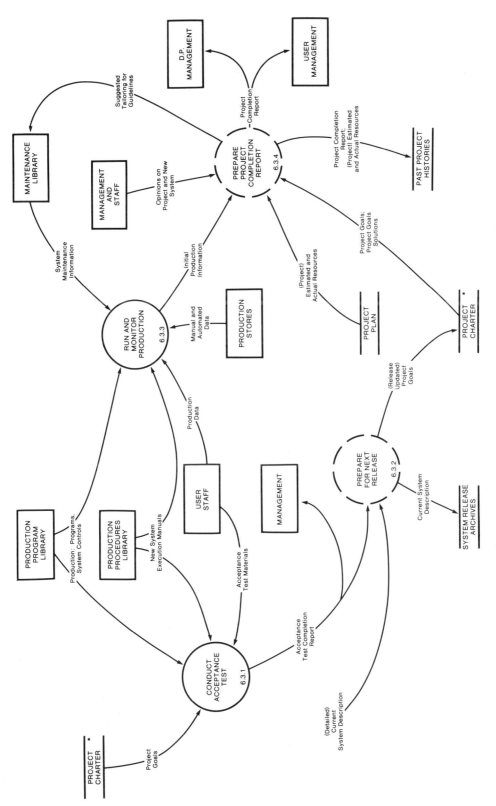

Activity 6.3   Accept System and Prepare Completion Report

INTRODUCTION TO
DATA DICTIONARY

The data dictionary is a set of definitions for the data in a leveled data flow diagram set, and it usually is the largest part of a structured specification. The data dictionary also contains definitions for data and control items on a structure chart and in application code. If I had developed this methodology's data flow diagrams to a more detailed level than that in Level 2, this dictionary would have been exponentially larger. However, one of my objectives was to make this book as compact as possible, so I have omitted definitions of component data items where I felt the name sufficed, for example, "Requestor's Identification of Project Request." In your company, the composition of this data item might consist of

> [Government Request Number |
>
> Department Number |
>
> Name + Title + Department] +
>
> Authorizing Signature + . . .

I have also included comments, occasionally with examples, to aid data item definitions. These are needed as the methodology covers a number of classes of systems: The actual value, and even components, of a data item may differ depending on the system being developed. Using the data dictionary format, you can define the necessary components for your company environment.

When accessing a data flow declared on the data flow diagrams in the data dictionary, observe the following rules:

1. Parenthetic words are adjectives, which are not documented in the data dictionary. Therefore, look up the name without the adjective. (The adjective will be described in or be obvious from the process description that creates and/or uses the data flow.) For example,

(Additional) Project Goals

2. A semicolon separates data flow names. Each name can be looked up individually. For example,

Customized Methodology; Activity 2 Plan

3. A colon is used after a word that qualifies all names following it. The names themselves are separated by commas. Look up the name with the qualifying name preceding it (unless the qualifying name is in parentheses). For example,

Conversion: Programs, System Controls

The following seven symbols are used to document entries in the data dictionary:

> = An equal sign means "is defined as" or "is composed of."
>
> + A plus sign means "and."
>
> [ ] Brackets mean "select one of the items enclosed."
>
> | An "or" bar is used to separate the items within the brackets.
>
> { } Braces mean "iteration of" or "occurrences of the item or items enclosed." Where the number of occurrences, upper and lower limits, is known, it can be written next to the braces, for example, 1 {ITEM} 5 or $_1${ITEM}^{5}. Note that where no limits are shown, the notation means "zero to any number of."
>
> ( ) Parentheses mean "optional." If more than one item is within the parentheses, the whole set is optional. Note that (A) can also be written as 0 {A} 1.
>
> * * Asterisks are used to enclose a comment.

The data dictionary symbols can be combined, as shown in the following example:

= ([DATA ITEM A | DATA ITEM B])   means   is composed of either DATA ITEM A
                                                or DATA ITEM B
                                                or neither.

= DATA ITEM A + ({ DATA ITEM B })   means   is composed of DATA ITEM A
                                                and optional occurrences of
                                                DATA ITEM B.

DATA DICTIONARY
DEFINITIONS

A

Acceptance Test Completion Report = * Documents the formal completion of all (or each major phase) of the acceptance testing for the new system *

= Estimated Support Resources for Acceptance Testing +
Support Resources Actually Used for Acceptance Testing +
(Problems Encountered During Acceptance Testing)

Acceptance Test Material = * The user-supplied, executable information for an acceptance test unit *

For composition, see "Test Material."

Access Description = Access Method +
Access Requirements

Access Method = * A description of a data access technique, such as sequential, direct, indexed, or a combination of these. For an automated portion of the system, additional multi-record accessing implementation may be identified, such as chains, rings, or inverted lists *

Access Requirements = * Data usage requirements that affect accessing *

= Security +
Frequency/Periodicity +
(Access Time Range)

Access Time Range = * The normal-to-maximum access time for a data object, access path, or record *

Accessibility Times = * The times of the day that a data processing environment can be accessed, for example, special security hours *

Activity X Estimated and Actual Resources = * The cost, time, people, and materials estimated and actually used to accomplish a particular activity *

Activity X Resource Approval = * Approval from appropriate management to use resources for the next major activity. Approval should be in the form of a formal memo *

Activity 1 Plan = * The plan for accomplishing the project initiation tasks *

For composition, see "Plan."

Activity 2 Plan = * The plan for accomplishing the preliminary analysis and design tasks *

For composition, see "Plan."

Activity 3 Plan = * The plan for accomplishing the general analysis and design tasks *

For composition, see "Plan."

Activity 4 Plan = * The plan for accomplishing the detailed analysis and design tasks *

For composition, see "Plan."

Activity 5 Plan = * The plan for accomplishing the tasks in Activity 5 that are not covered by an implementation plan *

For composition, see "Plan."

Activity 6 Plan = * The plan for accomplishing the tasks in Activity 6 that are not covered by an implementation plan *

For composition, see "Plan."

Additional Evaluation Data = Affected Systems +

Project Goals +

Resolutions/Priorities +

Gross Benefits

Affected Automated System = * An automated area that may be affected by the project goals *

= Affected System Identification +

(Affected System Representative)

Affected Manual System = * A manual area that may be affected by the project goals *

= Affected System Identification +
(Affected System Representative)

Affected Plans and Resources = * Existing data processing plans and resources that will be affected by this project, such as lower priority projects and available resources *

Affected System = [Affected Manual System |
Affected Automated System]

Analysis Goal Solution = * A project goal solution identified in analysis; that is, a project goal that can be accommodated by a new function/data content, or by a change in function/data content, or by a change to the manual/automated environment boundary *

= [Solution Description |
Solution Reference Point]

Application Maintenance Contact = * An individual or department to contact for support or maintenance of the automated portion of the system *

Application Module = * A unit of computer software that is developed in-house to support an application *

Application Program = * An executable unit of computer software that is developed in-house to support an application. Programs are normally defined as consisting of many modules *

Note: The application program could also be obtained as a vendor package.

Application System Controls = * The language used to control computer-executable software that is developed in-house to support an application, for example, JCL, sort/merge parameters, PSB GENS, and so on *

Note: Application system controls could also be obtained as part of a vendor package.

Automated Data Dictionary = * The data dictionary that defines data in the automated environment *

For composition, see "Physicalized Data Dictionary."

Automated Design Goal Solution = * A solution to the project goal relating to the design of the automated environment *

= [Solution Description |
Solution Reference Point]

Automated Documentation = * The subset of the system maintenance information that applies to the automated portions of the system *

For composition, see "System Maintenance Information," which acknowledges that what was identified as "new" becomes "current" for a system restudy.

Automated Logical Model = * A logical specification of the automated portions of the system *

= {Logical Leveled Data Flow Diagram} +
Logical Data Dictionary +
{Logical Process Description}

Automated Process Description = * The specification of a process in the automated environment *

= (Process Identification) +
Process Name +
Process Description +
(Frequency/Periodicity of Use) +
Executing Processor Type +
(Pseudocode) +
(Source Language) +
(Process Size/Complexity) +
Cost Per Execution +
(Special Characteristics)

Automated System Installation Procedures = * The procedures needed to support the installation of the new system's application software *

Automated System Installation Support = * The support needed for installation of the new system's application software, for example, development libraries, production libraries, utility programs, installation control procedures, and so on *

Automated System Model = * A physical specification of the automated portions of the system *

= {Design Chart} +
Automated Data Dictionary +
{Automated Process Description} +
System Flowchart

B

Back-up Environment Description = * A description of alternative hardware/software environments that can be used in case of a breakdown of regular hardware/software *

Bounded New Logical Specification = * Basically a logical specification with an extra, expanded data flow diagram showing the man/machine boundary. Optionally, there can be some physical interface characteristics shown on this man/machine boundary *

= Logical Leveled Data Flow Diagram +
Expanded Data Flow Diagram +
Logical Data Dictionary +
{Logical Process Descriptions}

Business Constraint = * A business-oriented limitation on the project, such as a budget or a government-stated deadline *

Business Documentation = * Any literature or publication, such as sales publications or presentation material, that describes the functions of the system *

Business Objective = * A reason for the project, for example, to improve customer service *

Business/Support Documentation = * The maintenance and support information identifying what is accomplished by the existing system *

= [Bounded New Logical Specification |
New Logical Specification |
Business Documentation] +
Training Specification +
Regression Test Specification

C

Change Request = * A change to the new system (or a release of the new system) that could not reasonably be accommodated during the development activities *

= Requestor Identification +
Change Requested +
Reason for Change +
Known Impact on Project Goals +
Date Requested +
Priority of Change

Change Requested = * A description of the required change, which should be in the form of a project goal *

For composition, see "Project Goal."

Changes Since Last Presentation = * Changes that were made to goals, data, functions, schedules, and so on, during each major activity *

Company Hardware Environments Chart = * A diagram showing the different hardware environments (hardware groupings) at the company and how they interface with each other through channels, controllers, modems, switches, card batches, and so on. This is a high-level view of all the hardware configuration charts *

Completion Reports = Hardware/Software Installation Completion Report +

Conversion Completion Report +

Training Completion Report +

System Test Completion Report +

Acceptance Test Completion Report +

Project Completion Report

Configuration Data = Hardware/Software Environments Data +

{Hardware Specification} +

{Software Specification} +

Expected Future Hardware/Software Updates

Conversion Completion Report = * Documents the formal completion of all (or each major phase) of the data conversion for the new system *

= Estimated Resources for Conversion +

Resources Actually Used for Conversion +

(Problems Encountered During Conversion)

Conversion Data Dictionary = * The definitions of all data referenced in the conversion procedures. It is a subset of the data dictionaries of the current physical specification and the new physical specification *

Conversion Objective = * An aim of the data conversion effort, for example, synchronizing the payroll and personnel common data as part of the conversion task. The conversion objective can be requested by the system user or the project manager *

Conversion Plan = * A description of how to accomplish the data conversion requirements identified in the conversion specification *

For composition, see "Plan."

Conversion Procedures = * The procedures required to convert data from the current to the new system, that is, from manual to manual, manual to automated, automated to manual, and automated to automated. For complex or large conversion efforts, the contents of the procedure may consist of a system model (showing data flow and functions) and a design model (showing the implementation of the functions and their data coupling) *

Conversion Program = * An executable unit of computer software that is developed in-house to support the data conversion effort *

Conversion Specification = {Conversion Objective} +
{Conversion Procedures +
Conversion Support} +
Conversion Data Dictionary

Conversion Support = * The support — except for people support — needed to perform data conversion procedures other than those declared in the conversion data dictionary, for example, tapes, disks, folders, forms, utilities, production and development libraries, and so on *

Conversion System Controls = * The language used to control computer-executable software that was developed in-house to support the data conversion effort *

Conversion Test Case = * A test case for validating any part of the conversion effort *
For composition, see "Test Case."

Corporate Data Dictionary = * A set of definitions for all company data items and their relationships, which are maintained by the data administration group *

= {Data Object +
{Object Relationship}}

Corporate Data Model = * A data model for the data-administration-maintained company data *
See definition of "Data Model."

Corporate Data Specification = Corporate Data Dictionary +
Corporate Data Model +
{Data Management System Option} +
Corporate Data Storage and Access Description
Note: At a general level of study, the corporate data storage and access description is optional.

Corporate Data Storage and Access Description = * The storage and access descriptions for all data-administration-maintained company data *

For composition, see "Storage Description" and "Access Description."

Cross Reference to Current Physical Definition = * A cross reference (pointer) to the original data and physical characteristics from which an item of data was derived, for example, current physical: data flow name(s), data store name(s) *

Cross Reference to Current Physical Process(es) = * A cross reference (pointer) to the original process or processes from which a function was derived, such as, current physical process reference number and/or hardware/software ID *

Current Logical Specification = * A logical specification of the current system as a whole without delineation of manual and automated areas *

= Logical Leveled Data Flow Diagram +
Logical Data Dictionary +
{Logical Process Description}

Current Operations Manual = * Existing operations documentation describing how to operate the automated portions of the system *

For expected composition, see "Operations Manual."

Current Physical Specification = * A specification of the current system (manual and automated) showing the design used to implement it *

= Manual System Model +
Automated System Model

Current Procedures Manual = * Existing user documentation describing how to use the manual and automated portions of the system *

For expected composition, see "Procedures Manual."

Current System Description = Current Physical Specification +
Current Logical Specification +
Current System Execution Manuals

Current System Execution Manuals = Current Procedures Manual +
Current Operations Manual

Current System Test Case = * A test case for a function or a piece of data in the current logical specification *

For composition, see "Test Case."

Customized Methodology = * This methodology, tailored to fit a particular project *

D

Data Administration Library = * A merged, centralized source of the supported corporate data resources *

Data Administration Management = * The head of the database group, usually known as the DBA (database administrator) *

Data Administration Staff = * The people responsible for modeling the company's data *

Data Capture Goal Solution = * A solution to a project goal relating to the gathering of data that will be inserted into the corporate data dictionary *

= [Solution Description |
Solution Reference Point]

Data Category = * A high-level grouping of data to support a business function, for example, employee information to support the personnel functions *
Also known as a "Candidate Object."

Data Dictionary = * A set of definitions for all data items declared on a data flow diagram. It will also contain definitions for data and control items on a structure chart and in application code *

= {Data Flow} +
{Data Element} +
{Data Store} +
({Data Originator/Terminator})

Data Element = * An indivisible data flow *
Also known as a "Data Primitive."

= Data Element Name +
Data Element Description

Data Element Description = * Described by a comment or by the values or range of values that it takes on *

Data Element Integrity = * A dependency placed on a data element, for example, "order total" in "order object" is equal to the sum of the "part amounts" in the "part objects" *

Data Element Physical Characteristics
= (Physical Data Element Identification) +
Data Format +
Data Representation +
List/Range of Values +
(Special Characteristics)

Data Flow
= * A pipeline of information between processes, data stores, or data terminators. A piece of information is no longer available in the pipeline once it reaches its destination *

= Data Flow Name +
Data Flow Description

Data Flow Description
= * A data flow can be made up of other data flows and/or data elements. Therefore, a description may point to these or may describe the data flow in comment form or by the values that it takes on *

Data Flow Diagram
= * A modeling tool used to represent a system (automated, manual, or mixed). Four components — data flow, process, data store, and data originator/terminator — are represented graphically to model the system and to show its partitioning *

Data Flow Physical Characteristics
= (Physical Data Flow Identification) +
(Sample/Layout) +
Media +
Data Flow Volume +
Frequency/Periodicity of Use +
(Security) +
(Special Characteristics)

Data Format
= * The make-up of a data element, such as six characters, numbers in two decimal places, twenty characters alphanumeric, and so on *

Data Goal Solution
= * A project goal solution identified in data modeling *

= [Data Capture Goal Solution |
Data Interface Goal Solution |
Data Management Goal Solution |
Data Usage Goal Solution]

Data Interface Goal Solution
= * A solution to a project goal relating to data interface between systems *

= [Solution Description |
Solution Reference Point]

Data Management Goal Solution
= * A solution to a project goal relating to the compatibility or use of data management systems *

= [Solution Description |
Solution Reference Point]

Data Management System
= * A set of programs (manual or automated) used to store, access, and support data. For example, in an automated portion of a system, IBM's IMS with fast path feature using DL/1; in a manual portion of a system, procedures required to use an index-card system referencing tub files *

Data Management System Options
= * The existing data management systems in use at the company, or the compatible systems not currently in use at the company *

Data Model
= * A modeling tool used to represent stored data. It graphically shows individual objects (as boxes) and their relationships (as directed lines), which make up the stored data *

Also known as a "Data Structure/Access Diagram" or "Data Structure/Access Schema."

Data Object
= * A stand-alone record structure, such as class, employee, or customer, that supports a business function or functions *

= Object Description +
{Data Elements +
(Data Element Integrity)}

Data Organization
= * A description of the physical organization of stored data, for example, consecutive, random, or parallel (consecutive and random) organization *

Data Originator/ Terminator
= * An area where data originates or terminates from the point of view of the system study. It identifies a boundary of the system study *

Data Preparation/ Distribution Schedule
= * The schedule of times for data preparation and distribution in both the manual and automated portions of the system *

Data Representation   = * The way in which the data is encoded (EBCDIC/ ASCII, and so on) *

Data Specification   = Data Model +
Data Management System +
Data Storage and Access Description

Note: At a general level of study, the data storage and access description is optional.

Data Storage and Access Description   = * The data storage and access description for the system's permanent data. It is a physical view of the data and its support *

= {Storage Description} +
{Access Description}

Data Store   = * A resting place or reference place for data flows. It can physically take the form of a tape file, index-card file, folder, database, and so on *

= Data Store Name +
Data Store Description

Data Store Description   = * A data store can be described by the data flows/ records that compose it or by a data model *

Data Store Physical Characteristics   = (Physical Store Identification) +
Sample/Layout +
Storage Description +
Access Description +
(Special Characteristics)

Data Structure Diagram   = * Signifies the data model for the system before validating it against the corporate data model *
For definition, see "Data Model."
Also known as a "Data Structure/Access Diagram" or "Data Structure/Access Schema."

Data Usage Goal Solution   = * A solution to a project goal relating to data usage, for example, a solution to security requirements, response time needs, or volume needs *

= [Solution Description |
Solution Reference Point]

Dependency Network   = * A schematic showing the order in which tasks must be performed based on the flow of data, for example, a data flow diagram from the customized methodology *

Design Chart = * A model that illustrates the partitioning, hierarchy, and communication of an automated portion of the system. It can be represented by a system flowchart (for high-level view), structure chart, Jackson data structure diagram, Warnier-Orr diagram, or, in the current environment, HIPO V.T.O.C. program hierarchy *

Design Goal Solution = [Manual Design Goal Solution |
Automated Design Goal Solution |
Hardware/Software Goal Solution]

Design Test Case = * A test case for validating part of the system solution (design) *
For composition, see "Test Case."

Developing Structured Systems Guidelines = * This book or company-tailored version of this book *

Development Support Groups Used = * The support outside the project team that is available for the system, for example, the database group, technical support group, training group, and so on *

Development Support Systems = * System development aids, such as ISDOS, TSO, MFS, BTS, and so on *

Development Test Library = * A repository of all executable test material for the new system *

= {Test Material}

Development Training Materials = * The executable materials used in the training effort for the new system. The contents of the materials will vary depending on the type of system and training effort but will consist of such things as brochures/ handouts, course/lecture presentation materials, audiovisual tapes, computer training programs, test materials for training, and so on *

D.P. Management = * The people who control and approve the data processing resources *

= [Application Systems Management |
Systems Programming Management] +
Data Administration Management +
(Operations Management) +
(Quality Control Management) +
(Data Processing Audit Management) +
(Training Management)

D.P. Staff = * The data processing support staff for manual and/or automated systems *

= Maintenance Staff +
Data Administration Staff +
Operations Staff +
(Training Staff) +
(Support Planning Staff)

E

Electrical Support = * A description of the electrical support in a hardware environment, such as power supply, telephone circuits, and cable connections *

Environment Characteristics = * Information concerning the area in which the system study and installation were conducted *

= Environment Type +
Extent of User Involvement +
Development Support Groups Used +
(Special Characteristics)

Environment Conditions = * A specification of the environment conditions (temperature, humidity, ventilation, and so on) needed to support the hardware and the staff *

Environment Costs Per Year = * An estimate of the cost for support of a hardware/ software environment (if required for a cost/benefit evaluation) *

Environment Support Staff = * A description of the support staff needed for an environment housing data processing hardware and software, such as security staff or total operations staff *

Environment Type = * The area in which the system study and installation were conducted, such as the local main office, statewide divisions, nationwide divisions, worldwide divisions *

Estimated and Actual Resources = * The cost, time, people, and materials estimated and actually used to accomplish each activity of system development and installation *

Executing Processor Type = * A description of the type of hardware needed to execute a process. Particular support software may be included *

Existing Configuration Data = * The description of an existing configuration used to support manual and/or automated production systems *
For composition, see "Configuration Data."

Existing HW/SW Environments Data = * Description of the environments (throughout the company) that house hardware/software for support of manual or automated systems *

For composition, see "HW/SW Environments Data."

Expanded Data Flow Diagram = * A composite data flow diagram produced from a complete level of a set of diagrams. The level is one on which the man/machine boundary can be drawn without cutting through a process *

Expected Future HW/SW Updates = * Describes the future changes to a configuration, such as phasing out old equipment, upgrading existing equipment, waiting for equipment on order, enlarging a hardware environment, and so on *

Extensibility Space = * A description of the extensibility space in a data processing environment *

Extent of User Involvement = * The support that the user supplied during development and installation of a system, such as having a user representative on the project team, allowing minimum time for data-gathering interviews, having no knowledgeable user available for automating the system, and so on *

F

Feasibility Report = * Documents the progress of the project, provides an overview of the system documentation, and documents the resources required for the next major activity *

= Estimated Resources for This Activity +
Resources Actually Used During This Activity +
{System Option Identification +
Summary of Project Goals +
Summary of Project Goals Solutions +
Overview of System Documentation +
Changes Since Last Presentation +
Cost/Benefit Analysis +
System Limitations +
Risk Assessment +
Estimated Resources for Next Activity +
Estimated Resources for All Future Activities} +
Issues That May Affect Further Development

Final Proposal = For comments and composition, see "Feasibility Report."

Frequency/Periodicity of Use = * A description of how often and when a piece of data or a process is used *

G

Goal Priority = * The priority or importance placed on a project goal in relation to other project goals *

Gross Benefit = * The advantages gained by meeting a project goal; for instance, savings of up to X dollars in maintenance costs could be attained or customer service will exceed that of the competitors, thereby attracting more customers *

Gross Size = * The classification of the whole project by size: small, medium, or large *

Growth Space Organization = * A description of the stored data overflow organization: in the automated part of the system — chained overflow space, distributed free space, or cellular splitting; in the manual portion — an extra storage file, organized in sequential order *

H

HW Compatibility = * The identification of the types of hardware that can be connected to an identified piece of hardware *

HW Configuration Chart = * A diagram, for one environment, showing individual hardware components and how these components interface with each other using channels, controllers, modem switches, card batches, and so on *

HW Description = * Hardware can consist of processors, peripherals, data preparation and distribution equipment, optical character recognition (OCR) equipment, microfilm/fiche equipment, measurement and communication equipment *

= Hardware Vendor +
Hardware Model/Identification +
{Hardware Function} +
(Storage Capacity) +
Volume Throughput +
Data Representation Requirements +
(Special Characteristics)

HW Function = * A description of the function that a piece of hardware satisfies, for example, that communication line xyz transmits business data between the main office and all branches. Performance can also be included in this function, such as main processor X providing the power to give three-second response time during peak periods *

HW General Availability = * The number of hours or times a piece of hardware is available for general use *

HW Specification = Hardware Description +
(Hardware Compatibility Requirements) +
Hardware Status +
Hardware General Availability +
Trained Operations Staff for This Hardware +
Vendor Support Availability +
(Hardware Cost) +
Hardware Support Costs Per Year

HW Status = * An indication of whether a piece of hardware is already installed and being used by other projects, already installed and being used by the current system, or is new hardware (indicate installed or on order) *

HW Support Materials = * Materials needed to support the new system hardware. This material is identified as support for installation of hardware but can be used for on-going support. Examples of hardware support materials are tapes, disks, printer ribbons, folders and storage for them, office furniture for operations, vendor support documentation, hardware cleaning equipment, moving equipment, and so on. (Support material is not already identified in the hardware/software specification.) *

HW Support Procedures = * Procedures needed to support the installation of the new system hardware, for example, arrangements for moving hardware, vendor hardware installation procedures, store and media identification, hardware testing procedures *

HW/SW Data = * Informal documentation of hardware and software, which a vendor can supply. This documentation is least specific at the preliminary level and most specific at the detailed level, for example, a range of vendor products at preliminary level versus specific documentation of a particular product at detailed level *

For possible composition, see "HW Specification" and "SW Specification."

HW/SW Environment Description = Environment Identification +
Site Description +
(Environment Support Staff) +
Back-up Environment Description +
(Environment Costs Per Year)

HW/SW Environments Data = Company Hardware Environments Chart +
{Hardware/Software Environment Description +
Hardware Configuration Chart}

HW/SW Goal Solution = * A solution to a project goal relating to the hardware and support software used for the new system *

= [Solution Description |
Solution Reference Point]

HW/SW Installation Completion Report = * Documents the formal completion of the installation of all (or each major phase) of the hardware/software for the new system *

= Estimated Resources for Hardware/Software Installation +
Resources Actually Used for Hardware/Software Installation
(Problems Encountered During Hardware/Software Installation)

HW/SW Installation Objective = * An aim of the hardware/software installation effort, which can be requested by the system user or the project manager; for instance, the hardware/software must be installed before the training effort begins so actual hardware/software can be used to train the users *

HW/SW Installation Plan = * A description of how to accomplish the hardware/software installation requirements identified in the hardware/software installation specification *

For composition, see "Plan."

HW/SW Installation Specification = {Hardware/Software Installation Objective} +
{Hardware/Software Environment Description +
Hardware Configuration Chart} +
{Hardware Support Procedures +
Hardware Support Materials} +
{Software Support Procedures +
Software Support Materials}

HW/SW Maintenance Contact   = * Identification of and access to the representative to contact for maintenance of the system hardware or support software *

HW/SW Order   = * A formal request for the purchase or lease of hardware and/or software *

HW/SW Proposal   = * Formal proposal to supply the new system's hardware and/or software needs *

HW/SW Specification   = * A specification of all the hardware and support software (not application software) needed to support the new system. This can be made up of existing or new hardware and software *

= {Hardware Specification} +
{Software Specification} +
Hardware/Software Data from Vendors

I

Implementation Goal Solution   = *A solution to a project goal relating to conversion, training, hardware/software and system installation or testing *

= [Solution Description |
Solution Reference Point]

Implementation Language   = * The software language used to program *

Implementation Plans   = System Installation Plan +
Hardware/Software Installation Plan +
Conversion Plan +
Training Plan +
Test Plan

Implementation Report   = * Documents the progress of the project and the resources required for the next major activity *

= Estimated Resources for Activity 5 +
Resources Actually Used During Activity 5 +
Changes Since Last Presentation +
(Initial Test Results) +
Estimated Data Processing Resources for Activity 6 +
Estimated User Resources for Activity 6 +
Issues That May Affect Further Development

Implementation Specifications	= System Installation Specification + Hardware/Software Installation Specification + Conversion Specification + Training Specification + Test Specification
Independent Review Report	= * The documentation of the results of an independent review * For composition, see "Review Report."
Initial Context Diagram	= * Basically identifies the boundary of the system by declaring the external areas that supply or receive system data *
Initial Production Information	= * A summary of monitored production information * = {Production Factor Identification + {Production Factor Problem} + Production Factor Summary + Production Factor Usage Pattern}
Initial Proposal	= * Documents the progress of the project, provides an overview of the system documentation, and documents the resources required for the next major activity * For composition, see "Feasibility Report."
Interview Note	= * The information-gathering documentation for the existing system. This can be in the form of a data flow diagram, design chart, graph, decision table or tree, structured English, narrative, report layout, record layout, and so on *

J

Job Backup/Recovery	= * The back-up procedures with the support materials and the procedures necessary to restart a job/job step from a system abend (including disaster recovery procedures) *
Job Environment	= * The support environment for an executable unit in the automated system, for example, hardware needs, support software needs, back-up environment options, and so on *

Job Schedules/Procedures   = * The run instructions for an executable unit in the automated system, for example, run times, operating instructions, system parameter updates, system action messages, and so on *

Job Security   = * The security requirements for each job/job step in the automated system, for example, that special tape files should be kept in the safe when not in use or that printed output be seen only by security-cleared personnel *

Job/Job Step Description   = * An overview description of an executable unit in the automated system *

K

No Entry

L

Logical Data Dictionary   = * A set of definitions for all data items declared on a logical data flow diagram *

= {Logical Data Flow} +
{Logical Data Element} +
Data Model +
({Logical Data Store}) +
({Data Originator/Terminator})

Logical Data Element   = * A data element with its physical characteristics removed *

= Data Element +
Cross Reference to Current Physical Definition

Logical Data Flow   = * A data flow with physical characteristics removed *

= Data Flow +
Cross Reference to Current Physical Definition

Logical Data Store = * A data store with physical characteristics removed *

= Data Store +
Cross Reference to Current Physical Definition

Logical Leveled Data Flow Diagram = * A leveled set of data flow diagrams that form a model of a system (manual, automated, or both). This model describes what the system is doing without regard to how it does it (that is, without physical characteristics or control) *

For comment, see "Data Flow Diagram."

Logical Modification = * An addition, change, or deletion of a current function and/or data content (including a complete new function and data). The modification is represented in logical form, for example, logical data flow diagram, decision table or tree, and so on *

= Identification of Modification +
{Data Flow Diagram Change} +
{Data Dictionary Change} +
{Process Description Change}

Logical Process Description = * The specification of a process or function, which is declared on a logical data flow diagram, with physical references and control removed *

= Process Description +
Cross Reference to Current Physical Process(es)

M

Maintenance Contact = * The identification of an individual or department to contact for maintaining or modifying the manual or automated portions of the system *

Maintenance Library = * The library containing the system maintenance information for the manual and automated portions of systems *

Maintenance Plan = * The plan for accomplishing any identified changes and for generally supporting the new system *

For composition, see "Plan."

**Maintenance Resource
Approval**

= * The approval from appropriate management for the use of resources for maintenance. Approval should be in the form of a formal memo *

Major HW/SW Used

= * The major configuration used to support the system, for example, large-scale processor, minicomputers, microcomputers, and so on *

Management

= User Management +
Data Processing Management

**Manual Design Goal
Solution**

= * A solution to a project goal relating to the design of the manual environment *

= [Solution Description |
Solution Reference Point]

Manual Documentation

= * The subset of the system maintenance information that applies to the manual portions of the system *

For composition, see "System Maintenance Information," which acknowledges that what was identified as "new" becomes "current" for a system restudy.

**Manual HW/SW
Operating Instructions**

= * The operating documentation (probably supplied by the vendor) for the hardware and support software used in the manual environment *

Manual Logical Model

= * A logical specification of the manual portions of the system *

= {Logical Leveled Data Flow Diagram} +
Logical Data Dictionary +
{Logical Process Description}

**Manual System
Installation Procedures**

= * The procedures needed to support the installation of the new system's manual activities *

**Manual System
Installation Support**

= * The support needed for installation of the new system's manual procedures, for example, office layout, new office furniture and equipment (including furniture and equipment needing relocation), moving equipment and support, and so on *

Manual System Model

= * A physicalized specification of the manual portions of the system *

= {Physicalized Leveled Data Flow Diagram} +
Physicalized Data Dictionary +
{Physicalized Process Description} +
(Organizational Hierarchy)

Min-Max Volumes = * An estimate of the number of minimum and maximum occurrences of data objects or records *

Module Name = * A verb-object name that states a module's function *

N

New Automated System Model = * The automated system model for the new system *

For composition, see "Automated System Model."

New Logical Model = * A logical specification of the new system as a whole without delineation of manual and automated subsystems *

= Logical Leveled Data Flow Diagram +
Logical Data Dictionary +
{Logical Process Description}

New Operations Manual = * The operations manual supporting the new system *

For comments and composition, see "Operations Manual."

New Physical Specification = * A specification of the new system (manual and automated) showing the design used to implement it *

= Manual System Model +
Automated System Model

New Procedures Manual = * The procedures manual supporting the new system *

For comments and composition, see "Procedures Manual."

New System Description = Bounded New Logical Specification +
New Physical Specification +
New System Execution Manuals +
Implementation Specifications

Note: The system execution manuals are optional at the preliminary level.

New System Execution Manuals = New Procedures Manual +
New Operations Manual

New System Test Case   = * A test case for a function, an item of data, or the validation of the man/machine boundary in the new system *

For composition, see "Test Case."

Number of New System Staff/Procedures   = * Intended to show the amount of manual effort required for the new system. The number of new system staff/procedures can be categorized as operations staff, data preparation staff, user staff, and so on *

Number/Type of Changes During Development   = * The number of changes within type that were accommodated during development of the system, for example, major project goal change, minor data format change, major hardware interface change, and so on *

O

Object Description   = * A description of the company policy for a data object/entity *

= Object Name +
Object Function +
Object Primary Key +
{Object Secondary Key} +
Object Integrity +
(Object Special Rules)

Object Function   = * A description of why a data object exists, that is, what the function of the object is. For instance, for a department object, department is a subdivision of the company that accomplishes a unit of work *

Object Integrity   = * A constraint placed on a data object. For example, between employee and department objects, each employee is assigned to only one department *

Object Primary Key   = * The data attribute (or combination of attributes) that is used to uniquely identify a data object, for example, department number to identify a department *

Object Relationship   = * An association or correspondence between objects, consisting of a description of the relationship. For instance, between company object and employee object, the relationship is that the company employs an employee *

Object Secondary Key = * A data attribute (other than the object primary key data attribute) that can be used for identification of a data object, such as social security number instead of employee number to identify or retrieve the employee object *

Object Special Rules = * Any special rules governing a data object, for example, that an employee may be full- or part-time staff but not an outside consultant *

Operations Manual = * The documentation needed for the computer operations staff to operate and control the automated portions of the system *

= System Overview +
Operations Support ⊢
System Flowchart +
Data Preparation/Distribution Schedule +
{Job/Job Step Description +
Job Schedules/Procedures +
Job Environment +
Job Backup/Recovery +
Job Security} +
Application Maintenance Contact +
Hardware/Software Maintenance Contact

Operations Staff = * The people who support/control the execution of the automated system *

Operations Support = * The support that the operations area needs to provide for the system, for example, number of support staff, staff skill level, staff availability, and so on *

Opinions on Project and New System = * Informal notes about the project activities and the resulting new system or about a release of the new system. The notes include all factors, such as communication difficulties, disruptions, smoothness of system installation, ease of training, usability of the new system, and so forth *

Organizational Hierarchy = * The chart or charts showing the superordinate-subordinate relationships of the people in the manual environments that are affected by the project *

Outside Support Required = * The services/materials required from outside the project team and its available materials, for example, text processing, machine time, special software support, and so on *

Overall D.P. Plans and Resources = * The current and long-term plans of the data processing department, showing the allocation of current data processing resources *

= {Project Identification +
Project Priority +
Project Status +
Project Plan Summary}

Overall Schedule = * A schematic showing the desired start and completion dates for processes and their deliverables *

Overall Strategy = * The technique by which a goal will be accomplished, for example, that testing will be accomplished using boundary-value analysis or that all training will be performed in-house with workshop courses *

P

Packaged Data Model = * A data model represented in a hierarchical structure, network structure, or relational structure. (Although the packaged data model has some physical characteristics, it still represents a logical view of the data.) *

Past Project Histories = * Documentation of past projects for use in evaluating and planning future projects *

= {Project Identification +
Project Characteristics +
System Characteristics +
Environment Characteristics +
Project Completion Report}

Physicalized Data Dictionary = * A set of definitions for all data items declared on a physical data flow diagram *

= {Data Flow +
Data Flow Physical Characteristics} +
{Data Element +
Data Element Physical Characteristics} +
{Data Store +
Data Store Physical Characteristics} +
{Data Originator/Terminator}

Physicalized Leveled Data
Flow Diagram

= * A leveled set of data flow diagrams that form a model of a physical manual environment. This model basically represents a logical view of the environment but is annotated with physical characteristics to aid verification by the user *

For comment, see "Data Flow Diagram."

Physicalized Process
Description

= * The specification of a process/function declared on a physical data flow diagram *

= Process Description +
Process Physical Characteristics

Plan

= * A generic definition for all plans *

= Overall Strategy +
Dependency Network +
Overall Schedule +
{Process Identification +
Completion Criteria +
Skill Level Required +
(Support Material Required) +
Outside Support Required +
Process Actual Start Date +
Process Actual End Date +
Estimated Person Days +
Actual Person Days +
Estimated Task Cost +
Actual Task Cost +
Person/Group Allocated}

Problem to Be Solved

= * Existing system fault to be solved, for instance, that system maintenance costs are too high, or that downtime is unacceptable *

Procedures Manual

= * The documentation needed to use the manual portions of the system. It is mostly a physical packaging of information in the manual system model and hardware/software specification *

= Manual System Model +
Data Management System +
Data Preparation/Distribution Schedule +
Manual Hardware/Software Operating Instructions +
Maintenance Contact

Process Description = * The specification of a process declared on a data flow diagram *

= Process Name +
[Process Notes |
Process Specification]

Process Notes = * Used for high-level data flow diagram processes until lower component processes are defined. They are informal descriptions used when component data flow diagrams have not been completed *

Process Physical Characteristics = [Process Performed By |
Job Title] +
(Skill Level Required) +
(Frequency/Periodicity of Use) +
Yearly Operating Costs +
(Special Characteristics)

Process Specification = * A formal specification of the business policy for data transformation. This can take the form of a decision table or tree, a graph, other nonlinguistic forms (such as a Nassi-Shneiderman diagram), structured English, narrative, and so on *

Processing Mode = * The method of computing such as batch, on-line, or real-time *

Production and Maintenance Libraries = Production Procedures Library +
Production Program Library +
Production Stores +
Production Hardware/Software +
Data Administration Library +
Maintenance Library

Production Factor Identification = * The identification of a factor for production monitoring. There will be many different factors depending on the type of project and its goals. Factors include performance, maintainability, security, usability of manuals, usability of hardware, accuracy of results, and down-time *

Production Factor Problem = * An individual problem found for a monitored production factor *

**Production Factor
Summary**

= * A summary of data from a monitored production factor. Its content will vary depending on the factor. Performance factors include slowest response time, mean response time, fastest response time. Security factors include ease or difficulty of use, number of violations, type of violations *

**Production Factor Usage
Pattern**

= * The usage pattern for a monitored production factor. The documentation for this usage pattern will vary depending on the factor; for instance, it can be formal for database usage and number of bugs per program, or informal, such as explaining the reluctance of users to operate a particular terminal *

Production HW/SW

= * The actual hardware and support software used in the production environment *

**Production HW/SW
Inventory**

= * A complete, up-to-date inventory of all data processing hardware and support software (not application software) and the support environments that are available in-house. The inventory consists of hardware and software to support both manual and automated production environments *

= {Configuration Data}

**Production Procedures
Library**

= * The library containing the support documentation for the manual procedures of systems *

= {System Identification +
Procedures Manual +
Operations Manual}

Production Program

= * An executable unit of computer software developed in-house to support an application *

Note: It could also be obtained as a vendor package.

**Production Program
Library**

= * The library containing the executable software of systems *

= {Production Program} +
{Production System Controls}

**Production Program
Listings**

= * The latest printouts of the production programs *

Production Stores

= * The stores that contain the manual and automated data in the production environment, for example, manual reports/tables, automated stored data, transaction form layouts, and so on *

Production System   = {Production Program +
                                          Production System Controls} +
                                          System Maintenance Information +
                                          Converted Manual and Automated Data +
                                          Relocated and New Hardware/Software

Production System   = * The language used to control the computer-executable
Controls   software of a system, for example, JCL, sort/merge
                                          parameters, PSB GENS, and so on *

Production System   = * The latest printouts of the production system con-
Controls Listings   trols *

Program Name   = * A verb-object name stating a program's function *

Project Actual Resources   = * The total money, time, people, and materials actually
                                          used for the project *

Project Characteristics   = * Project information for a system development effort *

                                          = Project Type +
                                          Gross Size +
                                          Risk Assessment +
                                          Project Methodology +
                                          Structured Techniques +
                                          Number of Walkthroughs/Reviews +
                                          Development Support Systems +
                                          Number of Project Team Members +
                                          Skill Level of Project Team Members +
                                          Estimated and Actual Resources +
                                          (Special Characteristics)

Project Charter   = * The project contract or objective, which includes the
                                          reason for doing the project *

                                          = 1{Project Goal +
                                          Goal Priority +
                                          {Project Goal Solution}} +
                                          {Gross Benefit} +
                                          Gross Size +
                                          Risk Assessment

Project Completion Report = * The material that documents the formal completion of the new system or a release of the new system *

= Summary of Project Goals +
Summary of Project Goals Solutions +
Initial Production Information +
Summary of Project Team Performance +
Project Estimated Resources +
Project Actual Resources +
Project Estimated Gross Size +
Project Actual Size +
(Recommendations for Future Projects)

Project Estimated Resources = * The total money, time, people, and materials estimated for the project *

Project Evaluation Data = Initial Context Diagram +
{Affected System} +
{Project Goal +
{Gross Benefit}} +
Gross Size +
Risk Assessment

Project Goal = * An aim or requirement of the system *

= (Goal Requestor) +
[Business Objective |
Business Constraint |
System Objective |
System Constraint |
Problem to Be Solved]

Project Goal Solution = * A solution to a project goal, identified during system development *

= [Analysis Goal Solution |
Data Goal Solution |
Design Goal Solution |
Implementation Goal Solution]

Project Initiation Report   = * Documents the progress of the project and the resources required for the next major activity *

= Initial Context Diagram +
{Affected System} +
Summary of Major Project Goals +
Summary of Gross Benefits +
Gross Size +
Risk Assessment +
Summary of Development Approach +
Estimated Resources for Activity 1 +
Actual Resources Used for Activity 1 +
Estimated Resources for Activity 2 +
(Estimated Resources for All Future Activities) +
Issues That May Affect the Project

Project Plan   = Customized Methodology +
Activity 1 Plan +
Activity 2 Plan +
Activity 3 Plan +
Activity 4 Plan +
Activity 5 Plan +
Activity 6 Plan +
Implementation Plans

Project Plan Summary   = * A summary of the plans for a project, showing which, if any, activity is in progress, the resources being used, and future resources needed *

Project Priority   = * The importance of a project in relation to all data processing projects and/or in relation to other projects of a requestor *

Project Request   = * The request for system support *

= Requestor Identification +
Date Submitted +
{Project Goal} +
{Gross Benefit} +
{Affected System} +
Project Priority +
(User Representative)

Project Status   = * The state of a project, for example, deferred start date, under review, active, and so on *

Project Type   = * A project designation such as new system, rewrite, conversion, modification, and so on *

Q

No Entry

R

Recommendations for Future Projects   = * Any recommendations from data processing personnel and users that can aid future releases or entire project development, such as recommending that a user representative be a member of the project team for future projects *

Regression Test Library   = * The library containing the minimum executable test materials required to validate the system's data and functions *

= {Test Material}

Regression Test Specification   = * The specification of the minimum test cases required to validate the system's data and functions *

= {Test Case}

Request for Proposal   = * A request for formal proposals to supply hardware and/or support software *

= [Hardware Description |
Software Description] +
([Hardware Compatibility Requirements |
Software Compatibility Requirements]) +
Type of Contract Required +
Delivery Schedule +
Delivery Location +
Vendor Support Requirements

Resolutions/Priorities = * Support information for conflicting or unprioritized project goals *

Reusable Test Materials = * The executable test units that can be reused from the current regression test library *

For composition, see "Test Material."

Reusable Training Materials = * The development training materials that can be reused from the current system or from the available company training materials *

For composition, see "Development Training Materials."

Review Report = * Documentation of the result of a review *

= Identification of Reviewed Material +
Review Data +
{Review Participant} +
Review Summary +
{Review Recommendation}

Revised Plans and Resources = * The affected overall data processing plans and resources updated to allow for the project's next major activity *

Risk Assessment = * A statement of the business-oriented and technical probability of meeting the project goals *

= Overall Assessment of Risk +
{High-Risk Project Goal +
High-Risk Reason}

S

Safety Precautions = * A description of the safety details for an environment, for example, fire exits, smoke and water detectors, sprinkler systems, first-aid equipment, and so on *

Sample/Layout = * An example of an item of data, for instance, invoice form, check, report/screen/record layout, transaction form, and so on *

Selected System Option(s) = * The identification of areas for further study *

= {Affected System} +
{System Option Identification +
System Option Priority}

Selected System(s) Plans = * The plans that apply only to the selected system option(s) *

Selected System(s) Project Goals = * The project goals that apply only to the selected system option(s) *

Site Description = * A description of the physical environment housing data processing hardware *

= Site Layout +
(Extensibility Space) +
Electrical Support +
Environment Conditions +
Safety Precautions +
Accessibility Times

Site Layout = * The physical layout of the hardware and the connective cables between pieces of hardware, as well as the work space needed within this location *

Solution Description = * A brief description of a solution to a project goal *

Solution Reference Point = * An identification — for example, page, diagram, or process reference number — in a specification (or specifications) in which the solution is incorporated *

Special Characteristics = * A general component in a definition, used for documenting any other relevant information *

Staff = * Staff comprises management, users, and data processing people. Staff can include management, but management does not include staff *

= Management +
User Staff +
Data Processing Staff

Storage Description = Storage Media +
Data Organization +
Min-Max Volumes +
(Storage Growth Space) +
(Growth Space Organization)

Storage Growth Space = * The amount of storage allowed for overflow data *

Suggested Tailoring for Guidelines = * Improvements to the system development methodology, which should be identified by type and size of project. Heuristics can be included. (A support group should evaluate these suggestions.) *

Support Material Required = * The material needed to accomplish a process (if not already identified in a specification), for example, review facilities, presentation materials, and so on *

Support Planning Staff = * A general category of people who provide support for the data processing area, such as for hardware/software planning or technical services *

SW Description = * A summary of the software, such as operating systems, compilers, optimizers, program generators, data management systems, report packages, general packages, utility programs, all development libraries, and so on *

= (SW Vendor/Supplier) +
SW Identification +
{SW Function} +
Data Representation Requirements +
(SW/SW Requirements +
(SW/HW Requirements) +
(Special Characteristics)

SW Function = * The function that the software provides, for example, packages providing the user of the system with the ability to do ad hoc inquiry. Performance can be included with the function, such as the interface software providing five-second response times at any terminal *

SW Specification = SW Description +
(SW Compatibility Requirements) +
SW Status +
SW Availability +
SW Support Staff +
(SW Cost) +
SW Support Costs Per Year

SW Status = * An indication of whether the software is already installed and being used by other projects, is already installed and being used by the current system, or is new software (indicate installed or on order) *

SW Support Materials = * Materials needed to back up the new system support software. The materials are identified as support for installation of the software but can be used for on-going support. Examples of software support materials are tapes, disks, index cards and storage for them, vendor support documentation, interface hardware/software simulators, and so on. (This is material not identified in the hardware/software specification.) *

SW Support Procedures = * The procedure needed to support the installation of the system software, for example, tape/disk initialization, vendor software installation procedures including SYSGEN, library creation/update, software testing procedures, and so on *

SW Support Staff = * A description of the support staff available for the software *

= (Vendor-Provided Support) +
In-House Support Available +
Support Availability Times

SW/HW Requirements = * Dependencies on any hardware used to support the software, such as a maximum number of terminals that can be hooked to a package or a minimum machine capacity of one-half megabyte to support software *

SW/SW Requirements = * Dependencies on any software interfacing with the software, such as needing DL/1 to interface application programs with IMS/DC or VSAM in order to use the package *

System Characteristics = * System summary information, which will vary for each type of system *

= System Type +
Processing Mode +
System Overview +
System Organization +
{Data Management System} +
Overall System Complexity +
Quality of Original Documentation +
Number of Affected Manual Systems +
Extent of Affect on Manual Systems +
Number of Affected Automated Systems +
Extent of Affect on Automated Systems +
{Implementation Language} +
Number of New System Programs/Modules/Lines of Code +
Number of New System Staff/Procedures +
Major Hardware/Software Used +
Number/Type of Changes During Development +
(Special Characteristics)

System Constraint = * A limitation on the system solution, for example, that IMS be used as the database management system or that the system must provide distributed, rather than centralized, processing *

System Controls = * The language used to control computer-executable software *

System Flowchart = * A diagram showing the control sequence for the separately executed processes in the automated environment *

System Installation Objective = * An aim of the system installation effort, which can be requested by the system user or the project manager, such as insuring that the installation of a system does not cause delays in customer service *

System Installation Plan = * A description of how to accomplish the system installation requirements identified in the system installation specification *

For composition, see "Plan."

System Installation Specification = {System Installation Objective} +
{Automated System Installation Procedures +
Automated System Installation Support} +
{Manual System Installation Procedures +
Manual System Installation Support} +
{System Maintenance Installation Procedures +
System Maintenance Information Identification}

System Limitation = * A characteristic of the system that could potentially reduce its effectiveness; for example, the upper volume of transactions before performance (response time) is degraded *

System Maintenance Information = * The information needed to maintain the system (manual and/or automated) in production *

= Bounded New Logical Specification +
New Physical Specification +
New System Execution Manuals +
Production Program Listings +
Production System Controls Listings +
Regression Test Specification +
Regression Test Library +
Maintenance Plan +
Training Specification +
Training Materials +
Production Hardware/Software Inventory

System Maintenance Installation Procedures = * The procedures needed to support the installation of the new system maintenance information *

System Objective = * A requirement of the system solution, for example, that the stock reordering function must be included in the automated system or that inquiry-response time must be within five seconds *

System Organization = * The processing of the system can be centralized, decentralized, or distributed *

System Overview = * A brief description of the system, which can be a subset of the new physical specification or a narrative description *

System Release Archives = * A store for documentation that is no longer in use *

System Simulators = * Hardware and/or software that simulates the actual new system hardware and software, including simulated application software *

System Support = * The identification of a portion of the actual new system, which will be used for support *

System Test Completion Report = * Documents the formal completion of all (or each major phase) of the system testing for the new system *

= Estimated Resources for System Test +
Resources Actually Used for System Test +
Problems Encountered During System Test

System Type = * The type of application that the system supports, for example, stock control, payroll, compiler, support package, and so on *

System/Interview Data = {Interview Note} +
{Transformation Note} +
{Project Goal} +
Acceptance Test Materials +
Production Data +
Opinions on Project and New System

T

Test Case	= * A generic definition for all types of test cases *
	= Test Identification + Test Case Objective + Test Input Definition + Expected Execution + Expected Output + (Test Dependency) + (Test Environment)
Test Case Objective	= * An aim of an individual test, such as a customer-delete transaction that should remove customer billing and accounting information but not history information *
Test Dependency	= * A factor that a test is dependent upon, such as a cross-edit test to be executed on valid data, where normal field edits must have been applied *
Test Environment	= An environment that a test is dependent upon, for instance, real or simulated hardware/software, stores, or support tools *
Test Input Definition	= * The definition of test input data. It should be specific enough to build executable test data from, such as a completed transaction form *
Test Material	= * The executable information for a test unit *
	= Test Set Identification + Test Set Data + Test Set Scaffold + (Test Instructions)
Test Plan	= * Description of how to accomplish the testing requirements identified in the test specification * For composition, see "Plan."
Test Set Data	= * The executable test data for a test unit. For the automated environment, it will be machine executable, such as transaction input data or test files *
Test Set Identification	= * The test case identification, if this is for one test case, or identification of the test cases which it was developed from *

Test Set Instructions = * The instructions for executing a test unit, for example, that the user terminal must be used at noon to enter a test set ten times *

Test Set Scaffold = * The executable support needed for a test unit, for example, stub modules, driver modules, JCL, dummy printed forms, and so on *

Test Specification = {Testing Objective} +
{Current System Test Case} +
{New System Test Case} +
{Design Test Case} +
{Conversion Test Case} +
{System-Test Test Case} +
Testing Support

Testing Objective = * An aim of the testing effort, which applies to the whole system or a major part of the system, for example, back-up/recovery procedures that should return the system on-line within one hour *

Testing Support = * The support (excluding people support) needed to perform the testing effort, for instance, tapes, disks, test data generators, test libraries, hardware/software simulators, and so on *

Training Category = * A group of people requiring training for the new system, such as employees in data preparations or operations, users, special hardware/software operators, and so on *

Training Completion Report = * The material that documents the formal completion of all (or each major phase) of the training for the new system *

= Estimated Resources for Training +
Resources Actually Used for Training +
(Problems Encountered During Training)

Training Distribution = * A description of the distribution of training for the whole training effort or for a unit of training, for instance, centralized in the company's main training facility or localized at each division's training facility *

Training Documentation = * The description of the materials needed to support a unit of training, for example, identification of execution manuals, new system overview, hardware/software manuals, note pads, and so on *

Training Facilities	= * The environment required for a unit of training, such as a classroom, lecture room, dining facilities, and so on *
Training Level	= * The level of training required to support the new system, such as an overview for management, an overall familiarity for supervisors, working detail for staff, and so on. It can include training an individual in totally new procedures or changing existing procedures *
Training Number	= * The number of people requiring training. It can be an overall estimate at preliminary level or a specific number in a specific course at detailed level *
Training Objective	= * An aim of the training effort, which can be requested by the system user or the project manager, for instance, that training support be provided at each major division of the company *
Training Plan	= * A description of how to accomplish the training requirements identified in the training specification * For composition, see "Plan."
Training Requirement	= Training Category + Training Level + Training Number + (Training Distribution)
Training Specification	= {Training Objective} + {Training Requirement + Training Support}
Training Support	= * The training support that will be provided for the new system, excluding people support * = Training Type + Training Unit Description + Training Documentation + Training Facilities + (System Support) + (System Simulators)
Training Type	= * The type of training provided to satisfy a training requirement, for example, lecture, workshop, audiovisual equipment, textbook, on-the-job training, training in a pilot project, and so on *

Training Unit Description = * A description of a unit of training, such as training objectives, the content of a course or lecture, instructor's procedures, and so on *

Transformation Note = * The interview documentation that confirms and supports the transformation from a physical to a logical model. This can take the form of an updated data flow diagram, graph, decision table or tree, structured English, or narrative *

Type of Contract Required = * The required terms of purchase, such as fixed-price purchase, special bulk-discount contract, long-term lease, and so on *

U

User Management = * The requestors and owners of the system and the people who control and approve the user resources. (User management may also be responsible for the approval of the total system resources.) *

User Staff = * The people who use the existing system or perform system functions or who will use or perform system functions for the new system, including data preparation and distribution staff *

V

Vendor = * An outside supplier of hardware, software, or training support *

Vendor Support Requirements = * The support expected from a vendor *

= [Hardware Support Materials |
Software Support Materials |
Vendor Training Materials] +
([Hardware Support Procedures |
Software Support Procedures]) +
Vendor Staff Availability

Vendor Training Materials = * The development training materials supplied by vendors of hardware/software or of training support *

For composition, see "Development Training Materials."

W, X, Y, Z

No Entry

ADDENDUM TO DATA DICTIONARY

To avoid repetitious definitions in the data dictionary, I have identified generic definitions for some of the more complex specifications that are cycled through in this methodology and have indicated the level of detail at which each component item is identified. These generic definitions should be used in conjunction with the data dictionary. When two or more levels of detail are indicated for the same item, refer to the appropriate process description (pages 143-301) that creates that part of the specification for further clarification. Generic definitions are specified in a table of contents format for the manual system model, the automated system model, and the logical specification on the following pages. The level at which the contents are complete can be preliminary, general, or detailed, and is indicated by a P, G, or D, respectively, in the right-hand columns.

Sample Table of Contents for a MANUAL SYSTEM MODEL

*Current/New Environment**

- ■ **Physicalized Leveled Data Flow Diagram(s):**

P	G	D

Levels developed incrementally: P G D

- ■ **Physicalized Data Dictionary:**
- □ For each major data flow (documents/transaction streams):

	P	G	D
○ Data flow name	P		
○ Data flow description (optional)	P		
○ Physical data flow ID (if different from name)	P		
○ Media	P		
○ Data flow volume	P		
○ Frequency/periodicity of use	P		
○ Security (if applicable to whole stream)	P		
○ Special characteristics (optional)	P		

  - □ For each component data flow (documents/transactions):

	P	G	D
○ Data flow name	P		
○ Data flow description (optional)		G	
○ Physical data flow ID (if different from name)		G	
○ Sample/layout (optional) (at detailed level in new environment)		G	
○ Media (if different from whole stream)		G	
○ Data flow volume		G	
○ Frequency/periodicity (if different from whole stream)		G	
○ Security (optional)		G	
○ Special characteristics (optional)		G	

    - □ For each data element (fields/attributes):

	P	G	D
○ Data element name		G	
○ Data element description			D
○ Physical data element ID (optional)			D
○ Data format			D
○ Data representation			D
○ List/range of values			D
○ Special characteristics (optional)			D

- □ For each major data store (files):

	P	G	D
○ Data store name	P		
○ Data store description	P		
○ Physical store ID (optional)	P		
○ Sample/layout (optional) (at detailed level in new environment)	P		
○ Media	P		
○ Organization	P		
○ Frequency/periodicity of use (if not governed by data flow)	P		
○ Access management system (optional)	P		
○ Min-max store volume (estimate)	P		
○ Security (if applicable to whole store)	P		
○ Special characteristics (optional)	P		

---

*P = Preliminary, G = General, D = Detailed

Current/New
Environment

☐ A data model (data structure diagram) (if available   **P**
in current environment) or for each record/document:
(See "For each component data flow," above)

   ☐ For each data field:
     (See "For each data element," above)

■ **Physicalized Process Descriptions:**
☐ For each major process (for example, departments):
  ○ Process name   **P**
  ○ Process notes (optional)   **P**
  ○ Yearly operating costs (estimate) **P**
  ○ Special characteristics (optional) **P**

   ☐ For each component process (for example, sections/groups):
    ○ Process name   **P**
    ○ Process notes (optional)   **G**
    ○ Yearly operating costs (estimate) **G**
    ○ Special characteristics (optional) **G**

     ☐ For each individual process (procedures/tasks):
      ○ Process name   **G**
      ○ Process specification   **D**
      ○ Doer of the process (his/her name or a title) (optional) **D**
      ○ Skill level required   **D**
      ○ Frequency/periodicity of use (if not driven by data flow) **D**
      ○ Yearly operating cost   **D**
      ○ Special characteristics (optional) **D**

■ **Organizational Hierarchy**
(optional) developed incrementally   **P**   **G**   **D**

Sample Table of Contents for an AUTOMATED SYSTEM MODEL

■ **Design Charts:**

□ Different types of design charts

■ **Automated Data Dictionary:**

□ For each major data stream (transaction/report groups):

□ For each stream component (transactions/reports):

□ For each data element (fields/attributes):

□ For each data store (files and intermediate files):

	Current Environment*			New Environment*		
	P	G	D	P	G	D
Different types of design charts	P	G	D	P	G	D
For each major data stream (transaction/report groups):						
Stream name	P			P		
Stream description (optional)	P			P		
Media	P			P		
Stream volume	P			P		
Frequency/periodicity of use	P			P		
Security (if applicable to whole stream)	P			P		
Special characteristics (optional)	P			P		
For each stream component (transactions/reports):						
Transaction ID	P				G	
Transaction name (if different from ID)	P			P		
Sample/layout (optional)		G				D
Media (if different from whole stream)		G			G	
Transaction volume		G			G	
Frequency/periodicity (if different from whole stream)		G			G	
Security (optional)		G			G	
Special characteristics (optional)		G			G	
For each data element (fields/attributes):						
Data element name		G			G	
Data element description			D			D
Data format			D			D
Data representation			D			D
List/range of values			D			D
Special characteristics (optional)			D			D
For each data store (files and intermediate files):						
Data store ID	P		D			
Data store name (if different from ID)	P			P	G	D
Data store description	P			P	G	D
Sample/layout	P					
Media	P			P	G	D
Organization	P					D
Min-max store volume	P			P	G	D
Access method	P				G	D
Security (if applicable to whole store)	P			P	G	D
Frequency/periodicity (if applicable to whole store)	P			P	G	D
Special characteristics (optional)	P			P	G	D

* P = Preliminary, G = General, D = Detailed

	Current Environment			New Environment		
□ A data model (logical and/or physical, if available) or for each record/document: ○ (See "For each stream component," above, reading transactions as records)	P			P	G	D
□ For each data field: ○ (See "For each data element," above)						

■ Automated Process Descriptions:

	Current Environment			New Environment		
□ For each automated job (batch/on-line, front-end processing, and so on):						
○ Job name	P			P		
○ Job description	P			P	G	
○ Job size/complexity (estimate)	P			P	G	
○ Frequency/periodicity (if not governed by data)	P			P	G	
○ Executing processor type (if applicable to whole job)	P			P	G	
○ Yearly operating costs (estimate)	P			P	G	
○ Special characteristics (optional)	P			P	G	
□ For each program:						
○ Program ID	P					D
○ Program name	P					D
○ Program description (optional in new environment)		G				
○ Frequency/periodicity of use (if not governed by data)		G				D
○ Executing processor type (if different from whole job)		G				D
○ Source language		G				D
○ Program size/complexity		G				D
○ Cost per execution		G				D
○ Special characteristics (optional)		G				D
□ For each module (routines):						
○ Module ID		G				D
○ Module name		G				G	D
○ Module description			D		G	D
○ Frequency of use (if not governed by data)			D			D
○ Pseudocode (for current environment − actual code listing)			D			D
○ Source language (if not same) for whole program			D		G	D
○ Special characteristics (optional)				D		D
■ System flowchart	P					D

Sample Table of Contents for a LOGICAL SPECIFICATION

	Current/New Environment*	
P	G	D

■ **Logical Leveled Data Flow Diagram(s):**
☐ Levels developed incrementally — P G D

■ **Logical Data Dictionary:**
☐ For each major data flow (originally documents, transactions, and report streams or time-delayed stores):
  ○ Data flow name — P
  ○ Data flow description (optional) — P
  ○ Cross reference to current physical definition — P

  ☐ For each component data flow (originally documents, transactions, reports, or records):
    ○ Data flow name — P
    ○ Data flow description (optional) — G
    ○ Cross reference to current physical definition — G

    ☐ For each data element:
      ○ Data element name — G
      ○ Data element description — D
      ○ Cross reference to current physical definition — D

■ **Data Model** (optional in manual and automated logical models):
  ○ Data categories — P
  ○ Informal data structure/access diagram — G
  ○ Formal data structure/access diagram — D

  ☐ For each data object (or group) (originally records/documents):
    ○ Data object name — P
    ○ Data object description — G
    ○ Cross reference to current physical definition — G

    ☐ For each data attribute (originally fields or elements)
      (See "For each data element," above)

■ **Logical Data Store** (for manual and automated logical models):
☐ For each (necessary) data store:
  ○ Data store name — P
  ○ Data store description — P
  ○ Cross reference to current physical definition — P

  ☐ For each data store component (originally records/documents):
    (See "For each component data flow," above)

    ☐ For each data element (originally fields):
      (See "For each data element," above)

---

* P = Preliminary, G = General, D = Detailed

*Current/New
Environment*

■ **Logical Process Descriptions:**

☐ For each major function (originally departments or automated jobs):
  ○ Process name — P
  ○ Process notes (optional) — P
  ○ Cross reference to current physical process(es) — P

  ☐ For each component function (originally sections/groups or programs):
    ○ Process name — P
    ○ Process notes (optional) — G
    ○ Cross reference to current physical process(es) — G

    ☐ For each functional primitive (originally procedures/tasks or modules/routines):
      ○ Process name — G
      ○ Process specification — D
      ○ Cross reference to current physical process(es) — D

PROCESS
DESCRIPTIONS

To insure that this methodology can be applied to a variety of environments, the Level 2, or detailed, activities are not functional primitives, which normally are the detailed specification level of a system. Therefore, I am going to support my diagrams with process notes instead of the detailed policy descriptions required by a structured specification. It is up to you as a user of this guideline to identify the detailed tasks (that is, to further decompose the Level 2 processes) that your environment requires to produce a particular deliverable. You then can describe your company methods for carrying out these tasks.

Process name: APPROVE REQUEST
Process reference number: 1.1.1
Process guided by: General department plan

Process notes: If the project request comes directly from a user without being reviewed by data processing management, verify the following:

- that your department is the appropriate one to act on this request

- that the requestor is authorized to initiate a project

- that the contents of the request are clear and complete (as declared in the data dictionary definition)

The most common problem encountered is that the need for the project is stated as a solution, "I want an on-line system to store and retrieve customer records," instead of as a business objective, "I want to improve customer relations with faster turnaround on inquiries." In analysis, you may find the turnaround problems were not due to storing and retrieving speed, but instead were due to unreadable reports. The on-line solution may just give *faster* unreadable reports. Analysis will identify the problem; therefore, finding a solution will best be left until after analysis.

After verifying the request, identify the following:

- whether the request conflicts with an existing request, duplicates an existing request, or conflicts with any restrictions, such as federal regulations or company policy

- whether further evaluation should be deferred, for example, whether the product that the request supports is likely to be phased out, or whether the project is an extension to an existing system that is going to be rewritten or that is in the process of development (which means the request can be accommodated only in the next release)

If the request is not rejected or deferred and if you have the resources available for an initial study, update the overall data processing plans and resources accordingly and develop a project plan. This plan should identify only the scheduling of resources for initial project evaluation.

Inform the project requestor (user management) of the outcome of this process.

Process name: IDENTIFY ADDITIONAL AFFECTED MANUAL AND AUTOMATED SYSTEMS
Process reference number: 1.1.2
Process guided by: Activity 1 plan

Process notes: Often, more than one user and/or automated system will be affected by a project request, and the initial requestor may not have identified all of the affected systems in the request. So, using the contents of the project request as a guide, extract additional affected systems from the production procedure library. The procedures manual or operations manual should identify departments that give or receive information, which may be affected by, as well as affect, interfacing systems. Supplement these with any departments identified by management, and identify possible representatives for affected departments and automated systems.

Then develop an initial context diagram by looking for an area of study for the project that will completely bound the functions and data that will be affected. Develop the diagram to understand where and how input data is produced and where and what happens to output data. The areas that bound the system should be identified as data originators and terminators on the context diagram. These originators and terminators indicate the points where you stop studying the system's data. Do not assume that output from an existing computer system is the point where you should lose interest in the data. (One user on a project said to me, "This is a good computer report, we can *type* directly from it!" Clearly, the output was not the product the user had requested if it was necessary to reformat or recalculate any data on it.)

Process name: IDENTIFY ADDITIONAL MAJOR PROJECT GOALS
Process reference number: 1.1.3
Process guided by: Activity 1 plan

Process notes: To maximize the benefits from a project, you should identify any other major project goals from the affected systems. These project goals should relate either to the original project request or to some function or data that would be affected by the request. However, some goals may come from areas that are not obviously related, such as database administration management or operations management. The database group might request, "Because most of the affected interface systems utilize our centralized database, we would like any new data capture to be on our database or at least to be stored and accessed with a compatible database management system." Operations management may also identify problems with the original or affected system: "The operating and set-up procedures for this system are very time consuming." Steps to satisfy such requests may be easily incorporated in the system solution.

Process name: RESOLVE ANY CONFLICTS AND PRIORITIZE PROJECT GOALS
Process reference number: 1.1.4
Process guided by: Activity 1 plan

Process notes: Conflicts are likely to arise if more goals have been added to the ones indicated in the original request. Therefore, identify any conflicts between project goals. Then, compare the objectives and constraints of all the project goals, and, if any conflicts are discovered, aid management in resolving them. Resolution of conflicts can be accomplished by identifying the gross benefits and assigning priorities to the various goals, which may result in some goals being modified or even deleted. However, be careful not to delete the main goals of the original request. (This would effectively mean you canceled or deferred the original request because you went looking for more important projects.) Some examples of goals or objectives and constraints follow.

Business objectives

1.   Reduce operating costs forty percent in the first year.
2.   Improve customer service.

Business constraints

1.   The project costs must not exceed $200,000.
2.   The project must be completed in six months.

System objectives

1.   The on-line portion of the system must have ninety-nine percent availability.
2.   Response time must be three seconds or less ninety percent of the time and must not exceed five seconds ninety-nine percent of the time.
3.   The system must minimize data redundancy.

System constraints

1.   IMS must be used as the database management system (DBMS).
2.   COBOL must be used as the programming language.
3.   IBM's 3601 must be used as the controller.
4.   The system must provide centralized processing, not distributed processing.

Given the above goals and constraints, there are a number of apparent conflicts:

Conflict 1. Business objective versus business objective. Improving customer service may require adding personnel, thereby increasing operating costs.

Conflict 2. Business objective versus business constraint. A cost reduction as large as forty percent may not be possible to achieve with a system to be built in six months.

Conflict 3. Business objective versus system objective. A system with ninety-nine percent availability could cost two to three times as much as one with ninety-five percent availability. The increased expense could reverse the forty percent cost reduction.

Conflict 4. Business objective versus system constraint. Centralized processing could increase the cost of data communications and therefore affect the forty percent cost-reduction goal.

Conflict 5. Business constraint versus business constraint. During the planning of a project, time optimization usually requires more people and therefore added costs, thus conflicting with the cost limitation.

Conflict 6. Business constraint versus system objective. A system with ninety-nine percent availability is fairly sophisticated and requires thorough design and testing. This would probably conflict with the six-month time constraint.

Conflict 7. Business constraint versus system constraint. If this is the group's first database project, then a steep learning curve must be expected, which could cause the project to exceed both the time and cost limitations.

Conflict 8. System objective versus system objective. A database system that tries to minimize data redundancy may require significant processing overhead, making a three-second response time impossible.

Conflict 9. System objective versus system constraint. The use of full IMS may not permit a three-second-response-time objective to be met. If the fast-path option is chosen, the implied restrictions on file organization may be too severe for the application.

Conflict 10. System constraint versus system constraint. The IBM 3601 does not support COBOL.

Process name: CLASSIFY PROJECT BY GROSS SIZE AND RISK
Process reference number: 1.1.5
Process guided by: Activity 1 plan

Process notes: The last technical activity the initial project team needs to do in evaluating this project is to estimate its size and determine the probability of meeting the project goals. The team can accomplish this task by considering factors such as the number of affected systems along with the project goals and gross benefits. (Remember you're just evaluating the project request here, not trying to do a full feasibility study — that's the task of the preliminary-level study, Activity 2.) The best estimate that can be given at this point is to classify the project as either small, medium, or large because no analysis or identification of a solution has been done yet. "Small," "medium," and "large" are relative terms and vary in meaning at each company. These terms can be generally defined as follows: small, fewer than six months elapsed time and fewer than two person-years; medium, six months to one year elapsed time and two to ten person-years; or large, greater than one year elapsed time and greater than ten person-years.

Of course, to evaluate gross size and risk, you must make some assumptions about the classes of possible solutions (on-line/batch, distributed, totally automated, and so on) that are most appropriate for this problem. (However, it is important not to commit to any solution yet.) Then, compare this project with project histories to find similar projects and use their cost, time, and size data (estimated and actual) for this evaluation task, along with your own experience and knowledge of the environment. (If your department hasn't got a store of project histories, start one today and beg, borrow, or steal histories.)

Risk assessment will be based on the clarity of the project goals as well as on possible solutions. For example, if the existing system is totally automated and requires rewriting, and nobody wants to act as representative of this maintenance nightmare, then the risk involved in producing a satisfactory new system is going to be high. On the other hand, if the existing system is mainly manual, if the user is friendly and truly wants the new system, and if people of adequate skills are available, the risk is low.

Other major risk factors are the time requested for the completed system and the complexity level of the environments being studied, which will also affect the plans. Again, the best you can do is to classify the project and each project goal as having low, medium, or high risk. Use any available resources to help with this process. If the request is for a database environment, a representative from the database support group or anyone in the system department who has worked on a similar project would be helpful. These final two items of evaluation data (gross size and risk) should be stored in the project charter. The charter now constitutes the project contract.

Process name: SELECT CUSTOMIZED METHODOLOGY
Process reference number: 1.2.1
Process guided by: Activity 1 plan

Process notes: Using the evaluation data gathered so far, reasonably identify the project strategy; that is, select a customized methodology. (I shall assume that if you've read this far, you have elected to customize *this* methodology.) As I mentioned in the introduction, this book presents a standard framework for developing systems, but you may need to tailor the deliverables and activities of the guidelines to fit a particular project. Such tailoring consists of the following:

1. **Identify the number of cycles of decomposition necessary.** If a particular project is very small, then you can compress Activities 2, 3, and 4 into one activity (in fact, for a very small project, these guidelines may be used just as a checklist). At the other extreme, for a large, critical project, you may identify more than the three levels of decomposition shown in these guidelines.

2. **Identify unnecessary deliverables and processes.** There will be many cases in which all deliverables are not needed, as in the hardware/software installation specification, in which an objective is to use existing equipment, or in the case in which an objective is to use a software package. In such situations, most of the design and coding deliverables and activities may be omitted from the methodology. However, I recommend that for first-time use of this methodology, you employ all activities and deliverables. Then, for future projects, customize where you see fit, documenting the reason for customization.

3. **Allocate roles for project members.*** Allocate major roles; for example, designate that all data modeling will be performed by the database group or that the analyst will be responsible for designing data stores. Other examples might be that the project leader will be a member of the development team or that the project leader will act as an interface between data processing and the user area, as well as coordinate development activities. (It may also be helpful to identify user roles; for example, describe what participation is expected from them.)

4. **Appoint independent reviewers of deliverables.** Identify people not on the development team who can act as independent reviewers. The reviewers should have been involved in similar projects and may be outside consultants.

5. **Identify the approach to development.** The meaning of "approach" here is based on the radical-to-conservative spectrum described by Yourdon.† The premise of the approach is that the activities of analysis, design, and implementation are carried out sequentially in the conservative approach (design not beginning until all of analysis is

---

*Individual activity roles will be allocated in the activity plans.
†E. Yourdon, *Managing the Structured Techniques,* 2nd ed. (New York: YOURDON Press, 1979), pp. 74-76, 225-27.

complete), or overlapping each other in the radical approach (design beginning for a functional unit that has been analyzed, even though all of analysis is not complete). In this methodology, there are explicit levels of development through analysis and design, so identify here the approach — called the "political" or "practical" approach in my introduction — to preliminary, general, and detailed development.

6.   **Determine the change-management (or change-control) procedure.** An incorrect decision on the procedure to use can really kill the system. If you decide to manage change by freezing a specification as soon as possible, then you run the risk of producing a system that the user doesn't want; on the other hand, if you allow changes without any control, the system may never reach completion. The latter is a case of the target being moved constantly, a common complaint. It seems the target gets moved much more than the target date, especially in the programming phase. Even though the tools used for development in this methodology accommodate change easily, you must still have realistic change-management procedures. I have identified some in the activities of "Refine Project Goals" (Activity 2.2).

7.   **Specify project standards.** Standards for the development effort should be based on the project goals; for example, if reliability is the most important goal, check all deliverables using walkthroughs and reviews, and perform testing using logic-coverage testing, boundary-value analysis, and cause-effect graphing, or produce the design specification using structure charts and Nassi-Shneiderman diagrams. (Note that standards effectively become additional project goals.)

Each of the decisions made based on the seven steps above should be documented, especially the action taken in Step 2. This will help future project teams in their selection activity.

Expect some of the customizing made as a result of this activity to be modified after preliminary analysis and design.

Process name: CREATE ACTIVITY 2 PLAN
Process reference number: 1.2.2
Process guided by: Activity 1 plan

Process notes: The Activity 2 plan is the most difficult one of all to prepare, again because no analysis of the complexity of the areas that have to be planned for has been done. However, four considerations can help, as follows:

1. You are not trying to plan for the whole development effort, just for preliminary analysis and design (feasibility level).

2. The deliverables and the activities for producing these deliverables are defined in the methodology (Activity 2), so you know what you are allocating resources to, that is, you have a definable product.

3. The evaluation data created so far will aid planning:

   - "Affected Systems" identifies the area of study, and possible representatives from these areas who may help the planning effort.

   - "Project Goals" and "Gross Benefits" help identify the main reasons for the study of an area (that is, key areas of study for allocation of most resources).

   - "Gross Size" aids in determining the amount of resources needed overall.

   - "Risk Assessment" identifies key areas of business, and level of technical difficulty in order to allocate individual skills.

4. The estimated and actual resources used in a similar past project — which are the biggest help in creating new plans — can help us repeat success instead of failure.

I have starved Bubble 1.2.2 from one input it may need: the overall data processing plans and resources identifying available resources. It is probably better to identify what resources you need to accomplish Activity 2 on time (although your request for them may be rejected), as opposed to altering the project to fit the available resources (wishful thinking).

In doing this or any planning activity, you may uncover additional risks, such as the staff's lacking needed skills for the development activities, a situation that will probably necessitate an update to the risk assessment for presentation to management.

Note: It is probably a good idea to allocate extra time during preliminary analysis for a "blitz"* to guard against making any assumptions about the system. At this stage of the planning, with the help of the user representatives, identify a functional area that is reasonably complex and allocate extra resources for studying this small area to a detailed level; that is, blitz it. To understand a blitz in terms of levels of detail, think of

---

*The concept of blitzing was suggested to me by Steve McMenamin, a YOURDON colleague.

the system as a lake. You already have an idea of the surface area of the lake (the number of affected systems), and you want to study the depth of the entire lake (through preliminary, general, and detailed analysis). However, there will be different depths — analogous to the complexity of individual functions — throughout the lake. Executing a blitz will help in future planning activities because it will give you concrete information — not just assumptions — about an area's complexity, from which you can plan.

Process name: CONDUCT INDEPENDENT REVIEW
Process reference number: 1.2.3
Process guided by: Activity 1 plan

Process notes: Before you go further, make sure you are taking the best approach for the project. You can avoid compounding any errors by holding an independent review: The people conducting this review should be independent of the project because the test is to determine if the project team is on the correct path; therefore, objective observers are the best reviewers. You should use reviewers who have worked on similiar projects, who can understand project plans, and who have a knowledge of the concepts of this methodology. The reviewers should verify the customizing of the methodology and the project plan for reasonableness, against the evaluation data gathered so far. (For a further description of reviews, see Appendix E.)

Process name: PREPARE PROJECT INITIATION REPORT
Process reference number: 1.2.4
Process guided by: Activity 1 plan

Process notes: Produce a project initiation report containing sufficient information to enable management to decide whether to approve the resources necessary for further study of the project. The report's importance, of course, depends on whether the project is necessary or optional. A project based on a government requirement probably *has* to be approved, whereas another project, merely desired rather than needed by the user, does *not* have to be approved. In either case, management will need a summary of resources actually spent compared with what was estimated, and will require an estimate of future resource needs at least through Activity 2.

Process name: PRESENT PROJECT INITIATION REPORT TO D.P. MANAGEMENT
Process reference number: 1.2.5
Process guided by: Activity 1 plan

Process notes: In addition to providing information for approval of resources and estimates, the initiation report also gives an overview of the information gathered to date and a gross size and risk assessment to help management evaluate whether to continue the project.

The formality of the presentation will depend on the environment. In some companies, this presentation is so informal that it is made while passing management in the corridor. (It seems the only time any presentation becomes formal is when the project is late and someone has to account for it!)

If the project is approved, you should get a commitment for all resources needed at least through Activity 2.

Process name: PRESENT PROJECT INITIATION REPORT TO USER MANAGEMENT
Process reference number: 1.2.6
Process guided by: Activity 1 plan

Process notes: This presentation should be used to make user management aware of your progress and to get a commitment for the resources needed for Activity 2 (if the user is responsible for approval of resources).

The user, as the receiver and owner of the new system, should be kept informed of the project's progress, especially in environments in which system development costs are paid for by the user. This presentation keeps communication lines open with user management, and can be formal or informal although management generally prefers a more formal approach. In either case, all the information in the project initiation report should be presented.

If resource approval is given, the overall data processing plans and resource estimates need to be revised to reflect the reallocation of resources.

Approved affected systems are shown as output in this process. This implies that you can reduce the area of study to gain acceptable resource approval. If this is done, you must realize that you cannot reduce your area of study without affecting the project goals as well. So, in this case, you must cycle back through most of Activity 1.

Note: The project initiation report has served its purpose as of this process, but it can be kept for reference and used as documentation for project histories, if you think it helpful.

Process name: VALIDATE AND/OR CREATE PRELIMINARY DESIGN MODEL
FOR CURRENT MANUAL ENVIRONMENT
Process reference number: 2.1.1
Process guided by: Activity 2 plan

Process notes: The main deliverable of this task is a physical data flow model of the existing manual portions of the system, showing the major data streams, files, and activities that act on this data. I have called this deliverable a design model, because it is physical and shows *how* things are being accomplished; that is, it depicts the existing design. The goals of this task are as follows:

1. Produce a communication model (a data flow diagram and supporting information) of the user area that may be affected by the project goals, so the user can verify the model as correct.

2. Familiarize yourself with the user environment and convince the users that you understand their environment — in other words, develop a working relationship, as well as understand the areas into which the new system must fit.

3. Gather cost/benefit information and performance data to be used in future tasks.

4. Produce a working model that can be used to derive a logical model, which describes *what* is accomplished by the system without detailing *how* it is accomplished.

Your objective in this task is to produce a physical model that is verifiable by the user, but a logical model annotated with physical characteristics such as department or group names or numbers, file IDs, and form numbers can serve your purpose as well as aid in the logicalization process later. Of course, if you are lucky enough to have an existing data flow model for any area you have to study, then your task here is to validate that model at a preliminary level.

Data collected during this task will be used as a source for other activities. For example, you need the current frequency and volume of use of the data in the data flow diagram for such applications as cost/benefit analysis and conversion. Also, such data as is shown in an organizational hierarchy chart will be useful in identifying where and from whom to gather information. Therefore, the task involves gathering information that makes up the manual system model for this level of study. (To identify preliminary data, see the sample table of contents for the manual system model in the addendum to the data dictionary.) This level of the manual system model can be completed by using

- information gathered from interviews (at this preliminary level of study, interviews should be held with managers responsible for departments, sections, and major business functions, and the interview notes should consist of sketched data flow diagrams with their supporting, preliminary data dictionary)

- any available maintenance documentation (for example, training materials for new employees)

- actual production procedures and information in a procedures manual

In this task, you may represent an automated procedure as a single bubble and produce one complete high-level data flow diagram or separate high-level data flow diagrams derived from different affected manual systems. In creating the high-level data flow diagrams and data dictionary, you may encounter different names for the same data item, but it is sufficient at the preliminary level of study merely to document this by use of an alias.

Note that preliminary-level processes will be described at the general level by the lower functions inside these processes, so an overview description or a meaningful process name will suffice for a process description at this level.

The odd-man-out of this task is the output "Production HW/SW Inventory," which is all of the hardware and support software available in the company, not just that used by the area you are studying (although this subset should be highlighted). This is the most practical point at which to gather such information, but only if it is available in a complete detailed state; otherwise, time should not be taken out of preliminary study to gather the general- and detailed-level information in this store. This data should be gathered when needed as input to a task. The data in the "Production HW/SW Inventory" store will probably not be the responsibility of the project manager or team members, but each must be aware of such data because it can greatly affect the cost/benefit study. For example, the cost/benefit study will be affected if extra equipment needed for this project necessitates construction of another data preparation room.

It may be difficult to identify exactly when sufficient study has been accomplished to satisfy the preliminary model for a particular project: A blitz can be useful in assessing the level of detail expected in this portion of the project.

Process name: VALIDATE AND/OR CREATE PRELIMINARY DESIGN MODEL
FOR CURRENT AUTOMATED ENVIRONMENT
Process reference number: 2.1.2
Process guided by: Activity 2 plan

Process notes: The deliverable of this task is a model showing the processes and data of the automated portions of the system and how they are controlled. The model provides a physical representation — such as design charts with supporting information like data and control parameters — showing how the automated functions are implemented. This data-gathering task is a little harder to perform than the manual equivalent as you can't validate code too easily with the users. So, make sure you understand the automated environment before beginning the next task. The logical equivalent of the deliverable for this process will serve as a validation document for the user.

Therefore, the aims of this process are

- to produce a communication model of the automated systems affected by the project goals (use the model for communication with maintenance and data processing staff members who are familiar with the current system)

- to gather cost/benefit information and performance data to aid future tasks

- to identify reusable resources (even reusable code) of the existing automated environment to aid in the implementation of the new system (there may be a project goal requesting use of existing programs)

To accomplish these aims, you must complete the information that makes up the automated system model for this level of detail. (To identify preliminary data, see the sample table of contents for an automated system model in the addendum to the data dictionary.)

If there are any design charts available in the automated system's maintenance documentation for a system or part of a system that must be studied, then the task here is to validate the charts at a preliminary level. The type of design chart that is appropriate at this level will be similar to a system flowchart; that is, it will be a diagram that shows the major jobs with programs in the system, and the files and data they use. The streams of data will be groups of transactions and reports or groups of reports.

This level of the automated system model can be completed by using the affected systems to point to any maintenance documentation available (possibly a HIPO hierarchy chart or high-level program flowchart) or to identify maintenance and operations personnel and even original programmers for data-gathering interviews.

The current operations manual (if available) should contain information for a system overview. If all else fails, you may have to gather a list of all programs and JCL and produce a system overview from the affected programs.

Resolving conflicting names (aliases) for the same data item is easy in the automated area because the item can be documented as an alias and be given a meaningful name during logicalization. However, the name choice should correspond to the business need for this data item. To avoid redundancy in the data dictionary, confirm that interfaces of manual systems to automated systems are documented only once. How difficult this is will depend on the plan for Activity 2. For example, there may be difficulty if one team is working on the manual system while another team is working on the automated system.

The process description for processes in an existing automated system can be the source code (if the source code is in a high-level language). However, pure coordinating modules (those that call upon other modules to do their job) will disappear in logicalization; for these, a meaningful process name or overview description should suffice.

The odd-man-out of this task is the output "Production HW/SW Inventory." Along with equivalent data gathered in the manual system, this output forms a specification of all hardware and support software available in the company, not just that being used by the affected systems (although this subset should be highlighted). This is the most practical process in which to gather this information, but only if it is available in a complete, detailed state (that is, documented in a support library or purchasing area); otherwise, time should not be taken out of the preliminary study to gather the general- and detailed-level information in this store. This data should be gathered when needed as input to a task. The data in the "Production HW/SW Inventory" store will probably not be the responsibility of the project manager or team, but each must be aware of it because it can greatly affect the cost/benefit analysis. For instance, the cost/benefit study will be affected if extra equipment needed for a project necessitates construction of another machine room.

In an automated environment, it may be very difficult to identify when sufficient study has been accomplished to satisfy a preliminary model for a project. Such identification will certainly be difficult if the systems being studied consist of classical 5,000-line programs. Therefore, you may want to do a blitz of an average subsystem to identify the level of detail expected in this portion of the project.

Process name: DERIVE PRELIMINARY LOGICAL MODEL
FOR CURRENT MANUAL ENVIRONMENT
Process reference number: 2.1.3
Process guided by: Activity 2 plan

Process notes: Derive the logical equivalent of the physical manual system model; that is, derive the actual business functions that the manual system model portrays without reference to how the functions are performed. The more you can divorce yourself from the physical characteristics and control of the current system, the better chance you have of understanding the actual system (the business view) and therefore of being able to develop a good solution for the new system. We accomplish this separation by performing logicalization. If there already is a logical model (from the maintenance library) for any areas to be studied, then the task here is to validate that model.

At this preliminary level, the task should not be too difficult, as most high-level departments or groupings within companies are reasonably functional. If we have a physicalized model as input, the task will be even easier.

The logical model is derived by removing all physical characteristics other than those needed for business reasons that are referenced in the manual system model. For example, there may be references in data streams to document numbers, colors, or media; references to the sequencing or control of major processes and to the department that performs them; and references to media used for major stores. (To identify preliminary data, see the sample table of contents for a logical specification in the addendum to the data dictionary.)

Note: Even at this level, you may find processes that seemingly do not need to be represented on a logical model (for example, data preparation/distribution or back-up processes), except that they are needed for business reasons (for example, customer history). Therefore, some repartitioning or regrouping of nonfunctional areas may be necessary. If you are in doubt about whether to repartition, it is better to postpone repartitioning until it is time to derive the logical model for the whole system (manual and automated), or until you undertake the general level of study. Logicalizing interfaces to and from automated systems can be delayed until the logicalization of the whole system. Any internal stores (those not interfacing with automated functions) can be investigated to see if they would be better represented as data flows. (Note that a data store is needed for data that cannot be obtained dynamically.*)

The derivation and validation of the logical model can be assisted by any business and support documentation in the maintenance library. Also, a large number of users should be able to validate this logical transformation, especially on the manual portions of the system.

In this process you are deriving a separate model, not modifying the manual system model. The manual system model will be needed for reference in future processes.

---

*See the discussion of model transformations in Appendix C for an example of data store cleanup.

Process name: DERIVE PRELIMINARY LOGICAL MODEL
FOR CURRENT AUTOMATED ENVIRONMENT
Process reference number: 2.1.4
Process guided by: Activity 2 plan

Process notes: Derive the logical equivalent of the physical automated system model in such a way as to isolate the description of the actual business functions contained in the automated system model from references to how the functions are performed. As I have mentioned in the previous, equivalent manual task, the more you can divorce yourself from the old design, the better chance you have of understanding the actual system (the business view) and therefore of being able to develop a good design for the new system.

The difficulty of this task will depend on the input, the automated system model, and how knowledgeable the user (or the data processing maintenance staff) is about the functions performed by the automated system. At the preliminary level, the difficulty arises only if code must be analyzed or interpreted to derive the major logical functions.

If you do have a valid automated system model, you should turn it into a logical data flow diagram by tracking the major flows of data and identifying the major functions that act on that data. At the same time, remove from this model all physical characteristics, other than those needed for business reasons, such as references in data streams to transaction numbers or media, references to sequencing or controlling major processes, and so on. (To identify preliminary data, see the sample table of contents of a logical specification in the addendum to the data dictionary.)

Note: Even at this level, you may find processes, such as back-up and housekeeping jobs, that do not need to be presented on a logical model. Some repartitioning (regrouping) of nonfunctional systems may be accomplished here. If you are in doubt about whether to repartition, it is better to wait until the logical model for the whole system (manual and automated) has been derived or until the general level of study has begun. Also, the logicalization of interfaces from and to manual systems can be delayed until the logicalization of the whole system is completed. Any simple intermediate stores (those not interfacing with manual functions) can be investigated to see if they should really be represented as data flows.* You should rely on this logical model to be your communication tool with the user because the design chart is not as readily understood by the user. You should also be able to enhance the derivation and validation of this logical model with any business and support documentation from the maintenance library.

In this process you are deriving a separate model, not modifying the automated system model. The automated system will be needed for reference in the future processes.

---

*See the discussion of model transformations in Appendix C for an example of data store cleanup.

Process name: DERIVE PRELIMINARY LOGICAL SPECIFICATION
FOR THE CURRENT SYSTEM
Process reference number: 2.1.5
Process guided by: Activity 2 plan

Process notes: Produce a logical model for the whole system (manual and automated systems combined). The reason for producing a complete logical model is similar to the reason for performing previous logicalization tasks: If you can remove the physical view of how manual and automated·processes are partitioned in the existing system, there is a better chance of developing a good partitioning of the new system. Since this process involves combining two logical models into one, it is similar to the process just completed for deriving the manual logical model, except that now the physical characteristics occur only at the interfaces between the manual and automated components. One task is to match the interfaces and remove their physical characteristics. This should be easy to accomplish at the preliminary level, because you are mainly dealing with streams of data and their components, and the major processes that transform this data.

If an interface in the manual model does not correspond to one in the automated model (allowing for aliases), you must investigate the missing interface by cycling back to the original design models. Any interfaces that were missed will require the same development effort as used to derive other interfaces, such as looking for repartitioning problems with new functions. (To confirm the data required for general-level study, see the sample table of contents for a logical specification in the addendum to the data dictionary.) As with other logicalization tasks, you should

1.   remove all physical characteristics from the interfaces (other than those needed for business reasons) and develop logical names for those remaining business-related characteristics that are physical

2.   identify interface stores that are really data flows, such as those that are just used for time delays

3.   look for partitioning problems, for example, functions that are performed partly in the manual system and partly in the automated system; although rare, incomplete functions may also be discovered at this point

Even though this process is performed at a high level of detail, it should give a reasonably useful overview of the current system. This system model should show the major functional processes and their data. The only parts of the model that may not be functional are the stores, which should now be investigated for "kitchen sink" stores (stores that contain data for many different high-level functions) and redundant data present in many stores, a common problem on the boundary between the manual and automated environments. These stores should be split and regrouped into high-level categories (for example, from master file into employee data, client data, and project data), and re-incorporated into the logical system model, with the correct data flows connected to them. Adding this information should improve the readability of the model and should also remove the final physical characteristics of the current design (except those needed for business reasons, such as personnel data being updated before payroll uses it).

Process name: CREATE PRELIMINARY TEST CASES FOR CURRENT SYSTEM
Process reference number: 2.1.6
Process guided by: Activity 2 plan

Process notes: Identify the test cases needed to validate the current logical specification at a preliminary level. If you are lucky enough to have a regression test specification in the maintenance library for any of the automated or manual systems in question, use it to help form the preliminary test cases. For systems that don't have a regression test specification, review the current logical specification and develop test cases that will validate the current logical specification's completeness and correctness. The tests will validate the information contained in the specification, such as major streams of data, stores, and functions.

Of course, the best source to use for identifying and defining test cases is the data dictionary of the current logical specification, with the data flow diagram serving as a guide for identifying inputs and outputs. The test cases at this level of detail will probably be specified informally in narrative form, as follows:

Test objective:	validate that payroll exception-monies are accounted for in the general ledger
Test input:	payroll update transactions
Expected execution:	flow of data through payroll-exception-update processing into general ledger updating and reporting functions
Expected output:	payroll exception check and equivalent amount on general ledger update report

Since the user is obviously a good source of information, the user or his representative should help to create test cases to validate the current system, and can be particularly helpful in identifying invalid (negative) tests.

Process name: CONDUCT REVIEW OF PRELIMINARY CURRENT LOGICAL SPECIFICATION
Process reference number: 2.1.7
Process guided by: Activity 2 plan

Process notes: Use this review to identify any problems, inaccuracies, ambiguities, and omissions in the current logical specification at a preliminary level of detail. Since the specification will be used as the basis for the new system, it must be correct. A walk-through should have been conducted for each intermediate deliverable up to this point. Now, since the system can be viewed in total, with both manual and automated portions combined, a formal quality control inspection should take place. This review should include the project manager, user or user representative, and project analysts. The current system test cases can be used in the validation of the current logical specification.

Process name: IDENTIFY ADDITIONAL PROJECT GOALS
Process reference number: 2.2.1
Process guided by: Activity 2 plan

Process notes: Now that you have a logical view of the whole system that should be sufficiently clear for the user to understand, compare it with the current physical view(s) to identify any additional project goals. Goals that may already have been identified during system study should also be included here. The removal of physical characteristics may reveal new goals or modifications to existing goals; for example, new hardware/software goals may be revealed because of the elimination of physical interfaces between manual and automated systems. You may identify additional goals at this point because this is still preliminary study. However, you must be realistic; *any* major project goals discovered may affect your area of study, so don't add them unless they are essential to the success of the project.

Any new project goals requested at this stage should be compared with existing goals to assure that they are not duplicates. If not, the new goals should be highlighted so they can be identified as having been introduced after approval of the project initiation report.

Note: Activity 2.2 processes are not repeated at the general and detailed levels, even though more project goals would probably be found as a result of the detailed study. The additional project goals resulting from this activity require different processing because they are identified later in the project. If a new goal is actually a refinement of an existing goal, and has little or no impact on the project, then it can probably be accommodated directly. But if the goal is completely new or is a major change to an existing goal, then it may affect our area of study or conflict with an existing goal. If this is the case, the new goal may be processed by the change-management mechanism and documented as a change request to be included in the next release or to be put into effect during maintenance. If a project goal is discovered in a later activity, we must cycle back to redo this process (possibly even returning to Activity 1, if our area of study is affected) and at least reconsider the new goal's impact on every process performed between this and the process in which it was discovered.

Process name: CORRELATE IDENTIFIED PROBLEMS AND OBJECTIVES
Process reference number: 2.2.2
Process guided by: Activity 2 plan

Process notes: The identification of what the new system must accomplish depends upon the system objectives; so, in this task, present all project goals in the form of system objectives.

For each project goal stated as a problem, determine the business and/or system objectives that must be achieved in order to solve it. If a project goal is stated as a business objective, determine what system objectives will achieve it. Combine them with project goals already stated in the form of system objectives.

(Conflicts between system objectives are addressed in process reference number 2.2.3 on the following page.)

Process name: RESOLVE ANY CONFLICTS AND PRIORITIZE PROJECT GOALS
Process reference number: 2.2.3
Process guided by: Activity 2 plan

Process notes: Now that additional project goals have been found and/or new business objectives have been identified, prioritize them and resolve any conflicts that may have arisen. This task is similar to that in process reference number 1.1.4 in Activity 1. You may need to cycle back to process reference number 1.1.4 if the new goals affect the area of study and must be included in this development effort. This is a good time to identify goals that cannot be satisfied completely by this system, as well as to inform the user of them so he can modify his expectations. Your knowledge of the system will allow you to help management to reorder the priority of the goals and to discuss the repercussions of any conflicts.

Any new goals (highlighted in process reference number 2.2.1), as well as deleted goals, should be identified during this process and indicated in the project charter, as they will need to be identified in the cost/benefit analysis and feasibility report.

Process name: ANALYZE PRELIMINARY PROJECT GOALS
Process reference number: 2.3.1
Process guided by: Activity 2 plan

Process notes: Looking at the new system, identify the project goals that can be satisfied in analysis at this level of detail. These goals will be of two types: those affecting data and functions in the current logical specification, and those requiring completely new data and functions. Such goals will mostly consist of business objectives and constraints. Your task is to identify the logical modifications (that is, the changes to business data or functions) necessary for the system to meet these goals. This process will require little effort if all goals relate to the design and implementation of the new system; for example, changing the current system from batch to on-line or from manual to automated. In fact, don't be surprised if there are no logical modifications in the new system.

On the other hand, this process can require great effort if the current study identified only interface systems with a new business function and new data. In such a case, analyzing some of the preliminary project goals can be equivalent to a complete current design and logicalization process for the new functions and data. The amount of work depends on how the new data and functions are identified; for example, there will be a great amount of work if the necessary data and functions can be obtained only at another company. Also note that project goals may identify changes or deletions to data and functions, which may require validating physical-to-logical transformations of the data and functions. At this level of detail, however, the task will probably be relatively easy, as you are identifying only major streams of data and their major functions.

For those project goals that can be completely or partly satisfied in this process, document the solutions to analysis goals in the project charter.

(To identify preliminary data, see the sample table of contents for a logical specification in the addendum to the data dictionary.)

Note: If there are no completely new data and functions but only changes and deletions to data and functions, this process can be merged with process reference number 2.3.2.

Process name: DERIVE PRELIMINARY LOGICAL MODEL FOR THE NEW SYSTEM
Process reference number: 2.3.2
Process guided by: Activity 2 plan

Process notes: Produce the new logical model by applying the logical modifications to the current logical specifications. This process may involve adding, updating, and deleting portions of the data flow diagrams and data dictionary that make up the current logical specification. (Actually, you are developing a separate model here, not modifying the current logical specification, which will be needed for reference in future processing.) If any partitioning problems result from new functions being added, you can probably eliminate them in the next process, when you repartition the model into manual and automated functions. If new stores were introduced into the model, investigate to see if they satisfy many functions or if they contain redundant data. If the same data exists in more than one store, split the stores and regroup them (possibly in combination with existing stores) into high-level groupings.

One of the aims of studying the current system is to assure that all modifications fit inside the current model and are completely bounded by the area of study. If not, the study is not complete. This process should be relatively easy at the preliminary level, because you are dealing mainly with streams of data and their components and with the major processes that transform this data. In fact, the modifications may not be completely identifiable in the model at this level, making it necessary for you to give an estimate of the percentage of change to functions and data. It is useful to indicate the modifications in the new system model so that you can identify them easily in the future. A simple way to do this is to highlight them with a colored pencil.

Process name: IDENTIFY PRELIMINARY MAN/MACHINE BOUNDARIES
FOR THE NEW SYSTEM
Process reference number: 2.3.3
Process guided by: Activity 2 plan

Process notes: Identify the specific portions of the new logical model that are to be manual and those that are to be automated. This process can be viewed as one of physical change, whereas the previous two processes were involved with logical change; both types of change together make up the area of change in analysis. (There may be no area of change of analysis in some projects, but there may be an area of change of design, such as a rewrite of an existing system.) Because the new logical model is completely logical, you derive the advantage of being able to identify the best partitioning for this system, if you are fortunate enough to have no constraints. However, even if there are constraints, you still should identify the *best* man/machine boundary as one of the options.

To identify the man/machine boundaries, develop an expanded data flow diagram by connecting the data flows of the lowest-level diagrams. Then, simply draw on this diagram one or more lines to represent the boundary between automated and manual functions and data. Avoid using this expanded diagram for management presentations because it has more detail than management needs to see. Along with deciding the best partitioning, your task is to develop other man/machine boundary options by identifying the project goals, especially the cost and time constraints that affect the bounding of the manual and automated portions of the system. Such project goals must state requirements for the physical environment. For example, "Department X must not be affected in any way." In this example, the current physical specification must identify which parts of the logical model represent department X. This identification can be accomplished by using the cross-reference feature in the logical data dictionary.

You may also want to use the current physical model to help identify the position of the man/machine boundary for areas that have not yet been considered. In this case, using the current boundary will be the least disruptive. Also, the current physical characteristics of a data flow may help to identify the man/machine boundary; for instance, frequency of use may be a significant factor because you may not want to automate a function that is performed only once a year. (The use of the current physical model in this instance will depend on the project goals; therefore, this process has been starved of the current physical specification so that the current design will not negatively influence the new design unless the current physical is necessary in a project goal.) At this level of detail, since you may not be able to clearly define the man/machine boundaries, you may have to give an estimate of the percentage of automation of a function and its data. For boundaries that are clearly defined, you can do some repartitioning: Put automated functions and data together, and manual functions and data together.

You may find it helpful to identify some physical characteristics of the interfaces between the man/machine boundary, such as the media used for interface data flows or for interface stores. Identifying these characteristics will probably make the diagram easier to read from the new system perspective. Also, any interface stores introduced because of the boundary definition may be of use for data modeling, especially if a project goal requires their inclusion in the corporate data model. If the physical characteristics are introduced during this process, note that the bounded new logical specification becomes somewhat physical. Also note that the man/machine boundary is a physical characteristic. The physicalization of the interfaces will be one of the first tasks in design, if it is not done now.

For any project goals that can be completely or partly satisfied in this process, document the analysis solutions in the project charter. It is useful to indicate the modifications in the new system model so that you can identify them easily in the future. A simple way to do this is to highlight them with a colored pencil.

Note: Remember that the man/machine boundaries defined in this process represent the system options for later presentation. Consequently, development work from this stage on will expand: All processes until the end of Activity 2 will be performed *for each option*. This is necessary to identify an honest cost/benefit analysis and feasibility report. The amount of work involved may seem considerable, but realize that there will be overlap between tasks (in fact, one option may be completely bounded by another), and that you are working at only a preliminary level of detail.

Process name: CREATE PRELIMINARY TEST CASES FOR THE NEW SYSTEM
Process reference number: 2.3.4
Process guided by: Activity 2 plan

Process notes: You already have test cases for the current system; they can be used to help develop the new system test cases. How much they will help depends on how much modification was made to the current logical specification. If there were no modifications, all of the test cases can be used. If modifications were made, the test cases will need additions and/or changes depending on the modifications. You can think of such tests as logical tests, which do not pertain to the design or implementation of the system, but which verify whether the system accomplishes the logical functions using the logical data. These test cases can be employed later to develop system and acceptance test cases.

Note: Care should be taken in the selection of test cases as they are candidates for further decomposition and will be used finally for development of executable tests.

As with preliminary current system test cases, new system test cases will probably be specified informally in narrative form (see process reference number 2.1.6).

Process name: CONDUCT REVIEW OF PRELIMINARY BOUNDED NEW LOGICAL
SPECIFICATION
Process reference number: 2.3.5
Process guided by: Activity 2 plan

Process notes: Identify any problems, inaccuracies, ambiguities, and omissions in the bounded new logical specification, which is the final deliverable of the analysis activities at the preliminary level. Since this specification is going to be used to develop the new design, it has to be complete and correct. Walkthroughs should have been conducted on the intermediate deliverables up to this review.

The agents reviewing the specification should be the project manager, user or user representative, project analysts, and, optionally, the designer. You should use the new system project goals and their solutions as well as the new system test cases to help validate the current logical specification.

(For standard review rules and procedures, see Appendix E.)

Process name: VERIFY OR REVISE PRELIMINARY CORPORATE DATA DICTIONARY
Process reference number: 2.4.1
Process guided by: Activity 2 plan

Process notes: Validate the data from the project — which consists at this level of files, records, and so on — by comparing it with the corporate stored data. Even if you are not using a central data administration group to coordinate data, you should compare the data you are storing with that in other systems in the corporation and attempt to synchronize all of the data. However, if you do have a system objective to use a corporate database, then you should identify any project goals that relate to data capture (the whole project may be based on the centralizing of data). Using these goals, identify which of the project data declared in the preliminary data dictionary need to be included in the corporate data dictionary and which need to be noted for later identification in the data categories. The data that may require capturing will consist mainly of the necessary stored logical data defined in the project data dictionary and possibly stores created because of packaging decisions, which, for example, are determined by the man/machine boundary. For any project goals that can be completely or partly satisfied in this process, document the data capture goals solutions in the project charter.

Note: If you can develop a company-wide data dictionary and maintain the data that it defines in a common database, then you can reduce (if not eliminate) redundancy, multiple updating, and inconsistency of common data between systems. This process, the others in Activity 2.4, and the equivalent general and detailed processes take a company-wide view, whereas all the other processes concentrate on the project's area of study.

This process may be performed by an agent outside the project team, such as a data administration team.

Process name: REFINE PRELIMINARY DATA CATEGORIES
Process reference number: 2.4.2
Process guided by: Activity 2 plan

Process notes: Compare the project groupings of data (data categories such as employ-ee data, project data, or accounts data) with the groupings of data in the corporate data model (data objects or data entities). Using the existing corporate data model along with the corporate data dictionary, check to see if the project data categories need modification — such as when the corporate data model has the accounts data split into accounts-receivable data and accounts-payable data. These categories should be used only if they present a correct view of the project data. The system data flow diagram can be used to show the functional reasons for creation of the data categories.

In this process, we are identifying the best functional groupings possible at this level of detail. The functional groupings are called "candidate objects," and they represent en-tities that define a specific function and are verifiable and recognizable in the company. Such groupings are not confirmed until more detailed study of their attributes has been accomplished. The new or modified data categories should be noted, especially those that require a change to the corporate data dictionary, as they will affect the cost/benefit analysis for the system.

This process may be performed by an agent outside the project team, such as a data ad-ministration team.

Process name: IDENTIFY PRELIMINARY RELATIONSHIPS BETWEEN CATEGORIES
Process reference number: 2.4.3
Process guided by: Activity 2 plan

Process notes: Identify the relationships that exist between the data categories for the project. The relationships between objects in the existing corporate data model can be used as clues to identify comparable relationships that can be readily supported between the same objects or data categories in your project. You can use this method of comparison to facilitate relationship identification, but using these relationships does not mean that they will be the *actual* relationships needed to support the system. Instead, they help us by showing the access capabilities of the data that are already supported.

Using your knowledge of the system, identify the relationships that are not already supported and that you may need (that is, ones that will affect the existing database), and indicate such nonexistent relationships on the data model. The system's data flow diagram can be used to help identify these relationships.

This process may be performed by an agent outside the project team, such as a data administration team.

Process name: CREATE PRELIMINARY DESIGN MODEL FOR NEW MANUAL ENVIRONMENT
Process reference number: 2.5.1
Process guided by: Activity 2 plan

Process notes: The design of the manual system is normally given little attention in data processing even though the manual system is just as important as the automated system for accomplishing business functions. The data flow diagram is an excellent tool for modeling the new manual environment, the design of which will be affected by the project goals. For example, if one project goal is to identify a better means of performing the business functions, then the functional partitioning on the data flow diagram should translate easily to the new manual design. However, if the goal is to develop an automated system with as little disruption of the manual activities as possible, the current manual system model may be used along with the cross reference in the bounded new logical data dictionary to identify original data and functions in order to satisfy the goal. (Usually, the manual environment will have much less flexibility for change than the automated environment. So, the current model may have to be used for a longer period of time than if it were used in an automated environment.)

In order to create a preliminary design model for a new manual environment, you first must identify whether the data categories in the bounded new logical specification required modification in the previous data modeling activity. If they did, use the data model to amend the logical stores that apply to the manual and man/machine interfaces on the data flow diagram of the bounded new logical specification. If no modification was required, ensure that all support characteristics on the man/machine boundary — for example, input/output media, physical store requirements, and so on — are identified. When identifying the man/machine boundary, look for environment modifications on the data flow diagram. Such modifications to the environment will be key areas of change on which to concentrate. In addition, concentrate on any project goals that can be satisfied at this point. In this preliminary-level study, you can do no more than identify the high-level design, which may be changed greatly in the general-level study, but which will give a basis for estimating the cost/benefit analysis and feasibility of the system. To summarize, design at this level will consist of identifying boundaries — for example, departments with sections or groups — within the manual portion of the system, and then adding physical interface characteristics between these boundaries as well as on major streams of data within them.

Even at this high level, you may identify support functions that need to be inserted in the model, such as a data preparation section. The logical specification is being physicalized, so this process is basically equivalent to the reverse of logicalization. (To identify preliminary physical data, see the sample table of contents for the manual system model in the addendum to the data dictionary.)

For any project goals that can be completely or partly satisfied in this process, document the manual design goal solutions in the project charter. It is useful to indicate the areas of change in the new design model so that you can identify them easily in the future. A simple way to do this is to highlight them with a colored pencil.

Note that in this process you are developing a separate model, not modifying the bounded new logical specification. The bounded new logical specification will be needed for reference in future processes.

Process name: CREATE PRELIMINARY DESIGN MODEL
FOR NEW AUTOMATED ENVIRONMENT
Process reference number: 2.5.2
Process guided by: Activity 2 plan

Process notes: First, determine whether the data categories in the bounded new logical specification required any modification in order to develop the preliminary data model. If modification was necessary, use the data model to amend the logical stores that apply to the automated and man/machine interfaces on the data flow diagram of the bounded new logical specification. Identify the support characteristics such as terminals and report media on the man/machine boundary if they were not identified in the manual design activity. As with preliminary manual design, use the data flow diagram in the bounded new logical specification as a design chart by identifying physical boundaries within the automated portion of the system. At this level of detail, you cannot identify any definite program boundaries, classically done in preliminary design, because you do not have sufficient detail to know whether the functions in the preliminary logical specification are cohesive units. You should, however, identify a conceptual design with the aid of any project goals that apply to this automated design. The conceptual design may change in the general study, but it will serve as one of the factors for estimating the cost/benefit analysis and feasibility of the system.

The conceptual design consists of identifying a function or functions that might become a job or job step based on either hardware or software boundaries (front-end processors or software packages, for example) and/or based on time constraints or business cycles. These boundaries can be represented on the data flow diagram by drawing boundary lines separating functions, but there will probably be some overlap of these boundaries, such as a function that is performed both in weekly and monthly jobs.

The rest of this design activity will involve adding physical interface characteristics, such as intermediate stores, message queues, and transaction media between the boundaries. Depending on the project goals, you may want to use the current automated system model to identify any salvageable portions of the current design. The cross-reference feature in the logical data dictionary can be used as a pointer to the original physical processes and data, but you should not just copy the existing design. One of the reasons for logicalizing the model was to give you an objective view of the existing design so you could develop a good new design. You are physicalizing the logical specification, which is basically equivalent to the reverse of logicalization. (To identify preliminary physical data, see the sample table of contents for the automated system model in the addendum to the data dictionary.)

For any project goals that can be completely or partly satisfied in this process, document the automated design goals solutions in the project charter. It is useful to indicate the areas of change in the new design model so that you can identify them easily in the future. A simple way to do this is to highlight them with a colored pencil.

Note: The new design solution may depend greatly on your selection of automated support hardware and software.

Process name: CREATE PRELIMINARY HW/SW SPECIFICATION
Process reference number: 2.5.3
Process guided by: Activity 2 plan

Process notes: Identify the major hardware and software needed to support the manual and automated portions of the new system. You cannot do this in detail here but can identify the classes of equipment and support software (not application software) that are needed to support the preliminary design. It is necessary to identify hardware and support software for both the automated and manual environment, for example, by identifying the need for minicomputers for each division and typewriters with by-product optical character recognition (OCR) output. Such identification helps define the cost/benefit analysis and feasibility of the new system. You may have a project goal stating that you must use the existing system hardware/software or company hardware/software, which means that this process will be very simple (it will involve just allocations of preliminary hardware/software) as the design will have had to accommodate this goal, too. Otherwise, you should use the new physical specification along with any hardware/software goals to estimate needs — for example, new hardware or software must be compatible with that of a central division. Identify any project goals that can be completely or partly satisfied in this process.

The "Production HW/SW Inventory" process identifies all company hardware/software, the current system hardware/software being a subset. If you do not have project goals that dictate hardware and software requirements, proceed as follows:

1. Identify reusable portions of the existing system hardware/software.

2. Identify reusable portions of the company hardware/software.

3. For those requirements not satisfied as a result of the previous two steps, research the purchase of new hardware/software by using an internal company planning group, appropriate technical journals, and/or by obtaining preliminary hardware/software data from applicable vendors. This data should be stored in the hardware/software specification.

Although you may not have a project goal stating it, you should insure compatibility of all hardware/software in the system. The data flow diagram of the bounded new logical specification may be of use if the man/machine boundary was annotated with physical characteristics (this input is not shown on the methodology's data flow diagram). For any project goals that can be completely or partly satisfied in this process, document the hardware/software goals solutions in the project charter.

This specification is for all the hardware/software needs in the new system, regardless of where the hardware/software is acquired; but to aid in later processes, you should indicate in this specification whether the hardware/software is new, or already existing in the company.

Process name: CREATE PRELIMINARY TEST CASES FOR NEW DESIGN
Process reference number: 2.5.4
Process guided by: Activity 2 plan

Process notes: Identify the test cases needed to validate, at a preliminary level, the new physical specification and the hardware/software specification for the new system.

At this level of detail, you should be mainly concerned with tests that apply to the physical partitioning of departments and sections, the partitioning of jobs and job steps, and the man/machine boundary, as well as the hardware/software that supports them.

You can view these tests as physical tests — for example, data interface tests — that pertain to the design and implementation of the system and that do not affect the business operations. The new system test cases, already created from the bounded new logical specification, are the logical tests. You can build upon these to form physical tests. You can have two objectives for a test case: to test a business function and data and to test the implementation of that function and data. The best source to use for identification and definition of test cases at this stage is the data dictionary of the new physical specification with the physical data flow diagram (manual side) and design charts (automated side) as a guide for flow of data. The test cases at this level of detail will probably be specified informally in narrative form.

Note: Someone other than the designer(s) should create test cases, especially negative test cases, to insure the objectivity of the tests.

Process name: CONDUCT REVIEW OF PRELIMINARY NEW DESIGN SPECIFICATIONS
Process reference number: 2.5.5
Process guided by: Activity 2 plan

Process notes: Identify any problems, inaccuracies, ambiguities, and omissions in the new physical specification and the hardware/software specification for this level of detail. These specifications are the final deliverables of the design activities at this level. They will be used to develop the implementation specifications and, when completed at the detailed level, used to build the system (code and installation); therefore, they have to be complete and correct. Walkthroughs should have been conducted on the individual deliverables during and after development.

This process basically constitutes an internal data processing review for the project team or the project manager accompanied by an optional hardware/software planning representative, but you should try to keep the user or user representatives involved throughout all of the system development effort.

You should use the design project goals and their solutions and the design test cases to help validate the design specifications.

(For standard review rules and procedures, see Appendix E.)

Process name: PREPARE PRELIMINARY SYSTEM INSTALLATION SPECIFICATION
Process reference number: 2.6.1
Process guided by: Activity 2 plan

Process notes: In this process, identify procedures and support requirements needed for installation of the new system's application software and manual procedures, at a preliminary level. First, identify the area of change between the current and new systems. The area of change should already be indicated in the new physical specification, but if it isn't, the current physical specification can be used for comparison (the bounded new logical may also be helpful in this task, although not shown on the methodology's data flow diagrams). At this level of detail, you probably can only estimate the extent of change and therefore can only estimate the procedures and support needed for installation of the new system. For example, on the automated portion of the system, a complete transfer of software and operations procedures might be called for; on the manual side, a relocation of the data preparation department to a new environment may be required.

If the project is a rewrite of an existing system, then the installation can be identified easily (that is, with no change to manual environment and no replacement of automated procedures). Regardless of the type of project, you should identify any project goals that can be completely or partly satisfied in this process (for example, maintaining customer data accuracy during the installation period of the new system). For these project goals, document the implementation goals solutions in the project charter (for instance, document that a three-cycle back-up history will be kept during installation to preserve the accuracy of customer data). To do this task, you will have to rely on the conceptual design in the new physical specification and estimate the number of procedures and programs or jobs that you will need to install. The identification and estimation of installation procedures and support needs will form the preliminary system installation specification, because this is as much information as you can identify at the preliminary level of study.

Note: There will be overlap between the implementation specifications, but try to keep redundancy to a minimum.

Process name: PREPARE PRELIMINARY HW/SW INSTALLATION SPECIFICATION
Process reference number: 2.6.2
Process guided by: Activity 2 plan

Process notes: In this process, identify environment and support requirements needed for installation of the new system's hardware and support software, at a preliminary level. The hardware/software specification describes the major hardware and support software needed for the new system and also identifies the portions that are new. Focus attention on the new hardware/software as well as on existing environments that require modification.

If there are no new purchases or modifications, then this process will just involve estimating whether the existing environment can accommodate the new system's needs as well as identifying any support requirements, such as a need for extra operations staff for an increased workload on existing hardware/software. Otherwise, you should identify any project goals applying to installation that can be wholly or partly satisfied in this process, for example, that existing operations staff should operate the new hardware/software, and you should document the implementation goals solutions in the project charter.

Using these project goals, you should review the hardware/software environment's data in the "Production HW/SW Inventory" process and determine if an existing environment can be used as a base or a model for any new hardware/software. If so, this environment's documentation should be used as part of the hardware/software installation specification and should indicate the extent of change.

For the hardware/software that doesn't fit in an existing environment, identify the preliminary new environment description and configuration chart. Whether an existing environment can or cannot be used, the hardware/software installation support requirements should be estimated. You can give only estimates of installation needs because you have identified only major hardware/software in the hardware/software specification.

The agent performing this process may be outside the project team, such as a support planning group.

Note: There will be overlap between the implementation specifications, but try to keep redundancy to a minimum.

Process name: PREPARE PRELIMINARY CONVERSION SPECIFICATION
Process reference number: 2.6.3
Process guided by: Activity 2 plan

Process notes: Identify the procedures and support requirements needed in the conversion of data for the new system at a preliminary level.

The first task in this process is to identify the area of change between the current and new systems, as this is the focal point in this process (specifically, the change of stored data and input/output composition). The area should be indicated already in the new physical specification (in the data dictionary), but if it isn't, the current physical specification can be used for comparison. You should look for files containing data that will probably change or for new files that need to be created, in addition to files that will need a change of order, access, or media. At this level of detail, you only have identified the major stores and their records, for which you may be able to estimate the degree of change, if any (the whole reason for the project may be to convert stored data to an on-line environment). However, there may be other changes identified for these stores, as when a data structure diagram is produced or data modeling is performed in the general and detailed studies.

You should identify any project goals that can be totally or partly satisfied in this process; for example, all records in the personnel file that are not in the payroll file should be identified and deleted. For these project goals, document the implementation goals solutions in the project charter; for example, document that one centralized payroll/personnel file will be produced with an error file for non-matched records.

The conversion effort can be a system in itself if the data conversion is large and complex. If such is the case, a preliminary system model, showing existing data and the functions necessary to produce the new data, and a design model, showing the implementation of these functions and their data coupling, should be created. A conversion data dictionary should be developed so the conversion effort can stand alone.

For this preliminary level of detail, the identification and estimation of the data to be converted and of the degree and complexity of the conversion will form the conversion specification. Preliminary test cases can be identified to validate the conversion procedures and results.

Note: There will be overlap between the implementation specifications, but try to keep redundancy to a minimum.

Process name: PREPARE PRELIMINARY TRAINING SPECIFICATION
Process reference number: 2.6.4
Process guided by: Activity 2 plan

Process notes: Identify the requirements and support needed for training the users and the operations staff so that they can use the new system.

Producing the training specification is somewhat different from producing the other implementation specifications. The input to the training specification is untrained people who need training in some aspect of the new system; at this preliminary level, input or output is not more specifically defined. Therefore, you need to define your training requirements, which can be regarded as a further breakdown of the overall objectives.

The first task in this process is to identify the area of change between the current and new system, as this is the area you will concentrate on. The area should be indicated already in the new physical specification but, if not, the current physical specification can be used for comparison. Also, you should identify the area of change in the hardware/software specification. Look for changes in function, changes in interface with hardware/software, and/or changes in interface with data. This area of change applies to operations, as well as to users. At this level of detail, you may have to use a percentage of change for some areas. Identify any project goals that can be totally or partly satisfied in this process, for example, that training must be provided for management as well as staff. For these projects goals, document the implementation goals solutions in the project charter; for example, three levels of training will be provided: one for management, one for supervisors, and one for staff.

Using these project goals and the area of change, estimate the training requirements and training support needed to satisfy them. Some of the training support may be satisfied by vendors of hardware/software or by external trainers, but you should still identify the requirements and support needs in your training specification. For this preliminary level of detail, the identification and estimation of the training requirements and support will form the training specification.

Note: There will be overlap between the implementation specifications, but try to keep redundancy to a minimum.

Process name: CONDUCT REVIEW OF PRELIMINARY IMPLEMENTATION SPECIFICATIONS
Process reference number: 2.6.5
Process guided by: Activity 2 plan

Process notes: Identify any problems, inaccuracies, ambiguities, and omissions in the implementation specifications for this level of detail. These specifications document what is required to support the implementation of the new system, so they must be complete and correct for this level of study. Walkthroughs should have been conducted during and after development of each specification.

This review can involve a number of groups; for example, a planning group for hardware/software installation, the users and operations staff for training, the database group for conversion, and the project members for installation. Each group, as well as the developers of the specifications and the project manager, should be represented. Each specification can be reviewed individually with the agents concerned, but note that there will be overlap in these specifications, as stated in the process notes (for example, the training support may include part of the new system hardware/software or the actual system).

The project goals applicable to implementation and their solutions should be used to validate these specifications.

(For standard review rules and procedures, see Appendix E.)

Process name: IDENTIFY PRELIMINARY RELEASES (IF NECESSARY)
Process reference number: 2.7.1
Process guided by: Activity 2 plan

Process notes: In this process, determine whether there is a need to deliver the new system in releases. If so, identify them.

Remember that you have already identified preliminary man/machine boundary options for the new system. These options may correspond to the releases, or you may identify releases within these options. You can accept releases as equivalent to man/machine boundary options if you are delineating the system using the same factors, such as time, functions, and products.

Little detail is available at this level of study, but even so you should know the scope and complexity of the system, since you performed all the preliminary analysis, design, and support implementation activities. With such knowledge and preliminary documentation, you should estimate the amount of time needed for the project.

If for any man/machine option you estimate that it will take more than one to one-and-a-half years to deliver a product to the user, you should consider splitting the option into releases. Beyond this estimated time period, either the user loses interest, or the original request probably will have changed. If releases are necessary, you can use the bounded new logical specification, with its cross reference in the data dictionary to original physical details, to aid in identifying releases by current area or functions. Proceeding in this manner will be the least disruptive in implementation of releases but may need the most support effort from the point of view of the new system; for example, you may have to develop extra interface functions to accommodate each release's physical boundaries, such as in converting old data to new data and back to old again. Otherwise, you can partition by new functional boundaries or new time boundaries, for example, by monthly portion and on-line portion. You may even identify releases based on the area(s) that cause the user the most problems or based on one of the implementation specifications. The new system documentation as well as the project charter then should be annotated to reflect these releases. After management has approved them, you can partition this documentation by release. The system documentation will reflect them throughout the next level of study. You should define the first release as precisely as possible for this level of study and give your best guess for other releases.

If the system is very large, the general-level study may start with just the first release; otherwise, you may want to conduct the general study for the whole system and focus on the first release in the detailed study. The latter procedure is better because you can identify the releases more clearly, but doing so will delay producing the first release.

Note: The output data flow of this task is shown driving the development of the plans. This is an example of iteration in data flow diagrams, as these processes will probably rely on each other; for example, given x resources, y products and/or functions can be delivered by date z.

Process name: PREPARE AND SYNCHRONIZE PRELIMINARY
IMPLEMENTATION PLANS (BY RELEASE)
Process reference number: 2.7.2
Process guided by: Activity 2 plan

Process notes: Now that you have derived specifications containing implementation requirements and identified the releases, prepare the implementation plans, which detail
how the implementation will be conducted. Then, synchronize each plan with all others
for this preliminary level of detail. Although this is a large managerial task, at this level
it should not be too complicated.

Identify any project goals that can be partly or completely satisfied in this process, either
from the project charter or from the implementation specifications themselves. These
project goals affect how you implement the system (for example, designating the buying
department as the first to use the new system), and their solutions should be amended
to the original request document. Develop a strategy for meeting the project goals and
for performing each implementation specification that has releases identified. Indicate
all dependencies and schedules and provide as much detail as possible for a first release.
For example, system installation done using a pilot project in a specific department will
need to be synchronized with training that will be provided for the new system operation on a regular in-house basis, which in turn will need to be synchronized with the
hardware/software installation.

At this level of detail, you can only roughly identify the synchronization of these
specifications; for instance, new data entry hardware/software should be installed early
in order to aid training. A second example might be that conversion of all data must be
finished before the installation of the system in a main branch of the company can be
started. Along with the scheduling activities, the availability of any outside support,
such as a database group or vendor training, should be confirmed here.

Note: This task is identified as a managerial task because the agents performing it are
the project manager and higher management, but the project team should help with the
implementation plans because it is familiar with the effort involved since it has
developed the preliminary documentation.

Process name: PREPARE ACTIVITY 3 DEVELOPMENT PLAN (BY RELEASE)
Process reference number: 2.7.3
Process guided by: Activity 2 plan

Process notes: Having completed all of the development activities for analysis and design at a preliminary level and having identified releases for the new system, you are in a good position to prepare the development plan for the general-level study. Decide whether you will conduct the general-level study using just the first release or whether the complete system will be needed. Your decision will depend on the system's size and on the available time and resources, but you may not be the decision maker in this case. It may be the user management's decision. Therefore, you may wish to develop a plan for each option and release for presentation to management.

Having completed the preliminary study, you have five factors to help you develop the Activity 3 plan:

1. familiarity with the system

2. deliverables and processes already partly identified in the methodology

3. preliminary current system description and preliminary new system description, with releases defined and with the areas to study identified in more detail

4. figures for estimated and actual resources used in Activity 2

5. results from any blitz conducted during the preliminary study that are used to identify general-level detail required

Using these five factors, prepare the development plan for Activity 3. Include all tasks, resources, dependencies, and information about schedules needed to conduct the general-level analysis and design.

The plan should be as detailed as possible for Activity 3, but for cost/benefit analysis and feasibility purposes, you should estimate the plans needed for each release for Activities 4 through 6, excluding those releases already covered in the implementation plans. The plan may include the use of manpower resources from outside the project team, such as a database group, the user, and the operations staff (confirm their availability from management).

Note: Even though this is a managerial task because the agents are the project manager and management, the best source for identification of the effort involved in Activity 3 is the project team.

Process name: ANALYZE PRELIMINARY COSTS/BENEFITS
AND PREPARE FEASIBILITY REPORT
Process reference number: 2.7.4
Process guided by: Activity 2 plan

Process notes: Produce a feasibility report containing sufficient information to allow management to decide whether to approve the resources for further study. This report should provide

1. a summary of estimated and actual resources used in the preliminary study

2. an overview of the system documentation developed so far, with options and releases identified for the new system

3. a list of the project goals and preliminary solutions that apply to the preliminary study, noting any goals that have been added since project initiation

4. a cost/benefit analysis for the new system along with a summary of any limitations and risks associated with producing it

5. a detailed estimate of plans and resources needed for Activity 3 and an overall estimate of the plans and resources needed for Activities 4 through 6

One of the main reasons for doing the preliminary study was to produce this feasibility report. Item 1 above can be drawn from the project plan. Items 2 through 5 are documented by option — areas of change associated with man/machine boundaries, for example — with releases identified, if necessary. Item 2 is produced from the current and new system descriptions. Item 3 is produced from the project charter. Item 4 is produced from the cost data in the specifications of the current and new system descriptions and from cost/benefit information in the project charter. You should add any benefits and risks that you have identified yourself, such as improved documentation or a more maintainable system. Item 5 can be derived from the project plan.

In this process, you will be working with information gathered during the preliminary study. Therefore, the degree of accuracy in the cost/benefit analysis and plans is not very high. State this in the feasibility report, along with the notation that all estimates may be off by as much as fifty percent.

Process name: CONDUCT INDEPENDENT REVIEW
Process reference number: 2.7.5
Process guided by: Activity 2 plan

Process notes: Now that you have conducted a full preliminary study but are not too far into the project, this is a perfect time to confirm that the correct approach to the project is being taken and that the development tools are being used correctly.

You can avoid compounding any errors made up to this point by holding an independent review. The people conducting the review should not be project members because you want objective observers to verify that the project teams are on the correct path. You should enlist reviewers who have worked on similar projects, who can easily understand the form of documentation, and who have a knowledge of the methodology being followed.

(For standard review rules and procedures, see Appendix E.)

Process name: PRESENT FEASIBILITY REPORT TO D.P. MANAGEMENT
Process reference number: 2.7.6
Process guided by: Activity 2 plan

Process notes: The aim of this formal presentation is to make data processing management aware of progress, to inform them of the resources used, to advise them of the feasibility of the project, and, if the project is approved, to obtain approval of data processing resources for further study. You want to keep data processing management informed of project progress as this is one way of avoiding cancellation of resources if a schedule slippage is necessary. In the presentation, you may identify options that required additional data processing staff to be hired or brought in on contract.

Process name: PRESENT FEASIBILITY REPORT TO USER MANAGEMENT FOR SELECTION
Process reference number: 2.7.7
Process guided by: Activity 2 plan

Process notes: Design this formal presentation to accomplish the following: to inform user management of the resources used so far; to give an overview of the system documentation showing the options for the new system with any necessary releases identified; to present the feasibility and cost/benefit of each option; and to obtain approval and commitment for resources to study the selected system option or options. Include this last application if user management is also responsible for the overall resource cost. There is, of course, the possibility of the project being canceled at this stage, but you are presenting options (different areas of change, or man/machine boundaries), so it is likely that one of them will be accepted. The data flow diagrams and data dictionary used for development allow you to easily adapt your design to different options because of the partitioning of the documentation.

As you have completed only a preliminary study so far, you may want to recommend to the user that you proceed through the general study with more than one option (unless it is obvious which option is required, for example, if only one option falls within budget).

The project charter and project plan should be updated to reflect the option(s) selected, and the overall data processing plans and resources should be revised for reallocation of resources, including new hiring and contracting needs. (The feasibility report can be kept as reference and used as documentation for project histories.)

Process name: VALIDATE AND/OR CREATE GENERAL DESIGN MODEL
FOR CURRENT MANUAL ENVIRONMENT
Process reference number: 3.1.1
Process guided by: Activity 3 plan

Process notes: The first task in this general-level process is to use the selected system
option(s) to identify which portions of the preliminary manual system model will require further decomposition, while still allowing for study of areas that bound the system option(s). The aims in this process are the same as those of process reference
number 2.1.1 in the preliminary study, but now you are going to validate the existing
model or refine the preliminary model by producing more levels of detail in the data
flow diagram and data dictionary. So, at this general level of study, identify all documents and transactions within major streams of data and all records and documents
within major files. List all of the associated elements. Also, identify all streams of data,
stores, and processes that were not considered major in the preliminary study. (To
identify general-level data, see the sample table of contents for the manual system
model in the addendum to the data dictionary.) This general-level task is going to require much more effort than the equivalent preliminary-level task.

The data-gathering activity for this level of detail will be conducted in the same manner
as in the preliminary study except that the interviewees will probably not be managers,
but instead will be supervisors and staff. You can expect to uncover major flows of data
that were missed in the preliminary study. If this is the case, the cost/benefit analysis
and feasibility study may be affected. These major flows should be noted and communicated to management for correction in another release or in this release via change-
management. You should be able to eliminate most alias data names at this level, but
if you are not able to do so, you can resolve them at the detailed level. During this
process, you will probably receive additional project goals from the people you interview. (See process reference number 2.2.1 for how to process additional goals.)

Process name: VALIDATE AND/OR CREATE GENERAL DESIGN MODEL
                  FOR CURRENT AUTOMATED ENVIRONMENT
Process reference number: 3.1.2
Process guided by: Activity 3 plan

Process notes: The first task in this process of general study is to use the selected system option(s) to identify which portions of the preliminary automated system model are going to be studied further, while still allowing for study of areas that bound the system option(s).

Your aims in this process are the same as in process reference number 2.1.2 in the preliminary study, but now you are going to validate the existing model or develop the preliminary model by identifying program structure and support information. So, at this level of study, identify all transactions and reports within major data streams with a list of their elements, all records within data stores with a list of their elements, and all programs within major jobs showing the structure of modules within these programs. You must also identify all streams of data, stores (including transient and intermediate stores), and programs not represented on the preliminary design chart (system flowchart). (To identify general data, see the sample table of contents for the automated system model in the addendum to the data dictionary.) This task is going to require more effort than was required at the preliminary level. Gather data for the affected systems using any available maintenance documentation, the current operations manual, and interviews, but emphasize program structure and the data used by the processes in the structure.

You may discover major processes and streams of data that have an effect on the cost/benefit and feasibility analyses. These new processes should be noted and communicated to management for inclusion in another release or in this release through change-management. The additional information gathered at the general level should clear up any data interface conflicts uncovered during the preliminary study.

It may not be obvious where existing programs are partitioned into modules or functions, but you may find the common modular program with a "pancake" structure (one boss module with one level of subordinate worker modules). If there are no partitionable modules in the existing program, it is worthless trying to develop a design chart of module descriptions. Therefore, you may have to exert more effort in the logicalization task, working from the source listing (code analysis), to identify the business functions.

During this process, you will probably receive additional project goals from the maintenance or operations staff. (See process reference number 2.2.1 for how to handle these.)

Process name: DERIVE GENERAL LOGICAL MODEL
                    FOR CURRENT MANUAL ENVIRONMENT
Process reference number: 3.1.3
Process guided by: Activity 3 plan

Process notes: Using the general manual system model, derive or validate the manual logical model, representing the general business functions and their data. This level of detail requires a fair amount of effort because you are developing functional primitives, which you will specify in the detailed study. The general-level logical model is derived by removing all physical characteristics (other than those needed for business reasons) referenced in the general manual system model. An example of these would be references to document numbers, colors, or media; references to the sequencing or control of processes, indicating which sections or groups perform them; and references to the media used for stores. (To identify general data, see the sample table of contents for a logical specification in the addendum to the data dictionary.) This task is made easier if you have a physicalized model as the input. Remove processes that do not need to be represented on a logical model, for example, processes that change data from one medium to another, processes that distribute data, and processes for copying and backup. The preliminary manual logical model (high-level view) will be used as a guide, but be suspicious: The greater level of detail in this general-level study will help you to spot partitioning problems (poor grouping of functions).

One way to spot poor partitioning is to look for processes with many interfaces (data flows) or processes that are difficult to name logically. Good partitioning is indicated by processes that are easy to name and that have few interfaces. More repartitioning will probably take place when the automated functions are combined with manual functions to form the logical model for the whole system. If in doubt about repartitioning (especially if a suspect area interfaces with an automated function), it will be better to wait until combining automated with manual functions.

Any internal stores (those not interfacing with automated functions) can be investigated to see whether they should be represented as data flows. Note that a data store is needed for data that cannot be obtained dynamically.* This logicalization task is a good place to clean up alias names for data and create meaningful names to replace physical names, numbers, and so on. This may require a number of iterations for each name. The derivation and validation of the logical model can be supplemented with any business and support documentation in the maintenance library. Most users should be able to validate this logical transformation, especially on the manual portions of the system.

Note: You are deriving a separate model here, not modifying the manual system model. The manual system model will be needed for reference in future processes.

---

*See model transformations in Appendix C for an example of data store cleanup.

Process name: DERIVE GENERAL LOGICAL MODEL
FOR CURRENT AUTOMATED ENVIRONMENT
Process reference number: 3.1.4
Process guided by: Activity 3 plan

Process notes: Derive or validate the manual logical model at a general level, representing general business functions and their data and using the general-level automated system model. This level of detail requires you to develop a model down to the functional primitives, which you will specify in the detailed study. How much effort this task will take depends on the automated system model, input, and how knowledgeable the user or data processing maintenance staff is of the functions the automated system performs. If a reasonable automated system model could not be supplied as input to this task, you may have to do code analysis to derive the logical functions.

If you do have a reasonable design chart in the automated system model, transform it into a logical data flow diagram by tracking the flow of data and identifying the functions that act on this data. If the input to this process is a good design chart, many of the processes will be performing coordinating and manager tasks. As coordinating and manager modules are not represented on a logical model, the task here is to derive the logical data flow diagram by tracking the data flowing through the worker modules and through any actual data transformation contained in the coordinating modules. The transformations of this data will form the functional processes in the logical model.

Producing this logical model from the automated system model also involves removing all physical characteristics (other than those needed for business reasons), such as references to transactions and/or report numbers and media; references to the sequencing or control of processes, switches, end-of-file flags, and program numbers; and references to the media used for stores. (To identify general data, see the sample table of contents of a logical specification in the addendum to the data dictionary.)

There will probably be processes that do not need to be represented on a logical model, for example, processes that perform initialization or termination, sorts or extracts, and any housekeeping routines not needed for business reasons. The preliminary automated logical model (high-level view) will act as a guide, but be suspicious: The greater level of detail here will help you to spot partitioning problems.

One way to spot poor partitioning is to look for processes with many interfaces (data flows) or processes that are difficult to name logically. Processes that are easy to name and that have few interfaces are an indication of good partitioning. More repartitioning will probably take place when the automated functions are combined with the manual functions to form the logical model for the whole system. So if in doubt about repartitioning, wait until combining the automated and manual functions.

Any internal stores not interfacing with manual functions can be investigated to see whether they should be represented as data flows. Note that a data store is needed for data that cannot be obtained dynamically.*

---

*See model transformations in Appendix C for an example of data store cleanup.

Use this logicalization task to create meaningful names to replace physical names, numbers, and so on. Alias names can be eliminated as well. You have a free hand at naming internal data flows, but you must be careful when renaming data flows that interface with manual functions. Expect to go through a number of iterations on some names before arriving at an acceptable name.

The derivation and validation of this logical model can be enhanced with any business and support documentation in the maintenance library. Also, it is hoped that the user and data processing maintenance staff will be able to help validate the transformation from the physical to the logical model.

Note: You are deriving a separate model here, not modifying the automated system model. The automated system model will be needed for reference in future processes.

Process name: DERIVE GENERAL LOGICAL SPECIFICATION FOR THE CURRENT SYSTEM
Process reference number: 3.1.5
Process guided by: Activity 3 plan

Process notes: Produce the logical model for the whole system, which is composed of manual and automated systems combined. The aim of this task is to remove the physical view of how processes and their data are partitioned in the existing system, along manual and automated boundaries. Having done this, you can develop the best partitioning for the new system, without being influenced by the existing partitioning. This process involves combining two logical models into one; therefore, it is similar to the process of deriving the general manual logical model. (To confirm the data required for the general level, see the sample table of contents of a logical specification in the addendum to the data dictionary.) However, in this process, the physical characteristics appear only on the interfaces between the manual and automated models.

All interfaces between these two models need to be paired and their physical characteristics removed. Any interfaces that cannot be matched need to be investigated by cycling back to the general-design models to determine whether they were missed during the design study; were documented as supported in the manual system but not in the automated system (which rarely happens); were phased out of the manual system but were still supported in the automated (which often happens); are aliases for other interfaces; or are components of another interface (for example, an automated model developed to a different level of detail than was the manual model).

The interfaces missed during the design study will require the same development effort as did the other interfaces identified prior to this task. The interfaces in which support discrepancies occur probably can be taken care of in this task, if you only have to delete and repartition functions and data.

Aliases can be handled as follows: Confirm that the interfaces are aliases and develop logical name(s) to replace the physical name(s). For those interfaces that are components of other interfaces, identify if they are too detailed for this general level. If they are, document them and exclude them from this model and include them later at the detailed level. If the interfaces have too little detail, cycle back to the design models and develop them further.

As with other logicalization tasks, you must do the following:

1. Remove all physical characteristics from the interfaces, other than those required for business reasons, while developing logical names for those that are physical.

2. Replace interface stores that are really data flows, such as those used just for time delays.

3. Look for partitioning problems, for example, functions that are performed partly in the manual system and partly in the automated system. With your current understanding of the system, you may be able to identify incomplete functions during this task.

The preliminary current logical specification (high-level view) will act as a guide in all tasks, but be suspicious: The greater level of detail in this general study makes it easier to spot partitioning problems that you could not identify in the preliminary study; you may have a smaller area of study at the general level. Finally, you should clean up the stores: With the amount of information you have at this level, you can probably develop a non-detailed data structure or data access diagram, which can be considered an informal data structure diagram or a data model or data subschema.* This data structure diagram can only be considered informal at this level because you don't know the business policy for the use of this data until the detailed study is completed. You do need to know the business policy to derive a good data structure diagram.

The data structure diagram is derived from all genuine system data stores on the logical model, which are those stores that remain after logicalization. The data structure diagram shows the functional entities of data in the system and their relationships. The entities can be viewed as small stores, and they should be plugged back into the general system model, and their applicable data flows should be connected. You may find stores that are supported but never used, data that is never updated, or use of data not identified as input to these stores. These occurrences obviously need to be investigated by cycling back to the design models. They may be signs of missed data flows, or the first two examples may indicate genuine faults of the current system. Re-inserting the data entities should improve the readability of the model. In addition, by doing this, you have removed the final physical characteristics of the current design except those needed for business reasons.

---

*For a detailed discussion of creating data structure diagrams, see T. DeMarco's *Structured Analysis and System Specification* (New York: YOURDON Press, 1979), pp. 233-55. Also, see P. Chen, "The Entity-Relationship Model — Toward a Unified View of Data," *ACM Transactions on Database Systems,* Vol. 1, No. 1 (March 1976), pp. 9-36.

Process name: CREATE GENERAL TEST CASES FOR CURRENT SYSTEM
Process reference number: 3.1.6
Process guided by: Activity 3 plan

Process notes: Identify and create the test cases needed to validate the current logical specification at a general level. If you have access to an existing regression test specification for any portion of the affected automated or manual system, you can use it to help form the test cases.

For systems without an existing regression test specification, review the current logical specification and develop test cases that will validate the completeness and correctness of the system's affected portions as well as of the complete system. These tests will relate to the level of information you have in your specification, for example, transactions within streams of data, records within stores, and general-level functions. Of course, the preliminary-level test cases will be good guides, but they must be validated for the area of study required at this level. If still applicable, they should be developed further.

Using the data flow diagram as a guide for inputs and outputs, you will find that the best source for further identification and definition of test cases is the data dictionary of the current logical specification. An example of a general test case follows:

Test objective:	validate that for a complete withdrawal, all accounts for a customer are closed out
Test input:	special complete-withdrawal transaction
Expected execution:	generation of savings, checking, and loan account close-out transactions, and the flow of these transactions through their respective processes to a special close-out reporting process
Expected output:	customer close-out report showing balances for savings, checking, and loan accounts

Since you are creating test cases to validate the current system and since the user is obviously a good source of information about the current system, the user or user representative should be one of the agents performing this task. The user can be especially helpful in identifying invalid (negative) tests.

Process name: CONDUCT REVIEW OF GENERAL CURRENT LOGICAL SPECIFICATION
Process reference number: 3.1.7
Process guided by: Activity 3 plan

Process notes: See process reference number 2.1.7 for notes on this review process.

Process name: ANALYZE GENERAL PROJECT GOALS
Process reference number: 3.2.1
Process guided by: Activity 3 plan

Process notes: Turn your attention in this process toward the new system to identify the project goals that can be satisfied in analysis at this level of detail. The goals relate to complete new data and functions and to changes to data and functions in the current logical specifications. Your task is to identify the logical modifications necessary to meet these goals.

You must also identify the preliminary logical modifications applied to the preliminary bounded new logical specification in order to decompose them. If the preliminary modifications are not indicated, use the analysis goal solutions in the project charter as a pointer. You will probably be able to identify most modifications at this level.

If your project goal requires that you add a major function, the task of analyzing the general-level project goals can be time consuming. You may have to study the physical design of a similar function at another organization and logicalize it, rather than conduct your own analysis. Other logical modifications consist of changes to and deletions from existing data or functions. For changes, you may have to validate physical to logical transformations of these data and functions. (To identify general data, see the sample table of contents for a logical specification in the addendum to the data dictionary.) There may be no logical modifications at all if the project is concerned only with design and implementation goals with no change to business data or functions.

For those project goals that can be partly or completely satisfied in this process, document the analysis goals solution(s) in the project charter.

Note: If there are no completely new data and functions, this process can be merged with the next process: deriving the new logical model.

Process name: DERIVE GENERAL LOGICAL MODEL FOR THE NEW SYSTEM
Process reference number: 3.2.2
Process guided by: Activity 3 plan

Process notes: Produce the new logical model by applying the logical modifications to the current logical specification. This may involve adding, updating, and possibly deleting portions of the data flow diagram, the data dictionary, and any process descriptions that comprise the current logical specification. The current logical specification will be needed for reference in future processing.

Most of the modifications will probably be made at this level. You should be able to use the modifications in the preliminary bounded new logical specification as a guide if major functions and data were affected. After the modifications are incorporated in the model, you may identify partitioning problems, which you can probably eliminate in the next process, when you repartition the area under study into manual and automated functions.

If any new stores were introduced into the model, investigate them to see if they can be completely replaced with an existing store. If not, derive another informal data structure diagram with this data included (see process reference number 3.1.5) and use it to plug the necessary stores back into the logical model.

At this point, you should see evidence of one of the advantages of studying the current system: Any modification should fit inside the current model; that is, the modifications should be completely bounded by the area of study. If they are not, you did not study far enough. If you find that the modifications "touch the edge" of your current model and you decide not to study beyond the modification, then according to Murphy's Law, that is where you will have the most problems. It is useful to indicate the modifications in the new system model to identify them easily in the future. A simple method is to highlight them with a colored pencil.

Note: You are developing a separate model, not modifying the current logical specification.

Process name: IDENTIFY GENERAL MAN/MACHINE BOUNDARY FOR THE NEW SYSTEM
Process reference number: 3.2.3
Process guided by: Activity 3 plan

Process notes: Identify the manual and automated portions of the new logical model. This process can be considered as distinguishing the area of physical change, whereas the previous two processes can be considered as distinguishing the area of logical change. The area of physical change combined with the area of logical change forms the area of change of analysis.

The area studied at the general level may have been determined by a man/machine boundary option that was specified at the preliminary level. It is at the general level of study that you can identify a *definite* boundary. You should attempt to settle on one and only one boundary: It would be expensive to proceed with more than one. Other factors to consider when determining the one definite boundary are the preliminary system option(s) selected by the user and the preliminary bounded new logical specification. Remember that this is an iterative process and that if a better option is discovered, you should bring it to the attention of management.

To summarize, the main source for identifying the final man/machine boundary is the project goals, especially those goals that apply to the requirements for the physical environment. (See process reference number 2.3.3.) As stated in the equivalent preliminary-level process, you may want to use the current physical specification as an overall aid, especially to identify some physical interface characteristics.

Some redundancy may have to be introduced regarding the stores between the manual and automated portions of the system. How much redundancy is introduced will depend on where and whether you split functions that are associated with one store. Splitting functions associated with *one* store does not necessarily lead to redundancy, as in the case of a manual function accessing data by a computer-assisted process. In this case, the data should not be duplicated in the manual and automated systems.

The bounded new logical specification is the new logical model with a man/machine boundary identified. Do not worry if this boundary forms many "islands" on the data flow diagram, as the next task is to repartition this model, separating the automated portion from the manual portions. Repartitioning should be done to facilitate both the presentation and the design of each of these areas. It may be useful to have an expanded data flow diagram showing the automated and manual portions together with the physical interfaces defined on the man/machine boundary.

For any project goals that can be partly or completely satisfied in this process, document the analysis goals solutions in the project charter.

Process name: CREATE GENERAL TEST CASES FOR THE NEW SYSTEM
Process reference number: 3.2.4
Process guided by: Activity 3 plan

Process notes: The test cases for the current system can be used in the development of the new system test cases. The extent to which they will be used depends on how much modification was made to the current logical specification. If there were no modifications, then all the existing test cases can be used.

If modifications were made, the test cases will need to be changed or added to accordingly. You can consider these tests as logical tests; that is, they do not pertain to the design or implementation of the system. Their purpose is to test that the system accomplishes the logical functions by using the logical data. These test cases can be used later to develop system and acceptance tests. The preliminary new system test cases will act as a guide for the general test cases, but they must be validated if the area of study for the general level was not the same as for the preliminary level. Most test cases will probably be developed in this process; they will need to be further developed at the detailed level of study, and finally, in Activity 5, they will become machine-executable tests.

The data dictionary of the bounded new logical specification will be the major source for the identification of test cases along with the data flow diagrams. The creation of new system test cases is the same as the creation of current system test cases (see process reference number 3.1.6).

Process name: CONDUCT REVIEW OF GENERAL BOUNDED NEW LOGICAL SPECIFICATION
Process reference number: 3.2.5
Process guided by: Activity 3 plan

Process notes: See process reference number 2.3.5 for notes on this review process.

Process name: VERIFY OR REVISE GENERAL CORPORATE DATA DICTIONARY
Process reference number: 3.3.1
Process guided by: Activity 3 plan

Process notes: Validate the system data dictionary against the corporate data dictionary. Based on the level of detail you have now in the current system data dictionary (records and elements) and on the project goals that relate to data capture — for example, up-to-date data is required; otherwise, client accounts are inaccurate — you can reasonably identify the data that needs to be included in the corporate data dictionary. You should review the corporate data dictionary and identify the data that requires inclusion or updating from the system data dictionary. This data should be noted for later identification in the data objects. The data that may require capturing will consist mainly of necessary stored logical data defined in the system data dictionary, and possibly will consist of data from stores created because of physical packaging, for example, because of the man/machine boundary or design boundaries in the manual and automated environments.

At this stage, you also should look for alias name problems that can be eliminated through clarification of the data definitions in the corporate data dictionary. For any project goals that can be partly or completely satisfied by this process, document the data capture goals solutions in the project charter; for example, document the solution to security problems or the synchronization of data.

Note: This process is designed to produce a company-wide dictionary of data that supports a common database, thus reducing or eliminating redundancy, multiple updating, inconsistency, and so on, of common data between systems. This process, the next two processes, and the equivalent preliminary and detailed processes take a company-wide view, whereas all other processes in this methodology concentrate on the project's area of study.

This process may be performed by an agent outside the project team, such as a data administration team.

Process name: REFINE GENERAL DATA OBJECTS
Process reference number: 3.3.2
Process guided by: Activity 3 plan

Process notes: At this level of detail, you have an informal data structure diagram (data model) of the project's data needs. Compare the data objects in this diagram with the ones in the corporate data model. (Note that you may have some extra data identified for capture because of preliminary packaging of functions.) Using the existing corporate data model along with the corporate data dictionary definitions, check to see if your project data objects need to be modified; for example, check to see whether data elements or attributes need to be assigned to different objects in the corporate data model. The system data flow diagram can be used to confirm the functionality of objects in your data structure diagram. Because you have not yet defined the data elements of the objects, they should be regarded as *refined* (candidate) data objects. You cannot update the corporate data model based on this level of detail, but you should still note any new objects (created out of existing objects) or updates to existing objects that are needed for the system, as this will affect the cost/benefit analysis for the system. You can bring in the preliminary data model as a guide, although it will not be of much use because the data administration activities really use only the most detailed data.

This process may be performed by an agent outside the project team, such as a data administration team.

Process name: IDENTIFY GENERAL RELATIONSHIPS BETWEEN OBJECTS
Process reference number: 3.3.3
Process guided by: Activity 3 plan

Process notes: At this level of detail, you should be reasonably able to identify the necessary relationships between data objects. The relationships can be identified from those that are already on the corporate data model and those on the informal data structure diagram. (There may be some relationships necessary to support extra data identified for capture because of preliminary packaging of functions.) The system data flow diagram can be used to confirm the relationships required in the data structure diagram for the system. You may modify these relationships after detailed study. However, continue to note any relationships identified on the corporate model but not in the system model to aid the cost/benefit analysis.

You can refer to the preliminary data model as a guide at this point, but the data administration activities really work on only the most detailed data. This process may be performed by an agent outside the project team, such as a data administration team.

Process name: IDENTIFY POSSIBLE PACKAGING OF DATA MODEL
Process reference number: 3.3.4
Process guided by: Activity 3 plan

Process notes: Now that you have a rough idea of the data objects and entities and their relationships as represented in the data model, you can begin packaging your data model into one or more hierarchical, network, or relational structures.* You should be able to decide which data management system can be used for support. Packaging decisions and data management support systems should be identified for manual storage and access systems as well as for automated systems; for example, identify that a manual system uses index-card files in tub files. The data model may show natural hierarchies and relational necessities that help identify the best packaging and management system. Also, consider that there may be project goals that control or restrict the choice of a management system (the whole reason for doing the project may be to put its data into a database environment and utilize an existing database management system). We may also have a limited choice of options stated to us by the data administration management, such as having to choose a system that is compatible with an existing or future environment. The data flow diagram and data dictionary are used as input to show the application of data, for instance, data needed only to support the man/machine boundary, or data used totally in the manual or the automated environment. The use of the data will affect the packaging of the data. Using the factors above, identify the proposed packaging of the data and the proposed data management system(s) to support this packaging. For any project goals that can be partly or completely satisfied in this process, document the data management goals solutions in the project charter.

Note: A review is not included in Activity 3.3 because the total activity is a form of review of data requirements. After completing this process, it is recommended that you show the proposed packaged data model(s) to the user and explain the advantages of the proposed data management system. As a result of the user presentation, there may be additional goals identified or solutions to some existing goals or problems because you will have a broader and clearer view of data. Again, you may need to cycle back through previous activities if new goals are identified.

This process may be performed by an agent outside the project team, such as a data administration team.

---

*For a description of such structures, see C.J. Date, *An Introduction to Database Systems* (Reading, Mass: Addison Wesley, 1977); or J. Martin, *Computer Data-Base Organization* (Englewood Cliffs: Prentice-Hall, 1977).

Process name: CREATE GENERAL DESIGN MODEL FOR NEW MANUAL ENVIRONMENT
Process reference number: 3.4.1
Process guided by: Activity 3 plan

Process notes: Develop the manual portions of the data flow diagram, which is located in the bounded new logical specification, into a design model that will show how the logical functions and data will be implemented in the manual environment. This involves adding physical characteristics to the model. You have enough detail in the bounded new logical specification to develop a good design, and you should be able to use the preliminary new manual system model as a guide. The first task is to use the packaged data model to amend or replace the logical stores that apply to the manual portions and man/machine interfaces on the data flow diagram of the bounded new logical specification. If not already refined, the support characteristics — terminals, message queues, report media — on the man/machine boundary may be refined here.

Identify any project goals that you can satisfy in this process, and, using the knowledge obtained so far about the system, validate (and, if necessary, modify) the preliminary new manual system model. Using this validated model, you can further identify allocation of functions and data to individuals within sections or groups through job roles and titles, for example. Depending on the project goals, you may want to aid the design effort by using the current manual system model. The cross-reference feature in the logical data dictionary will act as a pointer to the corresponding original specifications for physical processes and data. (Note that the manual system environment usually will have less flexibility for change than will the automated environment.) When the man/machine boundary was identified, any environment modifications should have been indicated — for example, functions that change from manual to automated — on the data flow diagram to signal that these are the key areas of change in which you will need to concentrate.

In this design activity, you will probably identify additional intermediate stores and support processes — as well as identifying some that were removed in logicalization — needed for the new design to support manual-to-manual boundaries, timing boundaries, and so on. There may be a project goal to include some of these intermediate stores in the corporate data model — whether including them will be necessary depends on the security, timing, and access requirements of this data. These intermediate stores can be accommodated in the detailed cycle for data modeling.

Also, as you are creating the new design, you should identify the control of the functions and data, that is, the organizational hierarchy of the new design. At this point, you are physicalizing the logical specification, a process basically equivalent to the reverse of logicalization. (To identify general physical data, see the sample table of contents for a manual system model in the addendum to the data dictionary.) Remember that you are developing a separate model in this process, not modifying the bounded new logical specification. The bounded new logical specification will be needed for reference in future processes.

For any project goals that can be completely or partly satisfied in this process, document the manual design goals solutions in the project charter. It is helpful for future processes if the areas of design change are color coded for easy recognition in the new design model.

Process name: CREATE GENERAL DESIGN MODEL FOR NEW AUTOMATED ENVIRONMENT
Process reference number: 3.4.2
Process guided by: Activity 3 plan

Process notes: Develop a first-cut design solution, such as a structure chart, for the automated portions of the system.

First, use the packaged data model to amend or replace the logical stores that apply to the automated portions and man/machine interfaces on the data flow diagram of the bounded new logical specification. Also, you should validate and possibly refine the support characteristics on the man/machine boundary; for example, validate the input/output media or physical store requirements. Use the automated portions of the data flow diagram in the bounded new logical specification first to validate and possibly to refine the job and job step boundaries identified in the preliminary new automated system model. Then, map these boundaries back onto the automated portions of the general-level data flow diagram in the bounded new logical specification. For each of these jobs and job steps, develop a design chart to identify how the functions and data will be implemented in the new automated environment.

Identify any project goals that can be completely or partly satisfied in this process; for example, identify that error processing should be standardized. Depending on the goals, you may want to use the current automated system model, perhaps to identify any salvageable portions. The cross-reference feature in the logical data dictionary can be used as a pointer to the corresponding physical processes and data in the original, but you should not just copy the existing design. One of the reasons for logicalizing the model was to assure objectivity about the existing design, so that a good new design could be developed.

Next, you should identify additional support functions such as sorts, error routines, input/output routines, and back-up routines, as well as additional data stores such as those between jobs or job steps. Note that there may be a project goal to include some of these intermediate stores in the corporate data model, depending on the security, timing, and access requirements of this data. These intermediate stores can be accommodated in the detailed cycle for data modeling.

The partitioned portions (jobs and job steps) of the general-level data flow diagram can now be investigated individually to see if they can be transformed into a design structure. There are a number of techniques that can be used to develop a design solution: For example, if you are processing data that has a strong (non-changeable) data structure, then you could use the Jackson or the Warnier-Orr technique.* Another approach would be to apply the Yourdon and Constantine technique to developing design charts by using transform or transaction analyses.† Transform and transaction analyses are techniques that advocate developing a hierarchical structure chart from a data flow diagram. For example, on a data flow diagram, the jobs and job steps may become pro-

---

*See M. Jackson's *Principles of Program Design* (New York: Academic Press, 1975); or K.T. Orr's *Structured Systems Development* (New York: YOURDON Press, 1977).
†See M. Page-Jones, *The Practical Guide to Structured Systems Design* (New York: YOURDON Press, 1980), pp. 181-222. Page 304 contains a DFD, parts of which can be used for the next-level breakdown of process 3.4.2; also see E. Yourdon and L.L. Constantine's *Structured Design: Fundamentals of a Discipline of Computer Program and Systems Design,* 2nd ed. (New York: YOURDON Press, 1978), pp. 171-222.

grams and the individual functions of the jobs and job steps may be modules within these programs. The data flow will become the data stored between programs or the parameters passed between modules.

It is probably best to use a combination of techniques to develop your design solution, depending on the characteristics of each part of the system. At this level of detail, you should produce first-cut design charts that will be refined in the detailed cycle. However, you should be able to identify the coordinating and control modules, which are not shown on a data flow diagram, and a majority of the worker modules that form the lower levels of the design charts. You are physicalizing the logical specification so this process is basically equivalent to the reverse of logicalization. (To identify general physical data, see the sample table of contents for an automated system model in the addendum to the data dictionary.) For any project goals that can be completely or partly satisfied in this process, document the automated design goals solutions in the project charter.

The new design solution may depend greatly on your selection of automated support hardware/software.

Process name: CREATE GENERAL HW/SW SPECIFICATION
Process reference number: 3.4.3
Process guided by: Activity 3 plan

Process notes: Here you will specify the hardware/software needed to support the manual and automated portions of the new system. First, you should validate (and, if necessary, modify) the classes of equipment identified in the preliminary-level hardware/software specification. Identify any project goals that you can partly or completely satisfy in this process. In fact, you may have a project goal stating that you must use the existing system hardware/software or the existing company hardware/software. In such cases, your task will be very small — just the allocation of hardware/software — as the design will have had to accommodate this goal, too. Otherwise, use the new physical specification along with any hardware/software goals; for example, one goal might be that the system must use IBM 3270 compatible terminals to further develop the hardware/software needs. This involves identifying the type or version within the preliminary hardware/software classes.

You will also identify additional, minor hardware/software as well as peripherals, interfaces, and communication needs. Support software as well as any general-purpose packages such as sort/merge or dump/restore programs should be identified. The proposed data management system input should be included in the hardware/software specification as well as the system support requirements, such as IMS/DL/1 with VSAM. The production hardware/software inventory identifies all company-wide hardware/software, the existing system hardware/software being a subset. If you do not have project goals dictating hardware/ software, proceed as follows:

1. Specify portions of the existing system hardware/software that can be reused for the new system.

2. Specify portions of the company hardware/software that can be used or reused for the new system.

3. For those hardware/software requirements not satisfied in 1 or 2, research the purchase of new hardware/software by using an internal company planning group, hardware/software journals, and by obtaining general hardware/software data from applicable vendors. This information should be stored in the hardware/software specification.

Although you may not have a project goal stating it, you should insure compatibility of all hardware/software in the system. The data flow diagram of the bounded new logical specification may be of use if the man/machine boundary was annotated with physical characteristics.* For any project goals that can be completely or partly satisfied in this process, document the hardware/software goals solutions in the project charter.

The information in this specification is built incrementally through preliminary, general, and detailed study. This specification is for all hardware/software needs in the new system, regardless of where the hardware/software is acquired. However, to aid later processes, indicate in this specification whether the hardware/software is reused, already owned by the company, or new.

---

*This input is not shown on the methodology's data flow diagram.

Note: For critical, long-lead-time hardware/software, you may have to attempt at this level to identify detailed characteristics and issue a request for a proposal or actually place an order with vendors. You should be able to reasonably estimate detailed hardware/software characteristics if it is necessary to indicate these at the time of ordering.

Process name: CREATE GENERAL TEST CASES FOR NEW DESIGN
Process reference number: 3.4.4
Process guided by: Activity 3 plan

Process notes: Identify the test cases needed at a general level to validate the new physical specification and the hardware/software specification for the new system.

Your first task is to validate the preliminary design test cases and modify them if the area of study or the preliminary boundaries (manual, automated, and man/machine) have changed. The preliminary test cases should be further developed in this process.

At this point, you can identify some test cases for the design structure of the automated portion of the system; for example, identify test cases for the correct operation of coordination and control modules, or for correct data coupling between modules including end-of-file and error conditions. In addition, you can identify test cases for any additional partitioning of both the manual and the automated portions of the system.

These physical tests pertain to the design and implementation of the system — for example, tests of response times for specified hardware/software or tests for error handling. These tests will also validate that such physical characteristics do not affect the business operations. Tests of the business functions can be taken care of by the new system test cases, which were already created from the bounded new logical specification. You can build upon these to form physical tests. To reiterate, you can have two objectives for a test case: to test a business function and data and to implement that function and data.

The best source to use for identification and definition of test cases is the data dictionary of the new physical specification, using the physical data flow diagram (the manual portion) and design charts (the automated portion) as a guide for the flow of data.

The specification of a test case will apply to the level of detail in the new physical specification and the hardware/software specification.

To insure the objectivity of the tests, a person other than the designer should create test cases, especially negative test cases.

Process name: CONDUCT REVIEW OF GENERAL NEW DESIGN SPECIFICATIONS
Process reference number: 3.4.5
Process guided by: Activity 3 plan

Process notes: See process reference number 2.5.5 for notes on this review process.

Process name: CREATE GENERAL PROCEDURES MANUAL
                  FOR NEW MANUAL ENVIRONMENT
Process reference number: 3.5.1
Process guided by: Activity 3 plan

Process notes: Identify the procedures that are necessary to use the manual portions of the system as well as to interface with the automated portions. The procedures manual is a support document totally governed by the physical design. (There is no preliminary procedures manual because the preliminary design is not specific enough. However, if the development of the procedures manual is going to be costly — for example, produced in foreign languages for distribution to overseas divisions — then the cost should be identified at the preliminary level, as the system's cost/benefit analysis and feasibility will be affected.) The general procedures manual is for all procedures in the manual system; that is, it documents all the manual tasks needed to accomplish business functions, including data interfaces to the automated system.

The physical data flow diagram and the data dictionary of the manual system model are good tools for describing the manual system. The data flow diagram shows a leveled view of the functions and data necessary to accomplish the manual business procedures, as well as the flow of data between physical departments and people boundaries and entities outside the system. You should use data flow diagrams as the basis for the procedures manual, especially because the user will already be familiar with these modeling tools. At this level of detail, you do not have any process descriptions for individual procedures, but you can use the manual system model and the hardware/software specification to identify the following:

1. individual flows of data through the manual system, such as transaction flows, and the data preparation and distribution procedures for them

2. operating instructions for interface hardware/software, such as terminals or remote printers, as well as for embedded manual hardware/software such as special typewriters and microfiche equipment

3. the physical packaging of the manual(s), including page formats

The information for this manual is in the new manual system model, except for operating instructions for manual hardware/software. So this task is mainly a re-formatting of information into a particular company's standard layout for the procedures manual. If it is available, the current procedures manual may be helpful as a guide for any reusable portions or to identify formatting conventions.

You may want to partition the data dictionary by transaction, putting together all fields and possible error messages for a particular transaction, in order to aid data preparation and entry procedures. Also, you may want to highlight the flow of each transaction through the entire system. Such highlighting can be done directly on the data flow diagram to aid the description of each transaction.

Although not shown on the methodology's data flow diagram, it is possible to have project goals that relate to this process, for example, that documentation for the system must be developed using new company standards.

Process name: CREATE GENERAL OPERATIONS MANUAL
                  FOR NEW AUTOMATED ENVIRONMENT
Process reference number: 3.5.2
Process guided by: Activity 3 plan

Process notes: Identify the documentation that the operations staff will need to operate and control the automated portions of the system. This documentation will comprise the operations manual, a support document totally governed by the physical design.

There is no preliminary operations manual because the preliminary design is not specific enough. However, if development of the operations manual will be costly — for example, because of distributed hardware or duplicate systems requiring multiple language versions — then the cost should be identified at the preliminary level, especially as the system's cost/benefit analysis and feasibility will be affected.

In addition to being governed by the physical design, the operations manual is also affected by the operations environment; for example, whether the environment is centralized or distributed with user control.

Most of the development of this manual is done at the detailed level, where the system flowchart that governs the executable units is developed. But, at the general level, you can use the automated system model and the hardware/software specification to identify the following:

1. operations support staff needs that are relevant to job and job-step groupings, such as batch or on-line processing or weekly or monthly processing, and hardware/software requirements for the new system

2. possible run schedules and procedures needed for such tasks as timing data preparation and distribution interface with operations

3. the physical packaging, such as page formatting or the number of manuals required

If the current operations manual is available, portions of it may be reused or it can be used to identify formatting conventions.

Although not shown on the methodology's data flow diagram, it is possible to have project goals that relate to this process; for example, goals requiring that documentation for the system be developed using new company standards.

Process name: CONDUCT REVIEW OF GENERAL SYSTEM
EXECUTION MANUALS FOR NEW SYSTEM
Process reference number: 3.5.3
Process guided by: Activity 3 plan

Process notes: The aim of this review is to identify any problems, inaccuracies, ambiguities, and omissions in the procedures and operations manuals for the general level of detail. These manuals will be used to support the system; therefore, if they are not complete and correct for this level of study, the system may not be accepted. Walkthroughs should have been conducted during development of the manuals.

The agents performing this task should be the project manager, user or user representative, developers of the manuals, and, optionally, other project team members.

If there were any project goals used in development of these manuals, they, along with their solutions, should be identified (this input is not shown on the methodology's data flow diagrams).

For standard review rules and procedures, see Appendix E.

Process name: PREPARE GENERAL SYSTEM INSTALLATION SPECIFICATION
Process reference number: 3.6.1
Process guided by: Activity 3 plan

Process notes: Specify procedures and support requirements for installation of the new system's application software and manual procedures, at a general level. The first task is to identify the area of change between the current and new system. This area of change should already be indicated in the new physical specification, but if it is not, you can use the current physical specification for comparison; the bounded new logical specification may also be helpful in this task, although it is not shown on the methodology's data flow diagram. You can use the preliminary system installation specification as a guide in this process, allowing for any changes in the area of study from the preliminary-level area of study.

At the general level of study, you should have a reasonable amount of information to help produce the system installation specification, but you will not have the process descriptions or programs, which may identify more changes from the current environment. You will need to estimate these procedures and programs from the general design in the new physical specification.

You should identify any project goals that can be partly or completely satisfied in this process; for example, one goal might be satisfied by stating that existing office equipment be used whenever possible, rather than be replaced with new equipment.

Then, using these goals, you should do the following:

1. For the manual portions of the system, review the area of change in the new physical specification and assess the type and degree of change: For example, there might be an environment change with the relocation of twenty staff members. After reviewing the area of change, specify the procedures and support necessary to accomplish this change.

2. For the automated portions of the system, review the area of change in the new physical specification and assess the type and degree of change: In this case, there could be a change to the operations department's job setup procedures, requiring a ninety percent change to the production libraries for the current system. Then, specify the procedures and support necessary to accomplish this change.

3. For the whole system, specify the installation procedures for the system maintenance information.

For any project goals that can be partly or completely satisfied in this process, document the implementation goals solutions in the project charter.

Note: There will be some overlap between the implementation specifications, but try to keep this redundancy to a minimum.

Process name: PREPARE GENERAL HW/SW INSTALLATION SPECIFICATION
Process reference number: 3.6.2
Process guided by: Activity 3 plan

Process notes: In this process, specify environment and support requirements for installation of the new system's hardware and support software, at a general level.

The hardware/software specification describes all hardware and support software needed for the new system and identifies the portions that are new. During this process, you will concentrate on the new hardware/software, as well as on any in the existing environment that requires modification.

If there are no new or modified portions of hardware/software, this process will just involve confirming that the existing environment can accommodate the new system's hardware/software needs, and identifying any support requirements, such as extra support materials for an increased load on existing hardware/software. Otherwise, the first task in this process is to validate, and if necessary correct, the preliminary hardware/software installation specification to use as a guide in this process while allowing for any change in the area of study.

Identify any project goals that can be partly or completely satisfied in this process; for example, a requirement might be that all new hardware/software should be housed in the data processing center. Using these project goals, review the hardware/software environment data in the production hardware/software inventory and determine if an existing environment or portions of it can be used as a base for new hardware/software. If it can be used, the environment's documentation should be updated to include the new system's modifications and, with these updates identified, the documentation should be included in the hardware/software installation specification. For hardware/software that can't be accommodated in an existing environment, specify the new environment description and configuration chart.

In either of the above cases, the hardware/software installation support requirements should be specified at a general level — that is, in sufficient detail to support the information in the hardware/software specification.

At this level of detail, you should have enough information to specify the basic environment but only part of the support requirement, which will be completed at the detailed level.

For any project goals that can be partly or completely satisfied in this process, you should document the implementation goals solutions in the project charter.

This process may be performed by an agent outside the project team, such as a support-planning group.

Note: There will be some overlap between the implementation specifications, but try to keep this redundancy to a minimum.

Process name: PREPARE GENERAL CONVERSION SPECIFICATION
Process reference number: 3.6.3
Process guided by: Activity 3 plan

Process notes: Specify procedures and support requirements needed at a general level in the conversion of data for the new system. The first task in this process is to identify the area of change between the current and new systems. Concentrate specifically on the change of stored data, an area that should already be indicated in the new physical specification; and concentrate on input and output composition, in the data dictionary. If the area of change of stored data is not indicated, the current physical specification can be used for comparison. Look for files containing data that will change, for new files that must be created, and for files that need a change of order, access, or media. At this level of detail you have identified records and their elements, but not the contents of the elements. However, you should be able to identify a reasonable conversion specification with this data.

You can use the preliminary conversion specification as a guide in this process if the area of study is the same at this general level as it was at the preliminary level. Identify any project goals that can be partly or completely satisfied in this process; for example a goal might be satisfied by archiving all customer file records that have been inactive for more than six months. For these project goals, document the implementation goals solutions in the project charter; for example, document that the initial conversion process will separate and save non-active customer records prior to converting data. If the conversion of data is a large and complex task, you already may have identified the conversion effort as a system in itself, at the preliminary level of study. Or, you may identify the complexity of data conversion at this level of detail because of the data modeling activity. In both cases, you have the current and new data defined already, and you can use both to develop a system model, design model, and conversion data dictionary, to form the conversion specification. If the data conversion is simple, you may be able to use utility programs to accomplish the conversion procedures, or, on the manual portion of the system, you may be replacing data from old forms to new forms. In either case, you should attempt to use the new system's processes for creating new files, for example, by using current data to form new transactions that will be input for a new update program to add records to a new file.

You may want to take a short listing or sample of the current production stores to confirm that the data formats are up to date (this input is not shown on the methodology's data flow diagrams).

Using the preliminary test cases as a guide and allowing for any change in the area of study since that level, you should develop general test cases to validate the conversion procedures and results.

The creation or updating of any database information may not be the responsibility of the project team. Instead, either task may be accomplished by a data administration team.

Note: There will be some overlap between the implementation specifications, but try to keep this redundancy to a minimum.

Process name: PREPARE GENERAL TRAINING SPECIFICATION
Process reference number: 3.6.4
Process guided by: Activity 3 plan

Process notes: Here you will specify, at a general level, requirements and support for training the users and operations staff to use the new system. (See process reference number 2.6.4 for an explanation of the special activities in this task.)

The first task in this process is to identify the area of change between the current and new systems. This area should already be indicated in the new physical specification, but if it is not, the current physical specification can be used for comparison. Identify the area of change in the hardware/software specification, and look for changes of functions, changes of interface with hardware and software, and changes of interface with data. The area of change applies to the operations area as well as to the user area.

At this level of detail, you should be able to specify basic training and support requirements. However, there are no process descriptions yet for your model, so you cannot identify changes in individual procedures or in methods of performing these procedures. You can use the preliminary training specification as a guide allowing for any change in the area of study at this level.

Identify any project goals that can be partly or completely satisfied in this process, for example, that of using existing company training materials wherever possible. For the identified project goals, you should document the implementation goals solutions in the project charter; for example, document the in-house training of staff using company training materials. Using these project goals and the general-level area of change, you should specify the training requirements and the training support needed to satisfy these requirements. At this level of study, you should be able to identify the number of people who need training for each training level in each training category. The general new system execution manuals should be used as part of the training support, and can also be used to help identify training requirements.

Where possible, the new application system itself, the hardware and software, and any reusable materials in the company maintenance library should be specified as training support. Specify training materials that must be created for this project, such as a special workshop or on-line instruction course. At this point, identify the availability of training support such as facilities, materials, vendor-provided training, and so on.

Note: There will be overlap between the implementation specifications, but try to keep this redundancy to a minimum.

Process name: CONDUCT REVIEW OF GENERAL IMPLEMENTATION SPECIFICATIONS
Process reference number: 3.6.5
Process guided by: Activity 3 plan

Process notes: See process reference number 2.6.5 for notes on this review process.

Process name: VERIFY (AND IF NECESSARY UPDATE) RELEASES
Process reference number: 3.7.1
Process guided by: Activity 3 plan

Process notes: As the process name states, you are going to verify the releases identified in the preliminary-level study (if releases were identified), and update them, if necessary. However, you may realize that releases are necessary only after general-level study.

Based on your knowledge at this level of study, you can verify the preliminary releases identified on the actual input documentation, and if necessary, update them. Obviously, you should avoid radically modifying the first release after the user has accepted the preliminary release strategy. However, you can expect modifications to the preliminary release boundaries.

As an aid later in detailed study, identify all release boundaries in as much detail as possible here. All new system documentation including the project charter should be updated to reflect any modifications to releases.

Process name: PREPARE AND SYNCHRONIZE GENERAL IMPLEMENTATION PLANS
(FOR THIS RELEASE)
Process reference number: 3.7.2
Process guided by: Activity 3 plan

Process notes: Using the increased detail in the implementation specifications at this level and taking into consideration the possible refinement of the releases done in the previous task, develop and synchronize the general-level implementation plans. Use the preliminary implementation plans as a guide if they still apply. In the project charter or in the implementation specifications, you should identify any project goals that can be completely or partly satisfied in this process, such as having the first release of a system by the end of the year; and should identify the implementation goals solutions, for example, a summary of the implementation plans. For each project goal and each implementation specification, with releases identified, you should develop the individual strategies, dependencies, and schedules for meeting them. The strategies, dependencies, and schedules should be specified in as much detail as possible for the first release. For other releases, give your best guess for dependencies and schedules. You will have to synchronize each of the specifications.

Synchronization can probably be attained by establishing one dependency network and schedule for all implementation plans; a possibly more detailed subset of these can then be used for each implementation plan. When developing a plan that requires support of materials or people from outside the project team, you should confirm the availability of the support from the appropriate area of management.

Note: Even though this is a managerial task, the agents being the project manager and management, obviously the project team is the best source for identifying the specific effort involved in the implementation plans.

Process name: PREPARE ACTIVITY 4 DEVELOPMENT PLAN (FOR THIS RELEASE)
Process reference number: 3.7.3
Process guided by: Activity 3 plan

Process notes: Now that you have completed all of the development activities for analysis and design at a general level and have confirmed the releases for the new system, you can prepare the development plan for the detailed-level study.

The results of the previous activities will help you to develop the plan. One beneficial result is that, after having done the general study, you are now very familiar with the system. Second, the deliverables and processes for which you are developing the plan are already identified in the methodology, although they are not at the functional primitive level. In addition, you have the general current system description and the general new system description, with releases specified, to identify the areas to be studied in more detail. Possibly of greatest value is having the figures for the estimated and actual resources used in conducting Activity 3.

As added input to developing the plan, use the estimated Activity 4 plan identified for the cost/benefit analysis in process reference number 2.7.3. Moreover, the results from any preliminary-level blitz defined in process reference number 1.2.2 should help in the process of creating this plan. Drawing on all of this information, prepare the development plan for Activity 4, including the tasks, resources, dependencies, and schedules needed to conduct detailed analysis and design.

The plan should be as detailed as possible for Activity 4, but for cost/benefit analysis and feasibility purposes, you should also estimate the plans needed for Activities 5 and 6, except for those areas already covered in the implementation plans.

The Activity 4 plan may include the use of people and resources outside of the project team, such as technical writers needed to prepare system execution manuals. Confirm the availability of such support from their management.

Note: Even though this is a managerial task, the agents being the project manager and management, obviously the project team is the best source for identifying the specific effort involved in Activity 4.

Process name: ANALYZE GENERAL COSTS/BENEFITS AND PREPARE INITIAL PROPOSAL
Process reference number: 3.7.4
Process guided by: Activity 3 plan

Process notes: Produce an initial proposal containing sufficient information to allow management to decide whether to approve the resources for further study of the system. This report will provide the following:

1. a summary of the resources actually used in the general study compared with what was estimated

2. an overview of the system documentation developed so far, with options and releases identified for the new system

3. a list of the project goals that apply to the general study and general solutions to these goals

4. an analysis of the costs and benefits for the new system, along with any limitations and risks in producing it

5. a summary of the plans for Activities 4 through 6 with a detailed estimate of resources needed for Activity 4 and a best-guess estimate of resources for Activities 5 and 6

Item 1 can be extracted from the project plan. Items 2 through 5 are documented by option (man/machine boundaries) with only necessary releases identified. Item 2 is produced from the current and new system descriptions, and item 3 is produced from the project charter. (Highlight any goals that have been added in the general-level study.) Item 4 is obtained from the cost data in the specifications of the current and new system descriptions and from cost/benefit information in the project charter. You should add to the proposal any benefits and risks that you have identified, such as a reduction in operating costs or an easy-to-use procedures manual, as well as any savings or increases in costs.

Item 5 can be extracted from the project plan. The degree of accuracy regarding costs, benefits, and plans will not be one hundred percent, because the information this is based on is from the general level of study. Since you are not working with precise figures, the initial proposal should state that estimates may be off by as much as twenty percent.

Process name: CONDUCT INDEPENDENT REVIEW
Process reference number: 3.7.5
Process guided by: Activity 3 plan

Process notes: This is the last opportunity in the project to hold an independent re-view, because after completing the general study, you will be too far into the project to change the development approach. Hence, before performing the detailed study, which produces the actual specification, you must confirm that you have selected the best ap-proach and that the development tools are being used correctly.

The people conducting the review should not be part of the project because an objective view is needed to verify that the project team is on the correct path. Therefore, you want reviewers who have worked on similar projects, who can easily understand the form of documentation used, and who have a knowledge of this methodology (former members of pilot projects are possible candidates).

(For standard review rules and procedures, see Appendix E.)

Process name: PRESENT INITIAL PROPOSAL TO D.P. MANAGEMENT
Process reference number: 3.7.6
Process guided by: Activity 3 plan

Process notes: In this presentation, make data processing management aware of the progress to date, specifying resources used, and get a firm commitment for the resources needed for Activity 4. This, therefore, should be a formal presentation of all the information in the initial proposal.

Keeping data processing management informed of project progress is a good way to avoid cancellation of resources, especially if a change in schedule is necessary and if the cost of the project is included within a data processing department's budget. You should also raise any issues that may affect the progress of the project — such as lack of support resources or coordination problems with outside groups — and, if possible, resolve them.

Process name: PRESENT INITIAL PROPOSAL TO USER MANAGEMENT FOR SELECTION
Process reference number: 3.7.7
Process guided by: Activity 3 plan

Process notes: This presentation serves many purposes: to inform user management of the resources used so far; to give an overview of the system documentation showing the various options for the new system with any necessary releases; to present the costs and benefits of each option; and to obtain approval and commitment of resources in order to study the selected system option. (The user management may also be responsible for the overall resource cost.) This should be a formal presentation of all the information in the initial proposal.

Although the project is not likely to be canceled at this point in development, it is possible that the option or options being presented will require modification. Since you are using structured development tools, you should be able to make modifications because of the partitioning of the documentation. However, you may have to cycle back through the design and implementation specifications in Activity 3 if the modifications cannot be accommodated in the detailed study.

You should help the user management select one option and any necessary releases, as it will be costly and time consuming to proceed into the detailed study with more than one option.

If releases are identified, you should proceed into the detailed study with the first release and then cycle back through all of Activity 3.7 in order to identify future releases. The project charter and project plan should be updated to reflect only the option selected and its first release. The overall data processing plans and resources should be revised for reallocation of resources, including new hiring and contracting needs.

Process name: PREPARE REQUEST FOR HW/SW PROPOSAL
Process reference number: 3.7.8
Process guided by: Hardware/software installation plan

Process notes: Upon management's approval of resources, you can now prepare the vendor request for proposals for hardware/software that cannot be provided in-house. To do this, prepare a list of qualified vendors for each piece or set of hardware/software, using the information contained in the hardware/software specification. Use the requirements found in the hardware/software specification and in the hardware/software installation specification, along with the schedule requirements in the hardware/software installation plan, to complete the formal request for proposals. Send these requests to potential vendors, and assign a project representative to review vendor responses. Note that sending requests for proposals at this level is mainly for major hardware/software.

For hardware/software that requires a long lead time, you can send out actual orders now, the request for proposal having been sent out when the preliminary specification was prepared. (If possible, you should wait until the detailed hardware/software specification has been prepared before placing any orders.) New hardware/software environments that need to be built as specified in the hardware/software installation specification may need to be started at this point.

This process may be performed by an agent outside of the project team, such as a planning support group.

Process name: VALIDATE AND/OR CREATE DETAILED DESIGN MODEL
                  FOR CURRENT MANUAL ENVIRONMENT
Process reference number: 4.1.1
Process guided by: Activity 4 plan

Process notes: As with the equivalent general-level process, first use the selected system option to identify which portions, if not all, of the general manual system model will require further decomposition while still allowing for the study of areas that bound the option. The aims in this task are the same as the equivalent tasks in the preliminary and general studies (see process reference numbers 2.1.1 and 3.1.1), but now you will validate the existing model or refine the general model by producing low-level data flow diagrams that show individual flows of data and the processes that act on this data.

The task of decomposition and validation involves defining in the data dictionary all of the fields within documents and transactions in streams of data, all of the fields within records and documents in files, and, probably the most time-consuming job, developing process specifications (mini-specs) for the lowest-level processes in the data flow diagram, functional primitives. (To identify detailed data, see the sample table of contents for the manual system model in the addendum to the data dictionary.) If a nonlinguistic means of representing a process specification — such as a decision table or graph for decision logic or a Nassi-Shneiderman diagram for both decision and nondecision logic — is acceptable to the user, use it. If a nonlinguistic means is not acceptable, as a last resort use structured English for a representation of process policy.* Of course, if a procedures manual is available for any portion of the system, use extracted portions of it as process descriptions, after validation.

The data gathering at this level of detail will be conducted in the same manner as in the preliminary and general studies, except that the interviewees will consist mainly of staff members, and greater emphasis will be placed on validation of process specifications.†

As I mentioned in my discussion of the processes of preliminary study, a logical model annotated with physical characteristics can serve the purpose if your users know or can understand *what* they are accomplishing in their activities instead of just *how* they perform these activities. So, in developing process specifications, you may have to embellish the process descriptions somewhat with physical characteristics to obtain validation; for example, it may be useful to recommend that a bank verify sufficient funds on Blue Form No. 986 by checking the bad customer list in the Red Book. If the customer has insufficient funds, then reject customer request using Form 12.

During full logicalization of the model, processes that are purely data transporters‡ and that do not perform any data transformation will disappear completely. Therefore, you

---

*See DeMarco's discussion of structured English in *Structured Analysis and System Specification* (New York: YOURDON Press, 1979), pp. 179-213. Also see Appendix C of this methodology for examples of formal and informal structured English.
†I recommend a maximum validation turnaround of 24 hours for a process specification, if validation cannot be acquired while gathering data. For example, while defining a process with a user, take the interview notes in the form of a data flow diagram and document the processes in decision tree format, and obtain validation using these communication tools.
‡The concept of data transporters was also developed by S. McMenamin and J. Palmer in two YOURDON seminars: *Structured Analysis and Design Workshop,* 6th ed. (New York: YOURDON inc.), October 1980; and *Advanced Structured Analysis* (New York: YOURDON inc.), October 1980.

do not want to produce process descriptions using such tools as detailed structured English for these. A process note will suffice as long as you are sure no real processing is being performed. Because this is the most detailed level, you should have already resolved most alias names for data; otherwise, full logicalization is the last chance to resolve names.

During this process, you will probably identify additional project goals. See process reference number 2.2.1 for instructions on how to process them.

Process name: VALIDATE AND/OR CREATE DETAILED DESIGN MODEL
FOR CURRENT AUTOMATED ENVIRONMENT
Process reference number: 4.1.2
Process guided by: Activity 4 plan

Process notes: As with the equivalent general-level process, first use the selected system option to identify which portions, if not all, of the preliminary automated system model should be studied further while still allowing for study of areas that bound this system option.

The aims of this task are the same as those in preliminary and general studies (see process reference numbers 2.1.2. and 3.1.2), but now you are going to validate the existing model or develop the general model until all modules (individual routines) and the data they use (coupling parameters) have been specified. Specification and validation involve studying and defining all fields within transactions/reports in major data streams, all fields within records in data stores, and all modules (routines) within programs in major jobs. You should also identify any significant internal program stores, such as working-storage tables and data parameters between modules. (To identify detailed data, see the sample table of contents for an automated system model in the addendum to the data dictionary.) In the module descriptions, you should include actual portions of code listings if they are written in a high-level language; otherwise, you may want to produce pseudocode (English-like, readable logic) or a decision table or tree to assist you in the logicalization and the new design process.

Data gathering for this level of detail will be conducted in the same manner as in the preliminary and general studies, but will be concentrated on individual modules and their data. As most of the lower-level modules are worker modules, they will be the main candidates for logicalization. Therefore, the clearer you make the module descriptions, the easier logicalization will be. As mentioned in the general-level study, if the systems contain non-modularized programs with non-partitionable functions, source listings may have to suffice as the process descriptions, and you may have to rely on the logicalization task to perform code analysis to arrive at a functional partitioning.

During this process, you will probably define additional project goals. See process reference number 2.2.1 for a description of how to handle them.

Process name: DERIVE DETAILED LOGICAL MODEL FOR CURRENT MANUAL
ENVIRONMENT
Process reference number: 4.1.3
Process guided by: Activity 4 plan

Process notes: Derive or validate the manual logical model at a detailed level of business functions and data, using the detailed manual system model. The reason for this task is the same as that for the equivalent preliminary and general tasks (see process reference numbers 2.1.3 and 3.1.3).

At this detailed level, you will complete the logical specification of the current manual environment. The detailed-level logical model is derived by removing all physical characteristics other than those needed for business reasons that were stated in the detailed manual system model. Such physical characteristics in the model might include, for example, references to field numbers, field codes, or physical format; references to the sequencing or control of processes and to the person who performs them; references to the media used for stores; and so on. (To identify detailed data, see the sample table of contents for a logical specification in the addendum to the data dictionary.)

Probably the greatest effort in this task will be devoted to producing process specifications of business policy, but you will be aided in this effort if you have a physicalized model as input. Look for processes that do no data transformation (that is, that do not change the status or composition of data). They should not be represented on a data flow diagram. The general manual logical model (higher-level view) will act as a good guide, but be suspicious: The level of detail in this study will help you spot partitioning problems, that is, poor cohesiveness of functions, which may not have been noticed at the higher level. Also, you may have a smaller area of study now at the detailed level causing the upper-level functions to be valid no longer. You may have to go back and repartition the higher-level diagrams. However, if you are in doubt about repartitioning, especially if a suspect area interfaces with an automated function, it is better to wait until the automated and manual logical models are combined into a logical system model.

All internal stores that do not interface with automated functions can be investigated to determine if they should really be represented as data flows. A data store is needed for data that cannot be obtained dynamically.*

At this point in development, you should have cleaned up most alias and physical data process names, with the exception of those occurring for matching purposes at interfaces between automated and manual functions.

Deriving and validating the logical model can be helped by referring to any business and support documentation in the maintenance library. Most users should also be able to validate this logical transformation, especially on the manual portions of the system.

Note: You are developing a separate model in this process, not modifying the manual system. The latter will be needed for reference in future processes.

---

*See model transformations in Appendix C for an example of data store cleanup.

Process name: DERIVE DETAILED LOGICAL MODEL
                   FOR CURRENT AUTOMATED ENVIRONMENT
Process reference number: 4.1.4
Process guided by: Activity 4 plan

Process notes: Derive or validate the automated logical model at a detailed level, using the detailed automated system model. The reason for this task is the same as that for the equivalent preliminary and general tasks (see process reference numbers 2.1.4 and 3.1.4).

At this level, you will complete the logical specification of the current automated environment. The amount of effort required to complete this task will depend on the automated system model input and the knowledge the user or data processing maintenance staff has regarding the detailed functions that the automated system performs. If you do not have a detailed automated system model, but instead have only program listings, you may have to do code analysis to obtain the logical model. If you have a significant amount of detail in the design chart in the automated system model, you can derive a logical data flow diagram by tracking the flow of data through the design chart and identifying each function that acts on this data. These functional primitives will be derived from the lower-level worker design modules, which may have to be split if they contain more than one function, or to be combined if two or more modules make up a function. Tracking the data flow will help identify complete functions.

Producing the detailed logical model from the automated system model also involves removing all physical characteristics other than those needed for business reasons, such as references to field numbers, field codes, or physical format; references to the sequencing or control of processes and to the routine that performs them; or references to the media used for stores. (To identify detailed data, see the sample table of contents for a logical specification in the addendum to the data dictionary.) There will probably be processes that do not need to be represented on a logical model, because they do no real data transformation. Examples include processes that read or write data and sort/merge, and backout routines. A large portion of the effort in this process is devoted to deriving process specifications, but less effort will be needed if the code is written clearly in the automated system model.

All internal stores not interfacing with manual functions can be investigated to see if they should really be represented as data flows. A data store is needed for data that cannot be obtained dynamically.*

By this stage in the development effort, you should have cleaned up most alias and physical data process names with the exception of those at interfaces between manual and automated functions for matching purposes. Deriving and validating the logical model can be made easier by checking any business and support documentation in the maintenance library. The user and data processing maintenance staff should also be able to help validate the transformation from the physical to the logical model.

Note: You are developing a separate model, not modifying the automated system model. The automated model will be needed for reference in future processing.

---

*See model transformations in Appendix C for an example of data store cleanup.

Process name: DERIVE DETAILED LOGICAL SPECIFICATION FOR THE CURRENT SYSTEM
Process reference number: 4.1.5
Process guided by: Activity 4 plan

Process notes: Produce a detailed logical model for the whole system (manual and automated systems combined). The aim of this task, as stated in the equivalent preliminary process, process reference number 2.1.5, is to remove the physical view of how processes and their data are partitioned (manual and automated partitioning) in the existing system. Having done this, you can develop the best partitioning for the new system, without being influenced by the existing partitioning.

Since this process involves combining two logical models, it is similar to that of deriving the detailed manual logical model. However, in this process the physical characteristics are only at the interfaces between the manual and automated models.

All interfaces between these two models need to be matched and their physical characteristics removed. At this detailed level, you may only need to validate that the contents of interfaces match between the manual and automated systems because an interface communicates by means of a transaction/report and these forms of communication will have been matched at the general level. (An exception would be an interactive system that communicates through individual fields.)

Any interfaces that do not match, except for aliases, need to be investigated by cycling back to the design models. New interfaces will require the same development effort as is required for other interfaces, such as looking for partitioning problems. As with other logicalization tasks, you need to

1.   remove all physical characteristics from interfaces (other than those required for business reasons), and concurrently develop logical names for those that are physical; at this level of detail, you should have resolved all alias names

2.   replace any remaining stores that are really data flows, for example, stores that are just used for time delays

3.   look for partitioning problems, such as detailed functions that are performed partly in the manual system and partly in the automated system; it should be relatively easy to identify incomplete functions at this level of study because of your knowledge of the system so far*

At this point, you should have completely specified the system. (To confirm the data requirements for the detailed level of study, see the sample table of contents for a logical specification in the addendum to the data dictionary.) The only parts of the model that may still reflect the current design are the stores. With the current amount of detail, you now can develop a formal data structure diagram for the current stored system data.† The data structure diagram is derived from all genuine system data stores on the logical model (that is, those left after logicalization), and it shows the functional entities

---

*See model transformations in Appendix C for an example of the derivation of a logical model.
†For information on data modeling, refer to T. DeMarco, *Structured Analysis and System Specification* (New York: YOURDON Press, 1979), pp. 233-55. Also see P. Chen, "The Entity-Relationship Model — Toward a Unified View of Data," *ACM Transactions on Database Systems,* Vol. 1, No. 1 (March 1976), pp. 9-36.

of data in the system and their relationships. These entities can be viewed as small stores, which should be plugged back into the detailed system model and their applicable data flows connected.

In developing the data structure diagram or after incorporating the stores into the model, you may find problems such as data (attributes) in stores that are supported but never used or data that cannot be updated. They will require investigation by your cycling back to the design models, since they may be signs of uncollected data or of genuine faults of the current system. Replacing physical stores with logical stores in the model as well as removing all final physical characteristics of the current design, except those needed for business reasons, should make the logical model more readable.

The whole process of deriving the detailed logical specification will be assisted by the general logical specification, but be aware that your area of study may be smaller than the general study. Also, the greater level of detail in this level of study may help identify partitioning problems that could not be identified in the general study.

Process name: CREATE DETAILED TEST CASES FOR CURRENT SYSTEM
Process reference number: 4.1.6
Process guided by: Activity 4 plan

Process notes: Identify all test cases needed to validate the current logical specification at a detailed level. If you have a regression test specification in the maintenance library for any of the affected automated and manual systems, use it to help form the test cases. Ones that can be reused in their entirety should be so indicated in the test specification.

For systems that don't have a regression test specification, you will need to review the current logical specification and develop test cases that will validate the completeness and correctness of the affected portions of the system, as well as the complete system. The test cases will be developed in detail, and may form one of the sources for the machine-executable development test library produced in Activity 5. The main guide for these test cases will be the general test cases. Note that you may have a smaller area of study at this level, so you may have an excess of general test cases.

Note that the test cases being developed are individual tests to validate the current logical specification. Other types of tests, including tests for the complete range and boundary value for the new system, will be generated from the new physical specification in a later process.

Using the data flow diagram as a guide, you will find that the best source for further identification and definition of test cases is the data dictionary of the current logical specification. The detailed test cases will specify transactions, fields, and so on. An example of a detailed test case follows:

Test objective:	validate that order status and discount are correctly updated on a late delivery order
Test input:	purchase order with express delivery date
Expected execution:	normal validation processes are successful; order-scheduling processing reveals late delivery is necessary, and late delivery processing is performed
Expected output:	approved purchase order with late delivery notice showing discount rate applied; customer-order store updated with late status
Test environment:	customer-order store indicating this customer is available and order status is normal

The user or user representative should be one of the agents creating test cases, especially to help identify invalid (negative) tests, because the user is a knowledgeable source for identifying test cases that can be used to validate the current system.

Process name: CONDUCT REVIEW OF DETAILED CURRENT LOGICAL SPECIFICATION
Process reference number: 4.1.7
Process guided by: Activity 4 plan

Process notes: See process reference number 2.1.7 for notes on this review process.

Process name: ANALYZE DETAILED PROJECT GOALS
Process reference number: 4.2.1
Process guided by: Activity 4 plan

Process notes: Turn your attention to the new system and identify all project goals that can be satisfied in detailed analysis. The goals on which you concentrate in this process concern both data and functions in the current logical specification and completely new data and functions. Your task is to identify the logical modifications necessary to meet these goals.

You must also identify and completely decompose the general modifications applied to the general bounded new logical specification (if modifications are not indicated in the specification, you can use the analysis goals solutions in the project charter as a guide). The task may be considerable if the project involves adding a major function, because you may have to perform a physical design study and logicalize for the new function. Adding any new function involves developing the process specifications, detailed data definitions, and data flow diagrams for the new functions.

Other logical modifications consist of changes to and deletions from data and functions in the existing system. For changes, you may have to validate physical to logical transformations of the affected data and functions. Probably the most difficult task at this level of detail is development or modification of process specifications. There may be no logical modifications if the project is concerned only with design and implementation goals, that is, if there will be no change to business data or functions. (To identify detailed data, see the sample table of contents for a logical specification in the addendum to the data dictionary.) For those project goals that can be completely or partly satisfied in this process, you should document the analysis goals solutions in the project charter.

Note: If there are no completely new data and functions, this process can be merged with the next process: deriving the new logical model.

Process name: DERIVE DETAILED LOGICAL MODEL FOR THE NEW SYSTEM
Process reference number: 4.2.2
Process guided by: Activity 4 plan

Process notes: Produce the new logical model by applying the logical modifications to the current logical specification. This may involve adding, updating, and possibly deleting portions of the data flow diagram, data dictionary, and process descriptions that make up the current logical specification. Actually, you are developing a separate model, not modifying the current logical specification, because the current logical specification will be needed for reference in future processing.

The general bounded new logical specification will be of major help, but you should be aware that a smaller area of study may exist at this level. This specification will show where general-level modifications were made, and one of your tasks will be to further decompose and define these modifications. After the modifications are incorporated in the model, you may identify partitioning problems, which can probably be handled in the next process, when the model will be repartitioned into manual and automated functions.

Possibly some minor stores will be introduced into the model in this process. If so, they need to be investigated to determine whether they can be completely replaced by existing stores. If they cannot be replaced, the formal data structure diagram should be derived again (see process reference number 4.1.5). Use the formal data structure diagram to plug back the necessary stores into the logical model. Any individual detailed modification identified — that is, one not part of a general modification — should fit into the current system; that is, the modification should be completely bounded by the area of study.

Note: It is useful to indicate the modifications in the new logical model to identify them easily in the future. A simple method is to highlight them with a colored pencil.

Process name: REFINE MAN/MACHINE BOUNDARY FOR NEW SYSTEM
Process reference number: 4.2.3
Process guided by: Activity 4 plan

Process notes: At this level of detail, you will mainly be identifying refinements to the man/machine boundary developed at the general level (see process reference number 3.2.3). For example, having developed detailed process descriptions, you may have found judgmental actions guided by no strong policy or systematic procedure, which you cannot or do not want to automate, so you may want to alter the man/machine boundary. You may even have a smaller area of study that necessitates a refinement to the boundary.

So, your task in this process is to use the greater amount of detail in the new logical model, along with any project goals that may affect this level of detail, to refine the man/machine boundary identified in the general bounded new logical specification.

For any project goals that can be completely or partly satisfied in this process, you should document the analysis goals solutions in the project charter.

Process name: CREATE DETAILED TEST CASES FOR THE NEW SYSTEM
Process reference number: 4.2.4
Process guided by: Activity 4 plan

Process notes: The major source for the detailed new system test cases will be the general new system test cases, except for those that may be outside your area of study at this detailed level. You should be able to use detailed current system test cases that have not been affected by any modifications to the current system.

Specifically, you must further develop the general new system test cases allowing for all data conditions, both normal conditions and exceptions. As with the creation of the general-level test cases, use the data dictionary as the source for further identification and definition of tests, including value range tests. You now are at a point in development at which you can develop all test cases that apply to the business data and functions, that is, that apply to what the system must accomplish, but not how it will accomplish it.* Therefore, detailed test cases can be developed to the level of fields and their contents. Later, you will add physical details such as record layouts, which will be used to form part of the machine-executable development test library.

---

*See T. DeMarco's description of acceptance testing in *Structured Analysis and System Specification* (New York: YOURDON Press, 1979), pp. 325-31.

Process name: CONDUCT REVIEW OF DETAILED BOUNDED NEW LOGICAL SPECIFICATION
Process reference number: 4.2.5
Process guided by: Activity 4 plan

Process notes: See process reference number 2.3.5 for notes on this review process.

Process name: VERIFY OR REVISE DETAILED CORPORATE DATA DICTIONARY
Process reference number: 4.3.1
Process guided by: Activity 4 plan

Process notes: Validate the data dictionary with the corporate definitions. At the detailed level of study, you can confirm the specification of the data, because it is only at this level that you know the detailed definition in the data dictionary and actual use of the data, as stated in the process descriptions constituting user policy. Identify any detailed project goals relating to data capture (for example, the security requirements for salary attributes of an employee object), and document the solutions to them in the project charter (for example, that field sensitivity is only allowed by the personnel department salary fields). In refinement of the man/machine boundary and creation of the general-level new design, you may have identified some extra data capture needs that were not identified in general-level data modeling. Include them here.

Review the corporate data dictionary and identify the data that requires updating with detailed data from the system's data dictionary. Include the result of this procedure in the corporate data dictionary. You may need to resolve some conflicting names of data (aliases) between the corporate data dictionary and the system's data dictionary. At this level of detail, the policy statements may clarify aliases or even identify new aliases.

Note: This process is aimed toward producing a company-wide dictionary of data that supports a common database to reduce, if not eliminate, redundancy, multiple updating, inconsistency, and other potential problems of having common data between systems. This process, the next two processes, and the equivalent general and preliminary processes take a company-wide view, whereas all other processes in this methodology have concentrated on the project's area of study.

This process may be performed by an agent outside the project team, such as a data administration team.

Process name: REFINE DETAILED DATA OBJECTS
Process reference number: 4.3.2
Process guided by: Activity 4 plan

Process notes: Using the formal data structure diagram or data model of the system's detailed data needs, identify any necessary modifications to data objects declared in the data structure diagram to make them correspond to the corporate data objects, or identify the necessary modifications to the corporate data objects declared in the corporate data model to make them accommodate the system's data. (Note that you may have some extra data identified for capture because of the general packaging of functions.)

The data dictionary input to this task contains the detailed definitions of data elements, and the system's data flow diagram can be used to confirm the functionality of objects in the data structure diagram. The resultant objects of this process will be normalized (refined) into what are called well-defined objects. These objects or their elements will be used to update the corporate data model and should be documented in the corporate data dictionary. You can refer to the general-level data model as an aid in this process, but the data administration function works with only the most detailed data. This process may be performed by an agent outside of the project team, such as a data administration team.

Process name: IDENTIFY DETAILED RELATIONSHIPS BETWEEN OBJECTS
Process reference number: 4.3.3
Process guided by: Activity 4 plan

Process notes: Identify all relationships between detailed data objects, including all dependencies and/or correlations between objects. The formal data structure diagram should identify all relationships necessary for the system's stored data. As a result of the general packaging of functions, there also may be some relationships necessary to support extra data identified for capturing. The system's data flow diagram can be used to confirm the relationships in the data structure diagram of the system. If there is a separate data administration library, it can be updated with the detailed objects, additional attributes, and relationships that are necessary to support the system. You also should identify any extra data integrity requirement resulting from these modifications to the corporate data model. (Data integrity relates to whether an item of data is dependent on other items of data, such as fields that are computed from fields in other objects.)

Finally, you should indicate on the data model any parts not already accommodated by the corporate data model to be used later for cost/benefit analysis. Refer to the general data model as a guide at this stage, but the data administration function is performed with only the most detailed data.

This process may be performed by an agent outside the project team, such as a data administration team.

Process name: IDENTIFY PACKAGING OF DATA MODEL
Process reference number: 4.3.4
Process guided by: Activity 4 plan

Process notes: You should now have enough information to identify the necessary packaging of the data model into a particular structure or structures — that is, hierarchical, network, or relational* — and to assign the data management system to support this structure. If you are not restricted to a particular packaging or data management system, the data model should be a good basis for the selection of one or more appropriate management systems. For example, there may be a natural hierarchical structure in the model — say, one root source with dependent objects. On the other hand, the model may contain a complex network that would introduce problems if forced into a hierarchical structure.

In the manual environment, for example, you may identify a system that uses multiple index files that point to data in tub files or in folders that are accessed using keys. The proposed packaged data model and management system will help in this task, especially if the model and system were developed using limited options of data administration. Other packaging considerations might be restricted by project goals such as a prime objective of interfacing with existing systems to centralize all branch data. The data flow diagram and data dictionary are inputs that show the use of the data; for example, one use might be that data is needed only to support the man/machine boundary or that data is used exclusively in the manual environment or automated environment. Data use will affect packaging. Using all of the factors just stated, you should identify the assigned packaging of the data and the assigned data management system to support this packaging.

For any project goals that can be completely or partly satisfied in this process, you should document the goals solutions in the project charter. Whatever management system is chosen, it should be documented and the documentation used to update the options for interfacing and for use with other projects.

This process may be performed by an agent outside the project team, such as a data administration team.

Note: A procedure for review has not been identified in this process, because the entire Activity 4.3 is itself a form of review of our data needs. However, you should show the packaged data model(s) to the user and explain the advantages of the assigned data management system, if these advantages were not already explained at the general level of study. Even at this point, talking to the user may reveal additional goals or provide the way to achieve some existing goals because of the broader and clearer view of data. Again, you may have to cycle back through previous activities if new goals are identified.

---

*For a description of such structures, see C.J. Date, *An Introduction to Database Systems,* (Reading, Mass.: Addison Wesley, 1977); or J. Martin, *Computer Data-Base Organization* (Englewood Cliffs, N.J.: Prentice-Hall, 1977).

Process name: DEFINE DATA STORAGE AND ACCESS
Process reference number: 4.3.5
Process guided by: Activity 4 plan

Process notes: Identify the storage of data on physical storage media and devices. In addition, identify the methods of accessing this data.

Your main concern in this process will be the use of access methods governed by the packaged data model, data management system, usage of the data, and any device characteristics that you can utilize. (Needing to identify the physical characteristics of the data before confirming storage requirements is a perfect example of the need for iteration. So, this task needs to be developed iteratively with the new physical specification in the next activity.) This process should basically identify whether any existing corporate data storage and access description will accommodate the system's data needs or whether the model will require updating. The packaged data model will identify the structure of the data, thus aiding its physical placement on media. The data management system will also determine physical placement and govern the accessing of data.

The data flow diagram and data dictionary, along with any project goals that apply to data usage, such as throughput volumes and response times, will also aid in identifying the physical placement of data on media and methods of access, such as physical adjacency, pointer chains, or a randomizing algorithm for direct addressing in the automated environment. You can also use the cross-reference feature in the data dictionary to identify volume and frequency of data in the current physical specification. The device that will store the data may govern access capabilities; for example, in an automated environment, a tape device requires sequential storage, but disks allow parallel organization for faster data recovery; in the manual environment, index-card files or display boards may speed data access. Hence, the general hardware/software specification may provide guidance on selection of particular characteristics of a device, and proposal data in the hardware/software specification may supply information on vendor data management systems. (Most probably, in checking the hardware/software specification, you will identify additional hardware/software support requirements for the data storage and access.)

The parts of the packaged data model that do not affect the corporate data are indicated in the packaged data model, which will be used to identify the parts for which you have to create project files and possibly identify conversion details. The data storage and access description output should indicate which parts are, or are not, accommodated by any corporate data storage and access description.

Note: You will need to update the data storage and access description later with new physical details, for example, field lengths, value ranges, and so on. Such details will be required at least for new data; but for existing data in the corporate storage and access descriptions, you can use the existing physical characteristics to aid identification of the new physical details. For any project goals that can be completely or partly satisfied in this process, document the goals solutions in the project charter. This task may be performed by an agent outside the project team, such as a data administration team.

Note further that in creating the storage and access description based on data usage, you may need to make some modifications to the packaged data model. If speed of access cannot be accommodated by the available means of storage or access methods, then data redundancy may need to be introduced; for example, this can be accomplished by introducing total amounts stored instead of recalculating at access time or by duplicating stored data in order to save accessing of multiple objects. Of course, the reverse may be necessary: to reduce overhead in pointers, you may access objects through other objects not needed by a particular request. These changes would cause data integrity constraints.

Process name: CREATE DETAILED HW/SW SPECIFICATION
Process reference number: 4.4.1
Process guided by: Activity 4 plan

Process notes: Complete the specification of the hardware/software needed to support the manual and automated portions of the new system.

The specification must be completed before detailed design, as the hardware/software used will greatly affect the detailed parts of the design; that is, it will affect the way in which you input and output data. For example, some support software may take care of error processing if an output device is not available, thus eliminating the need to show the detail of it on the structure chart.

In this process, you first should validate and, if necessary, correct the information identified in the general hardware/software specification. (You may have a smaller area of study at the detailed level, which may change this specification.) Next, identify any project goals that can be completely or partly satisfied in this process; for example one goal might be satisfied through a request for specific hardware, such as a dedicated communication line. In fact, you may have a project goal stating that you must use the existing system or company hardware/software. In such a case, your task — confirming availability and allocation of hardware/software — will be very simple, as the design and man/machine boundary will have had to accommodate this goal, too.

If you do not have such restrictive goals, you will use the following resources to complete the hardware/software specification:

1. the bounded new logical specification, which shows the refined man/machine boundary and possibly the physical support characteristics of the interfaces on the boundary, as well as the store volumes

2. the assigned database management system, for which you will need to specify support requirements; for example, a requirement might be that one megabyte of core will be needed to support the assigned database management system; the assigned database management system should be documented in the hardware/software specification

3. the data storage and access description, which will specify storage needs as well as access needs for the permanently stored data

4. the production hardware/software inventory, which identifies all company-wide hardware/software, of which the current system's hardware/software is a subset

The selection of hardware/software should be completed as follows by specifying

1. the detailed portions of the existing hardware/software that can be reused for the new system

2. the detailed portions of the company hardware/software that can be used for the new system

3. the purchase requirements for new hardware/software that was not specified in steps 1 or 2; this can be done by using an internal company planning group, hardware/software journals, and/or by obtaining de-

tailed hardware/software data from applicable vendors. (Include this hardware/software data in the hardware/software specification. Such data is mainly applicable for determining minor hardware/software needs — the requests for proposals should have already been sent out for major hardware/software purchases.)

Completing the hardware/software specification involves specifying the actual make and model of hardware and the name and release of software, and the interdependencies between them, plus the environment and support needs. This specification is for all hardware/software needs in the new system, regardless of how the hardware/software is acquired. However, you should indicate in this specification whether hardware/software is reused, new, or already owned by the company, because this information will aid later processes. For any project goals that can be completely or partly satisfied in this process, you should document the hardware/software goals solutions in the project charter.

Note: The creation of the hardware/software specification and of the new design, which includes identification of the man/machine boundary, are closely tied (you should iterate through both these activities together). The new design solution may vary greatly depending on the selection of support hardware/software.

Process name: CREATE DETAILED DESIGN MODEL FOR NEW MANUAL ENVIRONMENT
Process reference number: 4.4.2
Process guided by: Activity 4 plan

Process notes: Complete the design of the manual environment. The first task is to use the packaged data model to amend or replace the logical stores that apply to the manual and man/machine interfaces on the data flow diagram of the bounded new logical specification.

The portions of the data model that apply to the manual system should be included in the manual system model. If not already identified, the support characteristics on the man/machine boundary should be completed for the manual interfaces, such as identifying terminals and report media. Use this data flow diagram to verify that the general new manual system model is still valid and, along with any project goals that you can satisfy in this process, further refine the model to show how the detailed logical functions and data will be implemented in the manual environment. Refinement involves completing the allocation of functions and data to individuals (probably job roles and job titles), and adding detailed physical characteristics to the refined model. You also need to identify the implementation of the process descriptions that are contained in the bounded new logical specification; for example, identify how to process error conditions and access and storage of data in stores. The packaged data model and its storage and access description are input for this purpose. The hardware/software specification, which contains the data management system, is input also, but it is for permanent stores in the manual environment and for man/machine boundary stores. For these additional stores, you will need to identify the file layouts and the storage and access description, as well as the data management system. You may also identify additional intermediate stores and support processes.

Note that, depending on security, timing, and access requirements of this data, there may be a project goal to include some of the intermediate stores in the corporate data model. Including the stores correctly will require a cycle back to the data modeling activity. You can leave the operating instructions of any hardware/software for inclusion in the procedures manual. Depending on the project goals, you may want to aid the design effort with the current manual system model. The cross-reference feature in the logical data dictionary will act as a pointer to the original physical processes and data. Usually, the manual environment will have less flexibility than the automated environment in handling change: Changing programs is easier than changing people.

Concentrate in this task mainly on those areas that you highlighted when identifying the man/machine boundary on the logical data flow diagram, that is, the areas that required change from the current environment. Also, because you are creating the new design, you should identify the control of these functions and data; that is, identify the organizational hierarchy of the new design. You are thus physicalizing the logical specification, a process that is basically equivalent to the reverse of logicalization. (To identify detailed physical data, see the sample table of contents for a manual system model in the addendum to the data dictionary.)

The new design solution and its support hardware/software are closely tied (you should iterate through both these activities together). The new design solution may vary depending on your selection of manual support hardware/software.

For any project goals that can be completely or partly satisfied in this process, you should document the manual design goals solutions in the project charter. It is useful to indicate the modifications in the new system model to identify them easily in the future. A simple method is to highlight them with a colored pencil.

Process name: CREATE DETAILED DESIGN MODEL FOR NEW AUTOMATED ENVIRONMENT
Process reference number: 4.4.3
Process guided by: Activity 4 plan

Process notes: Complete the design of the automated environment. The first task is to use the packaged data model to amend or replace the logical stores that apply to the automated and man/machine interfaces on the data flow diagram of the bounded new logical specification. The portions of the data model that apply to the automated system should be included in the automated system model. Also, you should complete determination of the support characteristics on the man/machine boundary, such as determining all input/output media, physical store requirements, and terminal requirements. Then use the data flow diagram to verify that the job and job step boundaries in the general new automated system model are still valid. If they are not valid, use the diagram to refine them. The detailed data flow diagram and any project goals that you can completely or partly satisfy in this process can be used to complete the design charts.

Completing the design charts involves identifying functions that will become modules, and data flows that will become the data passed between these modules (data coupling). In addition, you will need to identify coordinating/control modules for the worker modules and control information, for example, transaction handler modules or sorts, and error flags or end-of-file flags. If you are using the Yourdon and Constantine structured design techniques, the completed structure charts should be refined using coupling and cohesion refinement criteria.*

Use the process descriptions in the bounded new logical specification to create the pseudocode for the modules that were developed from the functions on the data flow diagram. Writing the pseudocode involves adding instructions to the function for any initialization or termination, and for error, control, and end-of-file handling. For pure coordinating/control modules, you will need to completely create the pseudocode. Pseudocode is an intermediate step to final code; it should contain enough information to describe the function and validate how the function will be implemented, as well as provide a non-ambiguous document from which to code. Pseudocode is not retained for maintenance unless the language used for implementation is a low-level one.

You should identify how you are going to handle error processing in the design. This may affect the pseudocode, depending on how detailed and important the error processing is. For intermediate stores, error processing will probably not be complex; but for the information in the packaged data model, you may have to identify some backout or alternative processing. The packaged data model, which represents our logical view of stored data, and the data management system, described in the hardware/software specification, will help determine the processing necessary.

The packaged data model and the data management system may also be needed to identify storing and accessing requirements in the pseudocode, depending on how detailed you make the pseudocode. You can now identify program boundaries within these jobs and job steps (if necessary), and then develop the system flowchart that will be used for development of the job control language and system execution manuals. At this point,

---

*See M. Page-Jones, *The Practical Guide to Structured Systems Design* (New York: YOURDON Press, 1980), pp. 101-35. Refer as well to E. Yourdon and L. Constantine, *Structured Design: Fundamentals of a Discipline of Computer Program and Systems Design,* 2nd ed. (New York: YOURDON Press, 1978), pp. 76-126.

you will probably want to assign a physical identification to each executable unit, for example, an identification for jobs and recovery sets. Therefore, you can use these physical identifications for documentation in the system execution manuals. This step will introduce additional intermediate stores that you will need to document in the new automated system model. Such documentation will consist of items like file layouts, storage and access descriptions, and data management systems. Therefore, you will need to introduce additional read/write modules and possibly error routines to support these intermediate stores. Note that, depending on security, timing, and access requirements, there may be a project goal to include some of the intermediate stores in the corporate data model. Including stores will require cycling back to the data modeling activity.

Depending on the project goals, you may want to aid this design effort with the current automated system model; for example, to identify salvageable units of code or data packaging. The cross-reference feature in the logical data dictionary can be used as a pointer to the original processes and data, but be careful not to copy bad code or packaging designs. One of the reasons for logicalizing the model is to enable you to be objective about the existing design, so you can develop a good new design. You are physicalizing the logical specification at this stage, so this process is basically equivalent to the reverse of logicalization. (To identify detailed physical data, see the sample table of contents for an automated system model in the addendum to the data dictionary.)

For any project goals that can be totally or partly satisfied in this process, you should document the automated design goals solutions in the project charter. It is useful to indicate the modifications in the new system model to identify them easily in the future. A simple method is to highlight them with a colored pencil.

Note: The new design solution and its support hardware/software are closely tied (you should iterate through both these activities together). The new design solution may vary greatly depending on the selection of automated support hardware/software.

Process name: CREATE DETAILED TEST CASES FOR NEW DESIGN
Process reference number: 4.4.4
Process guided by: Activity 4 plan

Process notes: Identify all test cases needed at a detailed level to validate the new physical specification and the hardware/software specification for the new system.

The first task is to validate the general design test cases and modify them if the general boundaries (manual, automated, and man/machine) have changed. In addition, the general test cases should be further developed, including completing the test cases for the design structure on the automated side. For example, you will want to verify correct operation of coordination/control modules, and correct data coupling between modules including end-of-file and error conditions. You will also develop test cases for any additional partitioning on both the manual and automated portions of the system.

You should develop test cases to validate all processes — which, at this level, are probably pseudocode — including those introduced during design, such as access routines for stored data, error processes, and initialization or termination processes. The new system test cases should serve as test cases for the modules/procedures that were developed from the data flow diagram. All test cases developed here will be detailed individual tests with all physical characteristics identified so that machine-executable test sets can be developed from them. Therefore, the test cases developed in this process all are physical tests for the design and logical tests with the physical characteristics for implementation defined.

The best source to use for identifying and defining test cases is the data dictionary of the new physical specification, with the physical data flow diagram (manual side) and design charts (automated side) as guides for flow of data. The size of the testing effort, and the types of tests used — for example, range tests, boundary value tests, and so on — will depend on project requirements such as reliability, cost, and time.*

For objectivity, someone other than the designer should create test cases, especially negative test cases.

---

*For test case designs, see G.J. Myers, *The Art of Software Testing* (New York: John Wiley & Sons, 1979).

Process name: CONDUCT REVIEW OF DETAILED NEW DESIGN SPECIFICATIONS
Process reference number: 4.4.5
Process guided by: Activity 4 plan

Process notes: See process reference number 2.5.5 for notes on this review process.

Process name: CREATE DETAILED PROCEDURES MANUAL
                   FOR NEW MANUAL ENVIRONMENT
Process reference number: 4.5.1
Process guided by: Activity 4 plan

Process notes: Complete the procedures necessary for the users to work with the manual portions of the system and to interface with the automated portions.

The physical data flow diagram, data dictionary, and process descriptions of the manual system model, as well as the hardware/software specification, have now been developed to the detailed level. You should use all of them and the general procedures manual to complete the detailed procedures manual as follows:

1. Complete all individual flows of data through the system and complete the data preparation and distribution procedures for the flows.

2. Complete the operating instructions for interface hardware/software, such as terminals with program function keys, and for embedded manual hardware/software, such as special typewriters and encoding equipment.

3. Complete the physical packaging of the manual. The information for the manual is in the new manual system model, with the exception of operating instructions for manual hardware/software. So this task mainly involves a reformatting of information into a particular company's standard layout for the procedures manual. Then use the physical process descriptions and data dictionary of the manual system model to document the manual procedures and controls necessary to accomplish the manual business functions.

To complete these procedures and controls, you will need to use the data management system in the hardware/software specification along with the data storage and access description in order to describe how and where to access manual stored data. For example, a master set of index cards can be used to access central tub files which in turn contain folders in chronological order.

If it is available, the current procedures manual may be helpful for any reusable portions of it or to identify formatting conventions.

Process name: CREATE DETAILED OPERATIONS MANUAL
FOR NEW AUTOMATED ENVIRONMENT
Process reference number: 4.5.2
Process guided by: Activity 4 plan

Process notes: Complete the documentation required for the operations staff to operate and control the automated portions of the system.

This step is where most of the development of the manual is accomplished. The hardware/software specification as well as the automated system model that contains the system flowchart has been fully developed. The system flowchart identifies the executable units in the automated system and is used to identify run procedures. You should use all of these forms of documentation and the general operations manual to develop the detailed operations manual, as follows:

1. Complete the specification of the operations support needed (such as staff and skill level).

2. Complete the run schedules and procedures needed to control the system, for example, job and job step dependencies on tape and disk loads, parameter updates for system control, and security of system media.

3. Identify backup and disaster recovery.

4. Complete the physical packaging, that is, the formatting of the manuals.

If it is available, the current operations manual may be helpful in this process for any reusable portions of it or to identify formatting conventions.

Process name: CONDUCT REVIEW OF DETAILED SYSTEM EXECUTION MANUALS
              FOR NEW SYSTEM
Process reference number: 4.5.3
Process guided by: Activity 4 plan

Process notes: See process reference number 3.5.3 for notes on this review process.

Process name: PREPARE DETAILED SYSTEM INSTALLATION SPECIFICATION
Process reference number: 4.6.1
Process guided by: Activity 4 plan

Process notes: Complete the procedures and support requirements for installation of the new system's application software and manual procedures.

The first task in this process is to validate and, if necessary, correct the general system installation specification, as you will be using it to form the detailed system installation specification. Next, you should identify the detailed area of change between the current and new systems (including changes to the way a function is performed). This area of change should already be indicated in the new physical specification, but if it isn't, the current physical specification can be used for comparison. The bounded new logical specification may also be helpful in this task, although not shown on the methodology's data flow diagram.

At this level of study, you have all the information necessary to complete the system installation specification, the main factors to consider being the process descriptions and detailed boundaries in the manual portion of the system and the pseudocode and program boundaries in the automated portion of the system, which are shown on the system flowchart.

You should identify any project goals that can be completely or partly satisfied in this process. Along with the goals in the project charter, you should develop your own system installation goals and document them in the system installation specification. Then, using the goals and the general system installation specification, do the following:

1. Review the detailed area of change in the new physical specification for the manual portions of the system and complete the procedures and support required to accomplish this change. The review includes installation of procedures manuals, relocation of staff and office equipment, placement of new staff and new office equipment, and collection of old documentation.

2. Review the detailed area of change in the new physical specification for the automated portions of the system and complete the procedures and support required to accomplish this change. The review includes changes to production library names, transfer of software and system controls from development libraries to production libraries, installation of operations manuals, and deletion of application software.

3. Complete the installation procedures for the maintenance information for the whole system. For example, transfer documentation and materials to the maintenance libraries.

For any project goals that can be completely or partly satisfied in this process, document the implementation goals solutions in the project charter.

Note: There will be overlap between the implementation specifications, but try to keep this redundancy to a minimum.

Process name: PREPARE DETAILED HW/SW INSTALLATION SPECIFICATION
Process reference number: 4.6.2
Process guided by: Activity 4 plan

Process notes: Complete the environment and support requirements for installation of the new system's hardware and support software.

The first task in this process is to validate and, if necessary, correct the general hardware/software installation specification, as you will be completing the specification in this process and forming the detailed specification. The hardware/software specification describes all hardware and support software needed for the new system, and identifies the portions that are new. During this process, you will concentrate mostly on the new hardware/software, and on any in the existing environment that requires modification.

For all remaining hardware/software (or all hardware/software, if no new portions or modifications are identified), you should confirm that the existing environment can accommodate the new system's hardware/software needs and identify any support requirements. (The hardware/software specification will identify the hardware/software needs: This task identifies the support environment needs; for example, it might identify that an operations night shift is needed to accommodate the new system, but no office access is currently available at night.)

You should identify any project goals that can be completely or partly satisfied in this process. In addition to these goals from the project charter, you should develop your own hardware/software installation goals and document them in the hardware/software installation specification. Using these goals, you should review in detail the hardware/software environment data in the production hardware/software inventory identified as reusable in the general study, and confirm its reusability. Use this detailed data to complete the information in the hardware/software installation specification. For environments requiring modification or for completely new environments, you should complete the information identified in the general-level study, including completing the configuration chart showing all interfaces between equipment: channels, controllers, modems, switches, and so on.

For all hardware/software, the installation support requirements should be completed; for example, vendor installation procedures and support documentation should be acquired and included in the hardware/software installation specification.

For any project goals that can be completely or partly satisfied in this process, you should document the implementation goals solutions in the project charter.

There will be overlap between the implementation specifications, but try to keep this redundancy to a minimum.

This process may be performed by an agent outside the project team, such as a support planning group.

Process name: PREPARE DETAILED CONVERSION SPECIFICATION
Process reference number: 4.6.3
Process guided by: Activity 4 plan

Process notes: Complete the procedures and support requirements needed in the conversion of data for the new system. The first task is to validate and, if necessary, correct the general conversion specification, as you will be using it to form the detailed conversion specification. Next, identify the detailed area of change (specifically, the change of stored data) between the current and new systems. This area of change should be indicated in the new physical specification (in the data dictionary), but if not, the current physical specification can be used for comparison.

You are looking for files containing data that requires a change of format, representation, or content; for new files that must be created; and for files that need a change of order, access, or media.

At this level of study, you have all information necessary to complete the conversion specification. Your main sources of information arc the detailed data dictionaries in the current and new physical specifications, and the data storage and access description, which is needed to show the physical view of the system's permanent data, some of which may be included in a corporate data store such as a central database. The data management system may also be of help in this process, although it is not shown on the methodology's data flow diagram. You should identify any project goals that can be completely or partly satisfied in this process; for example, identify that all old values for stock code should be corrected, and data integrity between name and address and payment branch should be validated. For these project goals, document the implementation goals solutions in the project charter, for example, that all data contents will be validated against new system values and data integrity will be validated where applicable. In addition to these goals from the project charter, you should develop your own conversion goals and document them in the conversion specification.

If you have been developing a system model and design model for conversion activities in the general conversion specification, they should now be completed by documenting the process descriptions and pseudocode, for example, for data calculations; or if conversion is simple, you should complete the documentation for the procedures, such as specifying parameters to be used in utility programs. In either case, you should complete the support information needed for these procedures as well as the conversion data dictionary, which is a subset of the current and the new physical data dictionaries.

Where possible, use the new system's application code and procedures to create new files. For example, use the current system data to create transactions that will run using new software to add records to the new file. You may want to take a short listing or sample of current production files to confirm that your data formats are up to date (these files are not shown as input on the methodology's data flow diagram).

Using the general test cases as a guide, develop detailed test cases to validate the conversion procedures and results. Preparing a detailed conversion specification may involve the specification of a new database or updating an existing database, neither of which may be the responsibility of the project team.

Note: There will be overlap between the implementation specifications, but try to keep this redundancy to a minimum.

Process name: PREPARE DETAILED TRAINING SPECIFICATION
Process reference number: 4.6.4
Process guided by: Activity 4 plan

Process notes: Complete the specification of the requirements and support information that are needed for training the users and operations staff for the new system. (Remember that the training specification is different from the other implementation specifications, as explained in process reference number 2.6.4.)

The first task in this process is to validate and, if necessary, correct the general training specification, as you will be using it to form the detailed training specification. Next, identify the detailed area of change between the current and new systems, as this is the area you will concentrate on in this process. The area of change should already be indicated in the new physical specification, but, if not, the current physical specification can be used for comparison. Also you should identify the area of change in the hardware/software specification. You are looking for changes of function, changes of interface with hardware/software, and changes of interface with data. This area of change applies to the operations and user areas.

At this level of study, you have all information necessary to complete the training specification; your main sources of information are the process descriptions in the manual area, the job descriptions (the system flowchart and support documentation) in the automated area, and the hardware/software operating instructions in both areas.

You should identify any project goals that can be completely or partly satisfied in this process. If, for example, it is a goal that each person trained should have his or her own training documentation, document the implementation goals solution in the project charter, indicating that each student be supplied with a copy of all course materials. In addition to these project charter goals, develop your own training goals and document them in the training specification. Using these project goals and the detailed area of change, you should complete the training requirements documentation — such as indicating the exact number of people to train at each training level and the training support needed to satisfy these requirements. The training support can be as major as a series of courses or a pilot project, or as minor as instruction in modifications to existing procedures.

The detailed new system execution manuals should be used as part of training support and can also be used to help identify training requirements. In fact, they will probably be used as the main documentation. Where possible, the new application system itself and the hardware/software, as well as any reusable training materials in the company maintenance library, should be specified as training support. Reusable materials may be drawn from the current system training materials and modified as necessary. Complete the specification for any training materials that must be specially created for this project, such as a lecture or an audiovisual course. In addition, it may be helpful to use actual system development documentation, such as the bounded new logical specification, to aid in training people to understand the new system.

As part of completing the training specification, you should confirm the availability of training support: facilities, materials, vendor-provided training, and so on.

Note: There will be overlap between the implementation specifications but try to keep this redundancy to a minimum.

Process name: COMPLETE TEST SPECIFICATION
Process reference number: 4.6.5
Process guided by: Activity 4 plan

Process notes: Identify and document any test cases that are not covered already in the test specification, and identify and document the test cases required for system testing.

The test specification identifies what tests need to be performed on the system. It is created incrementally throughout the developing effort; the current system test cases are identified and are used to help develop the new system test cases, after which the design test cases are added. All test cases are developed through the preliminary, general, and detailed cycles. At this point in development, you can view all of the test cases together, and consequently can identify test objectives as well as test cases that were not covered.

You should identify any project goal that can be completely or partly satisfied in the testing effort, especially the testing goals for the total system, such as that the system should be able to handle more than a quarter of a million transactions a day with the individual transaction response time of five seconds or less during peak periods. For project goals that do not have a solution identified, you should document the implementation goals solutions in the project charter. In addition to these system goals from the project charter, you should develop your own testing goals — for example, to test all execution paths in the system with at least one positive and one negative test — and document these in the test specification. Using these goals, you should review the test cases in the test specification and verify that they satisfy the testing of the new physical specification. While doing this, you should identify and document the test cases required for a system test (the new system execution manuals should be used for this task as well). Look for tests that satisfy criteria relating to volume, performance, security, recovery, interfacing, and so on for the system.*

These test cases are for manual environment testing as well as automated environment testing, with special emphasis on the interface between the manual and the automated environments, the manual-to-manual interfaces, and the automated-to-automated interfaces.

Having the total view of test cases, you should identify individual tests that can be satisfied by a single test case: One test case can satisfy testing a function, the design implementation of the function, and the function's hardware/software interface or manual-automated interface.

You must also specify the total testing support needed, which can be identified by the individual test dependencies in each test case.

Note: There will be overlap between the implementation specifications, but try to keep this redundancy to a minimum.

---

*For a more complete range of testing categories, see G.J. Myers, *The Art of Software Testing* (New York: John Wiley & Sons, 1979), p. 112.

Process name: CONDUCT REVIEW OF DETAILED IMPLEMENTATION SPECIFICATIONS
Process reference number: 4.6.6
Process guided by: Activity 4 plan

Process notes: See process reference number 2.6.5 for notes on this review process.

Process name: VERIFY AND UPDATE IMPLEMENTATION PLANS
Process reference number: 4.7.1
Process guided by: Activity 4 plan

Process notes: Verify and update the general implementation plans now that you have detailed knowledge of the system.

The first task is to confirm that the general implementation plans still apply; if any boundaries have changed, the implementation specifications will have been updated and these can be used to modify the implementation plans. Next, identify any project goals in the project charter or in the implementation specifications that can be completely or partly satisfied in this process — such as that no backlog of processing should occur during operations training — and document them in the implementation goals solutions; for example, document that two extra operators will be needed temporarily to support the operations staff during training.

Using these project goals and the implementation specifications, you should update the strategies as necessary, and complete the specifications of the individual detailed tasks, resources, dependencies, and schedules for meeting these goals and specifications. Then, confirm that the plans are synchronized with each other by

1.   reviewing the lists of tasks and identifying any tasks that can assist or replace tasks in other plans

2.   reviewing the detailed dependencies and schedules, confirming that there are no conflicts, and identifying any improvements that can be made

3.   reviewing the material and people support and confirming that there are no conflicts in allocation and availability

Finally, complete the estimate of cost for each task for cost/benefit purposes.

This process will need to be iterated through with process reference number 4.7.2, which produces the plan for coding the automated portions of the system. The iteration is necessary because you are estimating the schedule for coding based on the system installation specification, which used the pseudocode and system flowchart to identify the size of the coding effort. If this estimate must be changed as a result of the coding activities, you can build the change directly into the implementation plans.

Although you do not have any acceptance test cases to work from in the test specification, you need to allocate data processing resources to aid the user in acceptance testing. (You may also need to identify the user resources required.) Proper allocation, of course, requires knowing the level or amount of testing to be performed, as this may affect the project's schedule. If a user representative is a member of the project team, he or she may be able to provide reliable testing information; otherwise, you will need to consult with the user to get this information.

Note: This task is identified as a managerial task, because the agents performing the task are the project manager and management, but obviously the project team should help with the implementation plans as the team is familiar with the effort involved after having developed the detailed documentation.

Process name: COMPLETE ACTIVITY 5 PLAN
Process reference number: 4.7.2
Process guided by: Activity 4 plan

Process notes: Prepare the plan for the Activity 5 development processes that are not covered by the implementation plans. These are the coding, walkthrough, and management processes.

For the coding processes, use the following planning factors:

1. the new automated system model of the new physical specification, containing the flowchart, pseudocode, coding language(s), and so on

2. the figures for estimated and actual resources used for developing the pseudocode, which can act as a guide for determining coding complexity; if pseudocode is formed from the process descriptions that were produced in analysis, refer to the figures for the actual resources used to develop these

3. the system installation plan, which identifies the schedule needed for installing the automated and manual portions of the system

Using these three factors, prepare the plan for developing the code, the system controls, such as job control language, and the walkthroughs to be performed.

For the managerial processes in Activity 5, you can prepare the plan using figures for estimated and actual resources for similar activities in Activity 4.

Note: This process uses the system installation plan as an input. In fact, this process and the one that produces the implementation plans are performed together (you should iterate through both these activities together). Since you have done so much pre-coding development, you can, if necessary, make the coding effort fit the implementation plan. The system installation specification used the pseudocode to estimate what needed to be installed so the implementation plans could be developed and synchronized. However, if this was done without iterating through this process, you may need to modify the schedules. Using the design chart of the new automated model, you are able to delegate efficiently, because each module in the chart can stand alone. Hence, you have more flexible use of time and people.

Process name: ANALYZE DETAILED COSTS/BENEFITS AND PREPARE FINAL PROPOSAL
Process reference number: 4.7.3
Process guided by: Activity 4 plan

Process notes: Produce a final proposal containing sufficient information to allow management to decide whether to approve the resources for further study of the project. This report will provide

1. a summary of the actual resources used in detailed study compared to what was estimated

2. an overview of the system documentation developed so far

3. a list of the project goals that apply to detailed study and the detailed solutions to these goals (highlight any goals that have been added or modified at this level of study)

4. an analysis of the costs and benefits for the new system, along with any limitations and risks in producing it

5. a summary of the plans for Activities 5 and 6 with a detailed estimate of resources needed for Activity 5 and a best-guess estimate for resources needed for Activity 6

Item 1 can be extracted from the project plan. Item 2 is produced from the current and new descriptions. Item 3 is produced from the project charter, in which you may also list your own objectives; for example, you may wish to specify that structured techniques will be used for development. Item 4 is produced from the cost data in the specifications of the current and new system descriptions and from cost and benefit information in the project charter. Add any benefits and risks that you may have identified, such as a need for less operator intervention or the advantage of using state-of-the-art equipment, as well as any cost savings or increases. Item 5 can be extracted from the project plan.

Since the information in this final proposal is produced from your detailed study, it should be accurate. Estimates here are expected to be accurate within five percent; this degree of accuracy should be stated in the final proposal with a comment that the accuracy is true only for factors within your control. Factors that are uncontrollable are such ones as hardware/software being delivered on time, user availability at presentations and reviews, and so on.

Process name: PRESENT FINAL PROPOSAL TO D.P. MANAGEMENT
Process reference number: 4.7.4
Process guided by: Activity 4 plan

Process notes: The aim of this presentation is to make data processing management aware of the progress to date, to report on the resources used, and to get a commitment for the resources needed for Activity 5. This should be a formal presentation of all the information in the final proposal.

The presentation is part of keeping data processing management informed of the project progress so that if a slip in schedule is necessary, you may avoid cancellation of resources by data processing management. (If the project is an internal data processing project, such as a rewrite of an unmaintainable system, data processing management will be the same as user management. This presentation, therefore, would be the main presentation.)

In this presentation, you should also raise any issues that may adversely affect the progress of the project — for example, lack of computer time or hardware installation problems — and, if possible, resolve the potential difficulties.

Process name: PRESENT FINAL PROPOSAL TO USER MANAGEMENT
Process reference number: 4.7.5
Process guided by: Activity 4 plan

Process notes: The presentation of the final proposal to user management serves many purposes: to report on the resources used so far, to give an overview of the system documentation completed to date, to present a detailed cost/benefit report of the option or its release for which you have completed detailed study, and to obtain approval for and commitment of resources needed for Activity 5. As the name of this process indicates, this is the final presentation of the option or its release that you are going to implement.

This should be a formal presentation of all the information in the final proposal. It is possible that, using the information at this level of detail, you may have identified minor modifications to this option or its release. These modifications should be pointed out in the presentation if they have already been incorporated into the system documentation. Approval of these modifications should have been received from individual user managers during the detailed study. If any serious modifications are necessary to this final proposal, you should cycle back through the activities that are affected in the detailed study.

Since most of the new hiring and contracting needs should have been satisfied by this point, the overall data processing plans and resources should be revised for reallocation of resources.

Process name: PLACE HARDWARE/SOFTWARE ORDERS
Process reference number: 4.7.6
Process guided by: HW/SW installation plan

Process notes: When management has approved resources, you can prepare to send out the orders for hardware/software that cannot be provided in-house. The vendor hardware/software proposals should be evaluated along with that data contained in the hardware/software specification, and a vendor or vendors should be selected to supply the hardware/software. Then use the detailed requirements presented in the hardware/software specification, the hardware/software installation specification, and the schedule requirements indicated in the hardware/software installation plan to develop and negotiate a contract or order with the vendor(s). The contract or order will probably have to be signed by management before it is sent to the vendor(s).

Note: This process may be performed by an agent outside the project team, such as a planning support group.

Process name: PREPARE TEST MATERIALS
Process reference number: 5.1.1
Process guided by: Test plan

Process notes: Using the test specification, which contains the overall testing objectives and individual test cases, and the test plan, which contains the testing strategy and resources, you will develop the executable test sets and the scaffolding needed to support these test sets, which are formed from one or more test cases. For example, a top-down, incremental testing strategy may be identified for programs in the automated system. Therefore, you need to identify all test cases that apply to each module in each program and those for the whole system, and to form test sets for each of these units. Then, create the actual test data and scaffolding needed to support these sets, such as the job control language procedures and stubs. These test sets and scaffolding should identify the original test case(s) from which they were derived. The test sets are for manual procedures as well as automated modules or programs. They may be partitioned by the type of test, such as normal, exception, performance, and so on. You may have a test data generator to build the test cases. There may be reusable testing materials that require no change or only minor changes, available from a regression test library in the maintenance area; these materials will be identified in the test specification. Another process, such as initial conversion that produces test files, may supply part of the test materials. You should conduct a walkthrough for each of these test sets.

Note: Unless there is a separate testing group in the company, do not expect all test sets to be built in this process — just the input data and entry criteria for the first testing phase may be accomplished. The others can be developed iteratively during each testing phase at successive program testing levels.

Process name: PREPARE TRAINING MATERIALS
Process reference number: 5.1.2
Process guided by: Training plan

Process notes: In this process, you will prepare the training materials needed for the new system training effort. Such materials will also be used for on-going training; for example, the materials could be used to train new support staff hired during production of the system.

Using the training specification and, if necessary, the training plan that also guides this process, you should

1. obtain the reusable training materials from the maintenance library and, if necessary, modify them

2. obtain support materials, such as pre-course reading or handouts for vendor-supplied training

3. create any new training programs, such as an on-line training support program

4. create the presentation materials

5. create the student materials

The training specification should identify which portions are reusable, as well as identify those that are developed by other processes; for example, it should identify actual application programs, testing materials, system execution manuals, and so on.

Note: This process may be performed by an agent outside the project team, such as a training department.

Process name: WRITE APPLICATION CODE
Process reference number: 5.2.1
Process guided by: Activity 5 plan

Process notes: Create the compiled application code and the development and production system controls for the automated portions of the new system. All information for doing this task should be in the new automated system model, the Activity 5 plan, which also guides this process, and the hardware/software specification.

The new automated system model contains the pseudocode (physicalized process descriptions), the structure charts showing the data coupling (module parameters), and the source language to be used for coding. Also, the system flowchart and data dictionary will be used for creating the system controls.

The Activity 5 plan contains the strategy to be used for developing the modules, such as whether top-down or bottom-up development will be used. The hardware/software specification identifies any compiler requirements and operating software for system controls, and identifies the hardware for any necessary program documentation. Also, the hardware/software specification contains the packaged data model and the data management system; the documentation for these will be needed for data access syntax and control, such as segment search argument (SSA) and program specification blocks (PSB) in IMS.

Note: This process and the next two processes should be cycled through for each module specified in the new automated system model.

Process name: WALK THROUGH THE APPLICATION CODE
Process reference number: 5.2.2
Process guided by: Activity 5 plan

Process notes: The aim of this walkthrough is to identify any problems, inaccuracies, ambiguities, and omissions in the application code and system controls.

Look for readability and logic errors in the code. The new automated system model contains the pseudocode from which the code was generated, so the logic can be validated from it. Also, the code should be checked against code standards. Unlike manuals and specifications, code can be implemented without anyone's having examined it, so this process provides the last and possibly only time code can be confirmed as being standard. It is for this reason that this walkthrough is explicitly shown as a process of the methodology, although others are not.

The code and system controls have to be complete and correct because they form the actual automated system. Since the computer is incapable of finding logic errors, you have to rely on this walkthrough and the testing effort to detect any bugs.

The detailed test cases from the test specification that are applicable to this module can also be used for this walkthrough. If a subsystem is being examined, this can be a review instead of a walkthrough; for example, you might review a group of modules together that have been walked through individually.

The agents performing this task should be the coder of the material being examined and other coders on the project team. A designer and an analyst could also participate. The walkthrough can be held before compilation of code, but is probably better held after compilation to avoid participants' looking for minor syntax errors.

Process name: PERFORM TESTING OF APPLICATION CODE
Process reference number: 5.2.3
Process guided by: Test plan

Process notes: Test each application module and the system controls. You may also perform subsystem or integration tests after all modules composing the subsystem have been individually tested. You will perform mainly function testing, that is, normal (positive) testing and exception (negative) testing, but some performance testing can be done on critical areas. The main performance testing will be done on the complete system during the system test.

The application modules and their system controls will be tested using the testing materials, which contain test sets for each module, and the test specification, which contains such information as the individual test objectives and expected results. The test plan, which also guides this process, will identify the strategy for testing — which, for example, might be incremental, top-down testing with the edit subsystem tested first.

When tested, these modules and system controls will form the application programs and their supporting system controls.

Process name: CODE AND TEST THE CONVERSION PROGRAMS
Process reference number: 5.2.4
Process guided by: Conversion plan

Process notes: Write and test the programs and system controls needed to support the automated portions of the conversion effort. This process for conversion programs is equivalent to process reference numbers 5.2.1, 5.2.2, and 5.2.3, which are for application code; see them for more detail on this process.

If the conversion effort is large and complex, you probably will have developed an equivalent new automated system model for conversion. Using this model, the hardware/software specification, the test specification (for conversion test cases), the conversion testing materials, and the conversion plan that also guides this process, you should develop the conversion modules that compose the programs and their system controls.

Process name: COMPLETE ACTIVITY 6 PLAN
Process reference number: 5.3.1
Process guided by: Activity 5 plan

Process notes: Prepare the plan for the processes in Activity 6, which are not covered by the implementation plans. These processes consist of five tasks: creation of the regression test specification and library, preparation of the maintenance plan, updating of release information, monitoring of production, and preparation of the project completion report.

The implementation plans should be used to synchronize the total Activity 6 plan. The test specification and the test material can be used to identify the resources and other elements for creation of regression test material. The new system description should be used to identify the resources for creation of the maintenance plan and to aid in preparing the entire Activity 6 plan. Much of this plan will rely on your knowledge of the user environment.

If a fairly comprehensive Activity 6 plan was developed for the final proposal, it should be used as a guide in this process.

Process name: PREPARE IMPLEMENTATION REPORT
Process reference number: 5.3.2
Process guided by: Activity 5 plan

Process notes: Produce an implementation report that will provide management with a summary of the project's progress to date.

The main purpose of this report is to document the resources, especially the user resources, needed to accomplish Activity 6. This report will provide

1. a summary of the actual resources used in Activity 5 compared to the estimated resources; the summary can be extracted from the project plan

2. a summary of the plans for Activity 6 with a detailed estimate of the resources needed and the user resources highlighted; this summary can be prepared from the Activity 6 plan and the implementation plans

3. identification of any issues not included in a previous report that have and will continue to have an impact on the project's progress

If possible, you should show the user some test results from the program function tests. This point in development entails the least contact with the user, so the user would probably welcome any communication of the system's progress.

Process name: PRESENT IMPLEMENTATION REPORT TO D.P. MANAGEMENT
Process reference number: 5.3.3
Process guided by: Activity 5 plan

Process notes: The aim in this presentation is to make data processing management aware of your progress to date, to report on the resources used, and to get commitment and approval for the data processing resources needed for Activity 6.

This should be a formal presentation of all the information in the implementation report. Keeping data processing management informed of the project's progress is especially important now that you have given your final proposal to management. Any slip in schedule, as well as any issues that can affect future progress, should be explained. Whenever possible, you should make recommendations for the solution of potential problems.

Process name: PRESENT IMPLEMENTATION REPORT TO USER MANAGEMENT
Process reference number: 5.3.4
Process guided by: Activity 5 plan

Process notes: Your aim in this presentation is to make user management aware of your progress to date, to report on the resources used, and to get commitment and approval for the user resources needed for Activity 6, which is the primary presentation goal because this activity requires the most user participation.

This should be a formal presentation of all the information in the implementation report. You may also present some program test results to keep open the communication about the project's progress. Any changes or slips in schedules during Activity 5, as well as any issues that may possibly affect future progress, should be explained here. Whenever possible, you should make recommendations for the solution of potential problems.

The overall data processing plans and resources should be revised to reflect any reallocation of resources. You should also get commitment and approval for outside resources needed in Activity 6, such as trainers or hardware movers.

Process name: INSTALL HW/SW
Process reference number: 6.1.1
Process guided by: HW/SW installation plan

Process notes: Install the hardware/software required to support the new system. Whether you install all hardware/software or do it in stages by iterating through this process together with other implementation processes depends on the hardware/software installation plan that guides this process.

Using the hardware/software installation specification, you should confirm that all environments, new and reusable, are ready for the new and relocatable hardware/software. Referring to the hardware/software specification, confirm that the new hardware/software has been received from the vendors and is ready for installation. In addition, you should identify the existing hardware/software that requires relocating and confirm that it is ready. Install this hardware/software in the production area using the support procedures and materials identified in the hardware/software installation specification.

After the hardware/software is installed and tested, you should complete the hardware/software installation completion report and update the production hardware/software inventory for new, relocated, and reallocated hardware/software.

The agent performing this process may be outside of the project team, such as a planning support group with vendor engineers.

Process name: PERFORM DATA CONVERSION
Process reference number: 6.1.2
Process guided by: Conversion plan

Process notes: Convert current production data to a new format or storage and access technique, and create new data needed for the production execution of the new system. Whether you convert all data at one time or in stages (iterating through this process with other implementation processes) depends on the conversion plan that guides this process.

Using the data dictionary in the conversion specification, you should confirm that the data is available and, if necessary, gather the source data for the new data needs. Then, execute the conversion programs and procedures against the current automated and manual production data, using the procedures and support identified in the conversion specification. Some application programs may be used to assist data conversion; they will be identified in the conversion specification.

After the data is converted and confirmed as being correct, which can be achieved by conducting a walkthrough and/or testing, you should produce the conversion completion report.

Some of the agents performing this task may not be members of the project team. For example, they could be data administration members setting up a new database or adding to an existing database.

Process name: CONDUCT TRAINING
Process reference number: 6.1.3
Process guided by: Training plan

Process notes: Train the user and operations staff to run the new system. Whether you train all staff at one time or in stages by iterating through this process with other processes depends on the training plan that guides this process.

Using the training support identified in the training specification and the system development training materials, conduct the training for both staff and management. The major documentation for training will be system execution manuals, but you may also use the actual application programs and system controls, identified in the training materials.

After the training is accomplished, you should produce the training completion report.

Process name: PERFORM SYSTEM TEST OF MANUAL AND AUTOMATED SYSTEM
Process reference number: 6.2.1
Process guided by: Test plan

Process notes: Validate that the complete new system or this release of the new system meets the system and business objectives, which are translated into tests in the test specification. Remember that at this point not all objectives can be tested for, as in the case of reduced production costs. This process represents the data processing trial run, in which you completely test the system as a whole. In this process, you will want to perform both normal (positive) and exception (negative) tests. Since you have already performed individual function tests, concentrate on integration, performance, volume, and security testing as well as on the recovery capabilities of the system.

You should use the system execution manuals as the main guide for this testing effort. Also use the test plan for the testing strategy. The test specification will provide the individual test objectives for the test sets in the development test library. The trained data processing operations staff and all application programs and system controls are, of course, used. Whenever possible, you should use the actual production environments for this system test.

In addition to the operations staff, other agents performing this process should be analysts, designers who did not develop the system code or execution manual, and the project manager. User representatives can also help if they are members of the project team. After the system test is accomplished, you should produce the system test completion report.

Process name: PREPARE REGRESSION TEST SPECIFICATION AND LIBRARY
Process reference number: 6.2.2
Process guided by: Activity 6 plan

Process notes: Create a regression test specification and library that can be used to validate the systems functions after maintenance and after modifications are applied in production. The regression tests ensure that functions that were not part of a modification were not inadvertently affected.

You should identify the minimum test cases that can be used for regression testing. These can be identified by examining their individual objectives in the test specification and the corresponding test materials in the development test library. Using them and making necessary modifications, form the regression test specification and library. You may need to include additional back-up documentation in the regression test specification, such as expected hardware/software, to meet performance tests.

Process name: PREPARE AND PRESENT MAINTENANCE PLAN
Process reference number: 6.2.3
Process guided by: Activity 6 plan

Process notes: Prepare and present the maintenance plan* required to support the new system or the current release of the new system in production. To prepare the plan, you should proceed as follows:

1. Review any change requests received during system development and identify those that apply to the data, functions, or support equipment/material installed in the system or release, not those changes that are going to be included in another system or release.

2. Identify the on-going training support for the system or the release.

3. Identify the data processing maintenance contacts required for the system or release.

Following these three steps, prepare the maintenance plan with the aid of the new system description and the actual and estimated resources used in the project plan. Present this plan to management to get approval for resources. Note that part of the resources may be devoted to accommodate releases; for example, a resource may be required to maintain interfaces between old and new system areas until the old areas are developed.

---

*Since you are using structured techniques, your maintenance effort should be relatively small. While a maintenance effort can be reduced, it will never be eliminated because business requirements may change during development of the system.

Process name: TRANSMIT SYSTEM TO PRODUCTION
Process reference number: 6.2.4
Process guided by: System installation plan

Process notes: Install the developed software and system execution manuals; that is, actually transfer the new system into the production environments. Use the system installation procedures and support in the system installation specification to move the application programs and their production system controls and the new system execution manuals from development libraries to production libraries. Be sure to generate listings of these programs and system controls for maintenance purposes. (The system execution manuals may have already been transferred to the staff during training.)

Process name: TRANSMIT SYSTEM MAINTENANCE INFORMATION
Process reference number: 6.2.5
Process guided by: System installation plan

Process notes: Install the system maintenance information required in production to support the new system or a release of the system.

Use the maintenance installation procedures and support as described in the system installation specification to move the following to the maintenance library: the regression test specification and library; the training specification and materials (on-going portions); the maintenance plan; the hardware/software inventory, which may be either a complete replacement or update to the existing maintenance version; the bounded new logical specification; the new physical specification; the new system execution manuals; and the program and system controls listings.

Process name: CONDUCT ACCEPTANCE TEST
Process reference number: 6.3.1
Process guided by: Test plan

Process notes: The users of the system will be the main agents in this task because members of the project team may not create objective test sets; therefore, the test plan only identifies support resources for this process. This is the user's chance to completely test the system, that is, to "test drive" it. Therefore, normal (positive) and exception (negative) tests must be executed.

You should recommend to the users, that, along with good tests, they should create tests that will attempt to make the system fail. It is better to find any bugs that the user's data reveals at this point, rather than have the user later lose confidence in the system because too many production runs crash. The user's best source for identifying test objectives is the project charter and the new system execution manuals. Trained operations staff, who were not involved in the system development effort, should test the operations portions of the system to obtain objective results.

The user's task is to test production programs, production system controls, and new system execution manuals. You could include testing of the production hardware/software for usability at this point because the user may be testing it, too. Trained staff are the agents that execute this process. After acceptance testing is completed, produce an acceptance test completion report.

Process name: PREPARE FOR NEXT RELEASE
Process reference number: 6.3.2
Process guided by: Activity 6 plan

Process notes: In this process, you will prepare the next release, if any, and archive the old system documentation, as follows:

1.   Document that this release's project goals, as stated in the project charter, have been achieved.

2.   Identify the project goals for the next release and document them as being "active"; if a significant amount of time has elapsed since receiving these goals or if you feel it necessary because of a change in user management, you should confirm that these project goals are still valid.

3.   Archive this release's current system description; note that if you are running parallel production — that is, running the current and the new system together to confirm results — this part of the process will be performed after an extra acceptance period.

The acceptance test completion report can be saved, if necessary, in the project charter. It is input acting as a "prompt" to activate this process.

Note: Depending on the level of study at which you started working on a specific release (general or detailed), you should cycle back to the process in that level of study at which releases were identified. For example, if you started studying just one release at the general level, cycle back to "Identify Preliminary Releases," process reference number 2.7.1; or, if you started at the detailed level, cycle back to "Verify Releases," process reference number 3.7.1. However, if the next release's project goals have been modified during development of this release, you may have to cycle back even further in order to update the developed system documentation.

For development of plans in future releases, you should use the applicable portions of this release's plans as an aid.

Process name: RUN AND MONITOR PRODUCTION
Process reference number: 6.3.3
Process guided by: Activity 6 plan

Process notes: Monitor the new system or the release of the system during its initial months of production. This time period may be considered to be the system's warranty period, which is why it is included in Activity 6.

After the system's cutover to production, you should monitor the user's normal production execution of the new system, noting any problems with usability, performance, accuracy, security, hardware/software support, and so on. You should also note any changes in the system usage pattern; for example, because the new system is accessible by all members of the user department, the number of inquiry transactions has exceeded the estimated number, thus requiring a faster access technique. Another change could result, for example, from additional inquiry functions, which have been identified because of the increased usage of the system.

After this initial production period, prepare a summary of initial production information for use in evaluating the new system. The duration of this monitored production period depends on the periodicity of the system: A weekly batch system will be monitored over a longer period than an on-line system.

Process name: PREPARE PROJECT COMPLETION REPORT
Process reference number: 6.3.4
Process guided by: Activity 6 plan

Process notes: Now that you have accumulated production data during the monitoring period, evaluate the project and the new system.

This monitoring period should have allowed you to determine whether you accomplished any long-term project goals, such as ease of maintainability, lower production cost, or less system down-time.

Gather opinions on the project and the new system or the release of the new system from both data processing and user management and staff. Then, prepare the project completion report as follows:

1. Using these opinions, the initial production information, and the project goals and their solutions in the project charter, document how well the project and new system meet their goals.

2. Comparing these opinions with the initial production information, document how well the new system is performing in production.

3. Using these opinions and the data on estimated and actual resources used in the project plan, document how well the project team performed.

This report should document what happened in the project and why. For example, document that the project was completed successfully because of the techniques used and the cooperation of the users, or that the system was delivered late because of hardware and planning problems. You can use the opinions and the data in the project plan to suggest any tailoring to this methodology's guidelines as well as to any general project development methods.

You should distribute the project completion report to applicable management and also store a copy in the project histories together with other project information that may be of help to future projects. The information in the completion report must be honest and accurate. (You want to repeat your successes, not your failures.) You can also present the project completion report to management, just as you did the activity reports. In fact, saving the activity reports that were presented to management during development can help to develop the project completion reports.

AFTERWORD

As I believe that the development of a system should be iterative and so should accommodate change, I issue a call to those of you who are concerned with quality system development to provide me with input and suggestions concerning your experience with this methodology and other system development techniques.

Send correspondence to:

Brian Dickinson
c/o YOURDON inc.
851 Traeger Avenue, Suite 350
San Bruno, California 94066

APPENDICES

303

APPENDIX A
Overview of
the Structured Techniques

Structured analysis

Structured analysis is the activity of communicating system requirements from a user to an analyst and from an analyst to a designer. Such communication is accomplished by using models — a new kind of functional specification — and by using a limited set of tools, as listed below:

- data flow diagrams
- data dictionary
- data structure/access diagram
- mini-specifications

In effect, structured analysis reveals *what* we require of the system.

Structured design

Structured design is the activity of developing a solution to a well-defined set of system requirements. The solution is developed with an aim toward flexibility and maintainability. Structured design tools include the following:

- structure chart (or Warnier-Orr diagrams or Jackson data structure diagrams)
- data flow diagrams
- data dictionary
- pseudocode or Nassi-Shneiderman diagrams
- quality evaluation criteria
- packaging criteria

Structured design determines *how* we organize a solution that satisfies requirements.

Structured programming/coding

Structured programming or coding consists of the activity of implementing a solution in a readable, maintainable style. Coding tools include the following:

- three means of building programs in a nested manner:
    - ○   through implementation of sequential statements
    - ○   through implementation of binary decisions
    - ○   through iteration
- readable coding styles

This activity can be considered *building* from a given solution of a system.

Incremental implementation

Incremental implementation is a technique of successively building and testing versions of a computer system having a hierarchical design. Implementation tools include

- hierarchical design charts
- drivers/stubs (simulation modules)

This process is one of *putting together and testing* a system.

Structured walkthroughs/reviews

Structured walkthroughs and reviews are peer-group reviews conducted to find errors. They are performed for all deliverables of a system; moreover, they serve as *quality control* during development of a system.

Data modeling

Data modeling is the activity of organizing the essential data needs of an environment and representing them in the form of a data or information model. Tools for this activity include

- data dictionary (which for this activity contains a superset of the analysis and design data dictionaries as well as integrity constraints, usage, security requirements, and so on)
- data models (including informal/formal data structure diagrams, which show data objects/entities and their relationships)

Modeling shows *what* actual data the system uses and may also identify *how* the data is stored and accessed.

APPENDIX B
Installing a Methodology

Introduction

I look upon this methodology as a system to develop systems.* Because it is a system itself, albeit a manual one, a methodology should pass through the same development activities as any other system — from identifying the project goals to installing the system.

The main project goal for development of a structured methodology is to formally integrate all of the structured techniques into a set of practical guidelines — a system, if you will — for developing automated systems. Other project goals for this methodology include these:

- to provide accurate project estimates and improved system products
- to provide system quality control
- to provide tools for communicating new development techniques and for documenting systems
- to provide efficient use of development staff and other resources
- to provide effective responses to system change requests
- to offer guidance in the use of state-of-the-art techniques
- to identify and precisely determine the degree of project risk

In sum, the methodology, in standardizing the system development activities, should impose order on the development process and enhance communication between all members of the project team. However, more important than a formulation of project goals is the proper installation of the methodology. (If a system is not correctly installed, then it may not be used at all!)

There are four major factors to consider when installing a methodology. Listed in order of importance, they are

- political/psychological considerations
- installation and training

---

*This appendix is based on a talk, entitled "Implementing a Management Discipline: A Case Study," which I presented during a panel session at the 1980 National Computer Conference in Anaheim, California. A version of it was published as "Committing to a Systems Methodology," in *The YOURDON Report,* Vol. 6, No. 1 (January-February 1981), pp. 3-4, 7. Copyright © 1981. Reprinted by permission.

- the training medium
- on-going support and monitoring

Let me expand on these and offer some recommendations for controlling them.

Political/psychological considerations

Political and psychological factors can profoundly affect users' acceptance of the methodology. The most important consideration is high-level management's commitment to the installation of the methodology. In order to enlist their backing, educate managers in the advantages of a company-wide methodology. It is important that the methodology be adopted throughout an organization, because isolated groups using the methodology, or part of it, will not be able to communicate effectively.

The second consideration is the potential feeling of loss of freedom or power, as well as the natural resistance to change, on the part of new users of the methodology. To combat this resistance, the methodology must appear simple to use. This, of course, will depend on the training and the tools, such as an automated data dictionary, provided to support the methodology. The quantity of forms and control procedures that a company assigns to go along with the methodology will also affect complexity.

Finally, there is the possibility that users' acceptance of the methodology will go to an extreme, and that the methodology will be taken too literally. Some people may look upon it as a "cookbook" solution to all their problems, instead of as an aid to their own thought processes. This leads to the problem of the developers' having to support the methodology, instead of the methodology supporting the development process.

Aware of these considerations, you can take several steps to minimize their effects. First, you can classify the methodology as a guideline rather than as a standard, and allow users of the methodology to customize it whenever problems are found in its use. Thus, the methodology can be viewed as a help, not as a restriction. Of course, customization must be accompanied by an explanation; random customizing is not the goal.

Second, you can predispose acceptance of the techniques by setting up a review group that consists of managers whose departments will use the methodology. By doing so, you give them ownership in advance and a part in the decision to accept the methodology. Beware, however, that reluctant managers may make any meeting of this group their political battleground. In addition, you can prove that the methodology works by offering statistics from other users of the methodology or from the results of a pilot project.* Finally, carefully consider methods of training new users to apply the methodology, as discussed in the next section.

---

*If you decide to test the methodology on a pilot project, choose such a project carefully: It should not be critical to the company's business, nor should it be overly complex. Of course, the learning curve for users of the new methodology will compound the complexity and critical nature of the project and may prove fatal to the pilot project and so to the methodology. Even if not fatal, a too complex pilot project is not useful as an example for others to learn from.

Installation and training

There are four general strategies that I see regularly implemented to install a methodology and to train its eventual users: the pilot project approach, the top-down and bottom-up approaches, and the sheep-dip approach. I briefly discuss each in the following paragraphs.

☐ The *pilot project* strategy: The installation is tested by applying the techniques on a reasonably sized pilot project, and the resulting documentation from the project is used as support for adoption of the methodology. The developers of the pilot project are then used to assist or even train members of other projects by either being assigned permanently to the project or participating in its plans and reviews. These project members then can be appointed to aid other projects.

☐ The *top-down* strategy: Training in the methodology consists of teaching only those techniques that will be used immediately by the members of new projects. For example, a course in analysis techniques is held before analysis activities, a design course before design activities, and so on. This training is repeated for each new project team.

☐ The *bottom-up* strategy: Training courses are held for each category of employee (for example, analyst, designer, coder, or database developer), starting with the course applicable to the specific role and proceeding to courses on activities with which the employee may need to interface. A programmer, for instance, would take a course in coding techniques first, and a design overview course later. This is a realistic strategy for groups that are not scheduled for any new projects.

☐ The *sheep-dip* strategy: In this approach, so named by Gerald Weinberg, all available staff members are trained at the time a course in any of the techniques is scheduled, regardless of whether they will need to use the techniques in the near future. This term is also used for the strategy that advocates training every employee in all of the techniques at once (a version of the six-week in-depth training course of everything you wanted to know about "getting structured" but were afraid to ask).

Of course, as with any system development effort, a plan should be developed to monitor and control the installation of the methodology and its associated training. Realistically, a combination of the above strategies will be needed for most (large) environments. For example, using the first two strategies is probably the best combination, but it could take years to train all of the groups involved. Moreover, neither strategy takes into account the training of new employees and small maintenance groups. Therefore, the incorporation of the third or bottom-up strategy is necessary. In this regard, some people truly understand only those courses most applicable to their background. For example, to programmers, the concepts of structured coding can be appreciated readily. Then, when introduced to structured design, they can see how its concepts greatly aid the coding activity.

The sheep-dip strategy may be of some use, but only as an overview of different techniques to upper-level managers and other generalists. In general, it is best to give a person only the knowledge necessary to do a job well. For example, high-level management may require only an overview; middle management may require an overview and possibly an introduction to the deliverables or products; project leaders may require a working knowledge of the complete methodology; and technical project staff members may require a detailed working knowledge of the activities for which they are responsible and possibly an overview of other activities.

Of course, how the methodology is installed cannot be separated from the medium chosen for training, as discussed below.

Training medium

How the methodology is taught will greatly affect its understandability and, therefore, its acceptability. Although cost will probably determine the training medium used, some options include a workshop course, a lecture course, a self-study audiovisual course, and books or documents. Any and all of these training devices can be backed up with assistance from outside consultants and with on-the-job advice of experienced personnel. In my consulting work, I have seen the best results come from using a combination of training vehicles, such as a workshop course with follow-up visits from a consultant.

A workshop course is one of the best forms of training, as it provides staff with hands-on experience in applying a technique and with immediate feedback to questions. A lecture course also provides immediate answers to questions and is usually easier and cheaper to present, but doesn't offer participants the chance to practice using the techniques. A self-study audiovisual course allows a person to learn at his or her own pace.

A final point to be made about training media pertains to the importance of the packaging of the support material. Careful consideration should be given to the way in which documentation is stored and accessed, so that it is easily usable. Massive, multiple volumes containing a pilot project or sample documentation, tutorial material, and information about support tools are usually so difficult to reference that no one uses them.

On-going support and monitoring

The methodology, like any system, should be maintained to keep it from becoming out of date. A support group or possibly one person should be responsible for this task. The importance of the task should not be minimized, however, for the data processing industry is developing rapidly: New software development and support techniques are being introduced in virtually every phase. For the methodology to survive, it needs to accommodate pertinent innovations, but the process of incorporating them must be controlled according to the same principles used in the original methodology.

This rule also applies to any customizing of the methodology, either for the company as a whole or for a particular project. The effectiveness of the methodology should be tracked and compared with results using the old techniques to determine the cost-effectiveness of the methodology. Based on these results, adjustments to the methodology should be made when necessary. Consequently, data must be collected before total installation of the methodology has taken place.

Finally, a point I want to stress relates to the need for support consulting. An expert in the methodology — someone who has used the techniques, say, in a pilot project or in the original training group — should be available to help out on new projects to insure that the methodology is being used correctly. This can be accomplished simply by the advisor's being available during reviews or walkthroughs.

In summary, the installation and on-going support of any system requires a great deal of commitment of cost and effort. This manual system — this methodology — is no exception.

APPENDIX C
Model Transformations

In this methodology, I have provided a description of what activities and data are needed in system development. In this appendix I would like to present an example of an application to demonstrate how the methodology would actually be used. My example focuses on the transformation of a physical model to a logical model.

Although it shows the types of conditions and environments to expect when developing system models, this example is not a case study. I will give only diagrams, but in actual practice each one should be backed up with data dictionary entries and process descriptions.

Assume we are asked to study a small consultant services company for the following reasons (that is, project goals):

1. to bring into synchronization the automated and manual stored data and possibly dispense with the need for separate, duplicate data because the number of errors and business costs caused by it are becoming intolerable

2. to identify a way of reducing the computer time taken up by the customer billing run, which is steadily becoming the longest running job in the data processing shop and is increasing with each new project and consultant

3. to integrate the edits performed manually on the consultant time allocations with the existing automated edits; many times the automated edits overrule the result of the manual edits

4. to allow a different rate to be charged for a consultant depending on the projects that he or she works on; currently the rate is fixed for a consultant regardless of the project

The first model to produce is a context diagram (see Fig. C1) which identifies the area of study. It shows the net incoming and outgoing data flows of the system and the originators and terminators of these data flows. The company basically deals with customers (who request warm bodies to fill projects) and consultants (whom the company employs and contracts to the customers). The company is constantly searching for consultants who meet its high quality requirements. The company obtains new consultants from personnel agencies because doing its own recruiting was too troublesome. Collecting payment from some of the customers was also troublesome, so the customer bills are sent to the financial service division of the company's bank for collection and accounting.

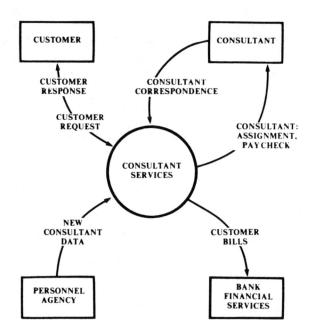

Figure C1.   Context diagram.

During the study of the design of the current manual environments, a number of physicalized data flow diagrams, which the users are able to validate, are produced. These data flow diagrams, when connected, form the diagram shown in Fig. C2. Note that when we create a set of data flow diagrams for a large system, it is not necessary to connect all the low-level diagrams to form a football-field-sized diagram; the intermediate-level diagrams can be used to get a complete picture of the system and to show the data flow from one diagram to another. The current physicalized diagram, backed up with its data dictionary and process descriptions, should be physical enough for the users to validate as being complete and correct.

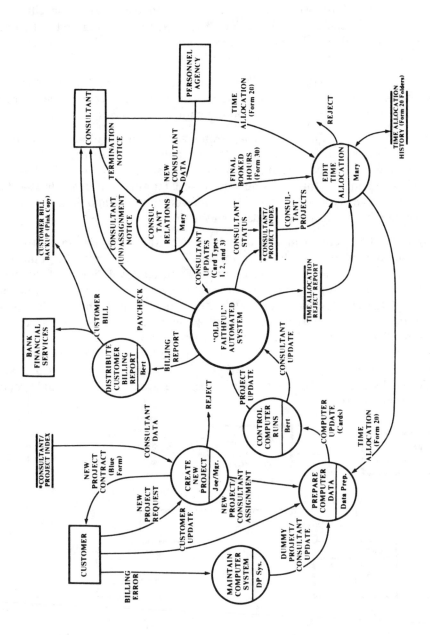

Figure C2. Current physicalized DFD for manual environments.

There are three characteristics to note in Fig. C2.

1.   Multiple functions: Many environments have people who perform more than one function. Therefore, we want to concentrate on data and its specific functions rather than on people and all the data that comes in to them and out from them. For example, in Fig. C2, Mary handles "terminations" in her consultant relations role, and edits the daily "time allocation" forms.

2.   Split functions: In contrast to multiple functions, some functions may be the responsibility of more than one person. For example, "create a new project" in the example is split between Joe and the company manager.

3.   Time delay stores: Pure time delay stores can be represented as data flows. For example, stores that are used to hold data between departments or between the manual and automated systems are time delay stores. In Fig. C2, the paychecks are produced in the form of one report — later they are separated — but here they are shown as a data flow. Also, reference stores and back-up stores have deliberately been left in the model for user validation purposes.

Other physical details remain in this model for user validation purposes (for example, back-up names like Mary, Joe, Blue Form, and Form 20 Folders). But others such as special locations and section names were removed during development of this model.

In the example, many of the manual functions interface with an existing automated system that the employees affectionately call "Old Faithful" because of its habit of blowing up regularly. In studying the design of this automated system, we can identify four programs that have varying qualities of structure, discussed as follows.

Program 1 has pretty bad structure: It was forced into a HIPO structure. There is no documentation other than a crude HIPO VTOC diagram (see Fig. C3), but it has been validated by the computer system maintenance group as a reasonable representation of the program structure.

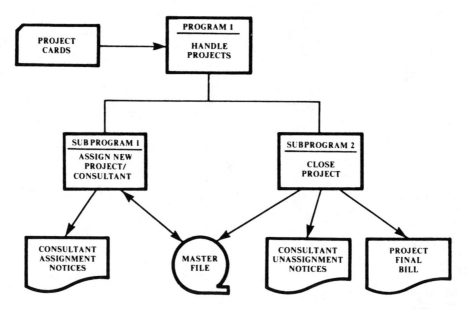

Figure C3. Current design chart for automated environment: daily batch program.

Program 2, depicted in Fig. C4, isn't too bad. It was developed during a modularization fad and had the typical pancake structure of the fad: one mainline module with all other modules immediately subordinate to it. It also typically didn't identify the data passing between the modules.

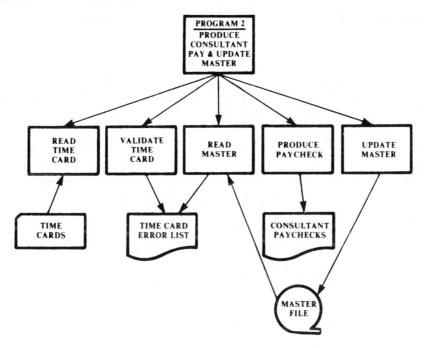

Figure C4. Current design chart for automated environment: nightly batch program.

Program 3 was developed with a report writer package and was driven with parameter cards, but it basically consists of only one function (see Fig. C5). Program 3 produces bills for any customers that had hours of consulting time booked to them in a given month. Unfortunately, because of the file structure (defined later in this example) and the processing to circumvent this structure, the program takes ages to run. It has to scan the whole master file (defined as a data dictionary entry on the following page) accumulating "hours billed this month" for a particular project from each consultant record.

Program 4 (see Fig. C6) has no structure at all and combines three functions scattered throughout the program. The functions are triggered by input card types. If card type 1 is present, an index list of all consultants and their assigned projects is produced. This index list is updated by hand until the next list is requested. If card type 2 is present, it is used to delete a consultant (actually a change of status) from the master file. If card type 3 is present, the specified new consultant data is used to add a consultant to the master file.

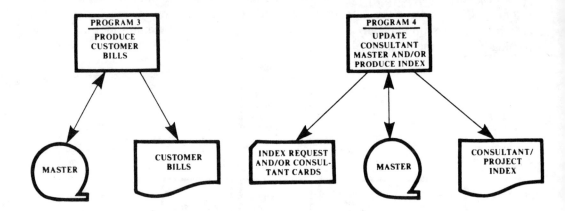

Figure C5. Monthly program.   **Figure C6. On-request program.**

Current design charts for automated environment.

The master file is defined in the current data dictionary as follows:

= {consultant name + consultant status + consultant address +

consultant skill + consultant rate + days per week available +

12 {pay period + pay hours + pay amount}12 +

5 {project ID + project status + project name +

project address + hours billed this month +

hours billed to date + amount charged to date} 5}

So, the master file consists of consultant information keyed on "consultant name" with two internal repeating groups; one for pay history (12 sets of history kept), and one for project (5 sets of project data kept). This data dictionary information is confirmed using the data flow in the data flow diagram. We produce the following data model from this information.

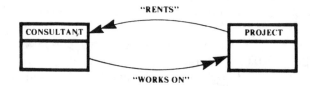

Figure C7. Current system data model.

From our system point of view, Fig. C7 states that the stored data consists of consultant information and project information, and that a consultant "works on" one or more projects and a project "rents" one or more consultants.

The data dictionary entries for these objects (functional stores) become

Consultant   =   {consultant name + consultant status +
consultant address + consultant skill +
consultant rate + days per week available +
{pay period + pay hours + pay amount}12}

Project   =   {project ID + project status + project name +
project address + hours billed this month +
hours billed to date + amount charged to date}

The entry for the "consultant" object, above, has an internal repeating group; that is, it is not fully normalized. The internal repeating group was not separated from "consultant" because it is not a stand-alone object; that is, there is no functional need for this data by itself. These objects (functional stores) can now be plugged into the logical models that use these objects.

Before going further, I want to present what I call the logical-physical spectrum (Fig. C8). I use the idea of such a spectrum to illustrate different degrees of logical and physical representations of models depending on the reason for a project. For example, if the aim of a project is to completely understand the underlying business functions of a system, then we will need to logicalize more than for a project that aims to identify better computer hardware for a system. In fact, this is why we should produce a physicalized model as our first model. There is precious little reason for developing a completely physical model when the aim is to ultimately produce a new system. Thus, the degree of logicalization should be considered before deriving physical or logical models.

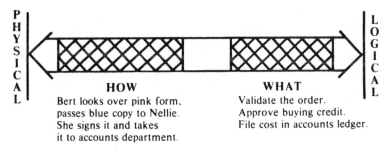

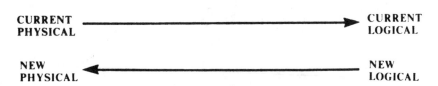

Figure C8. Logical-physical spectrum.

Further removal of physical characteristics from the model of the manual environment in Fig. C2 produces the diagram in Fig. C9.

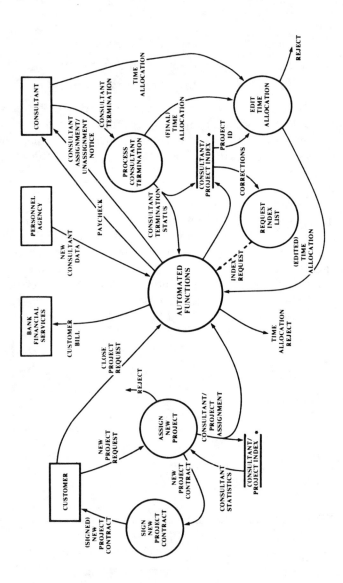

Figure C9. Current logical DFD for manual environment.

As it was derived from Fig. C2, the salient points of Fig. C9 are as follows:

1. Data transporter processes* have been removed because they perform no data transformation, that is, no change to data content or status. For example, in Fig. C2, the "prepare computer data" process changed just the input media and the "distribute customer billing report" process just moved data around.

2. Control/housekeeping processes and stores also have been removed. They are similar to the data transporters in that they are an added feature representing how the system is run. For example, in Fig. C2, "control computer runs" and "maintain computer system" processes and "customer bill backup" and "time allocation history" stores all formed a support to the system, but did not form the system itself.

3. Policy-related processes such as "sign new project contract" in Fig. C9 are physical tasks, but are shown because they are part of the company's business policy. The rule is "If the current implementation of a portion of the system cannot change, as far as the model is concerned, it's logical."

4. Aliases should be resolved, so resolution of any alias names was performed as the models were being produced. Data content and processing were also examined to reveal some of the unobvious aliases. For example, in Fig. C2, "final booked hours (form 30)" and "time allocation (form 20)" had the same data content and processing performed, so they became "(final) time allocation" in Fig. C9.

5. Judgmental processes may be difficult to specify in a process description and difficult to automate. In Fig. C9, "request index list" is based on the number of hand corrections on the current index list and on the agent's ability to judge the problems they may cause. The "consultant relations" process in Fig. C2 was mostly judgmental, but the only part of it applicable to our system was "process consultant termination" in Fig. C9.

6. Prompts are data flows that contain no actual data but serve as initiators of a process. For example, in Fig. C2, a card type 1 (part of "consultant updates") was identified. It had no data content but served as a request for an index list from the computer program. It is represented as a dashed line in Fig. C9 to indicate that it is a prompt.

7. Trivial reject processing — which does not require "backout" processing — was removed. For example, to derive Fig. C9, "time allocation reject report" was removed as input to "edit time allocation" because this was back-up processing for trivial time allocation rejects. Trivial processing is ignored because we are interested in the main flow of data and do not want to get wrapped up in the many trivial error paths that exist in all systems. They will be taken care of in the new design.

The model in Fig. C9 can be refined further when both automated and manual system models are combined.

---

*The concept of data transporter bubbles is also developed by S. McMenamin and J. Palmer in two YOURDON seminars: *Structured Analysis/Design Workshop,* 6th ed. (New York: YOURDON inc.), October 1980; and *Advanced Structured Analysis,* 2nd ed. (New York: YOURDON inc.), December 1980.

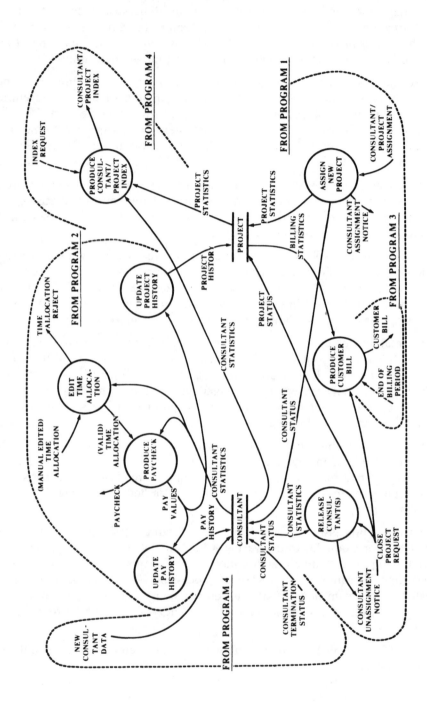

Figure C10. Current logical DFD for automated environment.

Removal of the physical characteristics from the design models of the automated system and the combination of resultant models produces the diagram in Fig. C10. The important characteristics to note in Fig. C10 are as follows:

1. Group stores should be partitioned. The most obvious group store in the current environment was the master file. This was really two stores (shown in the example) that were put together in the original automated system when that system only processed consultants' paychecks. The individual functional stores should be shown on the logical diagram. (The manual environment may have the same problem with its stores.)

2. References to the media used for the stores or data flows — for example, references to cards, tapes, working storage — should be removed, as was done in the diagram for the manual system.

3. Data transporters in the automated environment are processes such as read, write, or display. The data flow line itself serves to represent these activities.

4. As follows from the previous characteristic, do not worry if there is no actual processing shown on a data flow once the data transporters have been removed (for example, the data flow into the stores indicating updating of "consultant status" or "project status").

5. Control items (such as boss/coordination or back-up modules as well as their stores and data in a design chart) should be removed as in the manual environment. Also, if the control coupling — such as flags, switches, and end-of-file indicators — has been shown on the design diagrams, they should be removed.

6. If necessary, prompts can be shown using a dashed line as in the manual environment. For example, the customer billing process in Fig. C10 is prompted by the end of the month. I have labeled it "end of billing period" as it may change if it is not part of the business policy.

7. Functions should be separated. The model should show individual functions. For example, in Fig. C3, the subprogram that closed a project contained two functions: to release the consultants assigned to that project and to produce the final customer bill. These two functions are shown separately in the logical model.

8. As follows from the previous characteristic, the separation of functions may reveal duplicate functions that can be represented once. For example, in Figs. C3 and C5, the billing function is initiated twice in the system but should be represented once. (The code for producing a customer bill was therefore duplicated in the current automated system, which caused maintenance problems.)

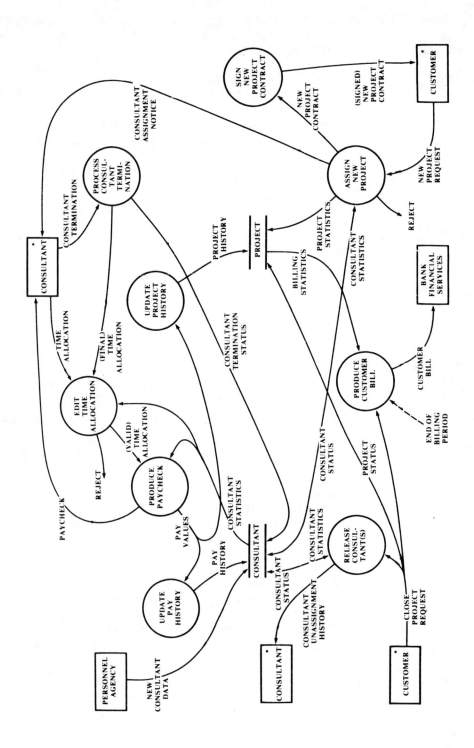

Figure C11. Current logical DFD for total system.

Combining the logical data flow diagrams for the manual and automated environments and, at the same time, removing any remaining physical characteristics produces the diagram in Fig. C11. The characteristics to note in Fig. C11 are the following:

1. Processes that are duplicated between the manual and automated environments may be common occurrences. They should be merged as we remove the final physical characteristics of implementation. For example, the assigning of consultants to new projects was performed in both the current manual environment against the index file and in the current automated environment against the master file.

2. Some control/back-up processes and stores may only support the separation of the manual and automated functions and should be removed in the development of the total system logical model. For example, the consultant/project index file and its updating were used for backup of the automated master file and should therefore be removed.

Next we look at the project goals and identify any logical modifications required. In the example of our consulting company, there are no logical modifications necessary to satisfy the project goals except a change to the data model. The user's goal — to be able to charge a different consultant rate for each project — requires adding "intersection data" to the data model, which results in the new data model shown in Fig. C12.

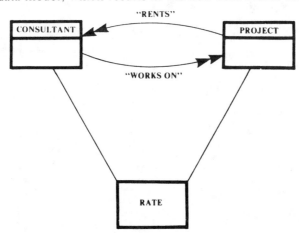

Figure C12. New system data model.

Figure C12 shows the same two objects and their relationships as does Fig. C7 but with the intersection data rate declared. This declaration states that rate is not dependent on just a consultant or on just a project, but on both. This does not change our data flow diagram stores because whether rate is stored in both the consultant and project objects or separately is implementation dependent. However, it will need to be noted in the data model and documented in the data dictionary.

The choice of a solution for the goal that requests bringing the automated and manual stores into synchronization will depend on the usage of the data and the cost-effectiveness of the solution. For example, a system providing on-line data access, eliminating the need for separate manual and automated stored data, would be one solution; producing more regular reports on stored data would be another. However, if the manual edits and new project assignment functions are automated, there is no need for a separate index file, which is the problem in the current environment.

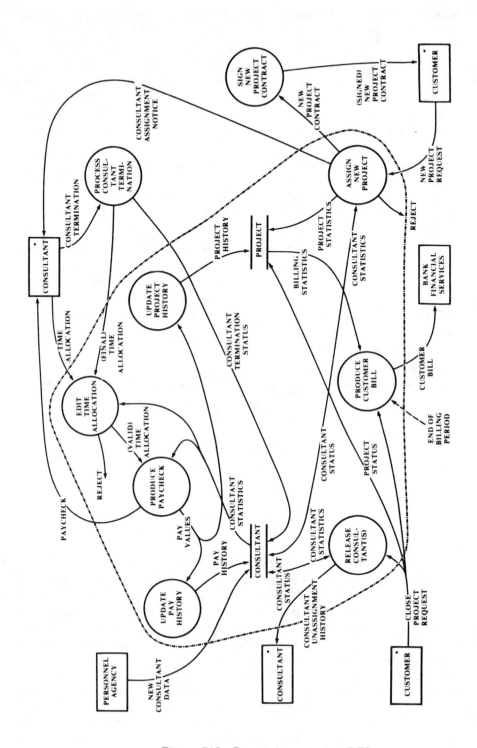

Figure C13. Bounded new logical DFD.

We can satisfy the goal to reduce the computer time used by the customer-billing run by a change in the physical file structure; that is, we can produce a structure that allows direct reference to project information without accumulating the data from each consultant record, as is necessary in the current environment.

Therefore, from the discussions above, it is apparent that because the goals require physical changes to the current system, the new logical data flow diagram is the same as the current logical data flow diagram. The bounded new logical specification consists of this data flow diagram with a man/machine boundary identified on it, as in Fig. C13. Note that the man/machine boundary indicated with a dashed, continuous line touches the edge of the area of study in most places, but all input and output data flows are known (declared in the data dictionary). However, it would be more reassuring to know what functions originally created and finally used our system data.

We can now begin to identify the new design by identifying the major job boundaries. In fact, the identification of the man/machine boundary is a design task. These boundaries will mainly be based on the periodicity of the functions. For example, the customer billing process will still be performed on a monthly basis because the user informs us that this is fixed business policy. So, the billing process becomes a separate job, but a customer will also receive a bill when a "close project request" is input. Therefore, we will make the process of producing a customer bill a routine that can be called from more than one program, thus overcoming the duplicate code that causes a problem in the current environment.

The only business requirement for the other processes is that they will be accomplished as soon as possible. Therefore, if it is cost effective to produce an on-line system, as stated earlier, then the rest of the system can be looked upon as a transaction center with a high-level design, as shown in Fig. C14.

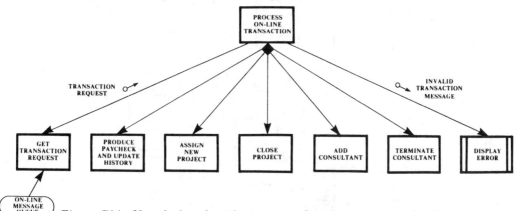

Figure C14. New design chart for automated environment: top levels.

The structure depicted in Fig. C14 can be implemented with the assistance of a vendor-supplied transaction processor, such as CICS. The structure shows a transaction-centered design indicated by the decision diamond under the "top boss" controlling module. This structure chart declares that a boss module calls a module to get a transaction request and then calls upon the appropriate sub-module to process this request, as the sub-module is one of the modules stemming from the decision diamond. If the request is for a transaction not supported — in other words, if the request is invalid — then an invalid transaction message is displayed by the library module "display error." Each transaction process module can be further decomposed, if necessary. For example, the module "produce paycheck and update history" performs a significant amount of work and is a good candidate for further development using transform-centered design techniques (see Fig. C15 on the following page).

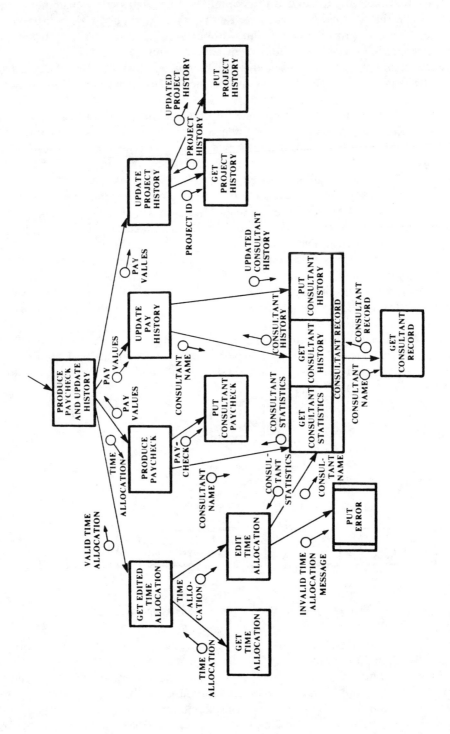

Figure C15. New design chart for automated environment developed using Yourdon and Constantine techniques: low levels.

Figure C15 is a first-cut design chart developed from the "produce paycheck and update history" portions of the data flow diagram. The "get" and "put" modules corresponding to the input and output data flows have been included. I have also shown an informational cluster because of multiple uses of portions of the consultant record. This is a protected/controlled temporary storage area for the consultant record that is available only to the modules shown spanning the data area labeled "consultant record."

Further refinement of this model will involve breaking down (factoring) modules: For example, the edit module can˙be broken down to show the types of edits performed; the addition of control information, such as error flags or record-not-found indicators; and the application of other refinement criteria such as investigating the chart to insure data is only passed between modules on a need-to-know basis. Each of the data items shown on the design chart should be defined in the data dictionary, and each module on the chart should have pseudocode developed for it if the analysis process description is not adequate.

In addition to showing model transformations for our consulting company example, I would like to discuss some support tools; specifically, an analysis process description — namely, structured English (formal and informal) — and a design module description — namely, pseudocode and a Nassi-Shneiderman diagram.

Structured English can be used, instead of ambiguous narrative, if no better form of specification — a decision table/tree for a decision-making process or a graph for calculation of variable rates — is available. For example, for the process "assign new project" in Fig. C11, we could develop formal or informal structured English as follows:

Formal structured English

```
        for each consultant in consultant store:
            if consultant days-per-week-available
                    greater than or equal to
                    project days-per-week-required
                and consultant-city equal to
                    project-city
                add 1 to available-consultants
        if available-consultants less than
                number-of-consultants-required in new-project-request
                issue project-request-reject
        otherwise
            for each available consultant repeat the following placement
                process until no further placements are necessary:
                    reduce days-per-week-available
                        by days-per-week-required in new-project-request
                    issue consultant-assignment-notice
                    if days-per-week-available equal to zero
                        set consultant-status to indicate unavailable
            set up a new project in the project list
            issue new-project-contract
```

Informal structured English

Check the consultant list to see if there are enough available consultants to fill the new project request. (An available consultant is one who has available a number of days per week equal to or more than the number of days requested for the project and whose city is the same as the project city.) If there are not enough available consultants, then issue a project request reject to the customer. If there are enough consultants, then do the following three steps for each available consultant until the new project request is filled: 1) reduce his or her days-per-week available by the days-per-week required in the new project request; 2) check to see if days-per-week available is now zero; if so, indicate that the consultant is no longer available by changing the consultant status; 3) send a consultant assignment notice. Finally, when the project request is filled, enter the new project in the project list and send out the new project contract.

Using the same process as in our example, we could have developed a design chart with one of the subordinate modules corresponding to part of the structured English, as shown in Fig. C16:

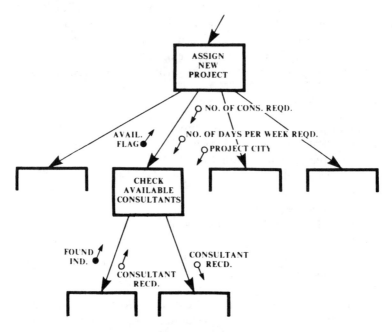

Figure C16. Design chart corresponding to structured English example.

The pseudocode for the module "check available consultants" will be dependent on the implementation details (such as sequential or on-line stored data), but one example of pseudocode is as follows:

```
module "check available consultants"
    *    This module identifies whether enough consultants are available
    *    to fill a new project request.  It uses the on-line consultant
    *    database for this purpose.
    *    input : no-of-cons-reqd, which is the number of consultants
    *                   required to fill the new project request.
    *              no-of-days-per-week-reqd, which is the number of days
    *                   per week that each consultant is required.
    *              project-city, which is the city where the consultant is
    *                   required to work.
    *    output: avail-flag, which identifies whether enough
    *                   consultants are available or not.

    set no-of-avail-cons to zero
    get consultant with status = "A," returning consultant-recd
                    and found-ind
    repeat while found-ind = yes and
            no-of-avail-cons < no-of-cons-reqd
        if consultant days-per-week-avail ≥ project
           no-of-days-per-week-reqd
            then if consultant-city = project-city
                add 1 to no-of-avail-cons
                put available consultant-recd
        get consultant with status = "A," returning consultant-recd
                    and found-ind
    endrepeat
    if no-of-avail-cons < no-of-cons-reqd
        set avail-flag = "NO"
    else
        set avail-flag = "YES"
endmodule
```

Or the same logic can be represented using a Nassi-Shneiderman diagram (with the same comments from the above pseudocode), as follows:

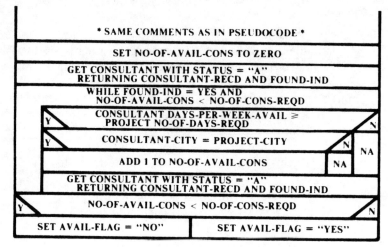

Figure C17.   Nassi-Shneiderman diagram.

APPENDIX D
Common Questions
and Answers

Q. *You state at the beginning of the book that this methodology works for maintenance and modification. How?*

A. The maintenance and modification effort can be classified as a small project. The existing documentation for the system to be maintained or modified will be the source for current study. If the system was developed using the structured techniques, then the documentation will just need to be verified as up to date. Then, all tasks needed for this project should be selected (Activities 2, 3, and 4 can be compressed into one activity if maintenance and modification are not extensive).

Q. *You state that this methodology can be used for software selection. How?*

A. Even though your intention might be to use a software package, you still need to identify your requirements, that is, to conduct analysis. You may also need to analyze the package itself if the documentation supplied is not adequate, and then judge whether the package fills these requirements. By using a package, you may save on design and construction of the system, but you may also have to modify or add your own programs to the package. The installation of the package will be the same as for any system built in-house.

Q. *Do we really need to study the current environment if we already know what the new system must do? or, the manual environment if we are just rewriting the automated system? or, the current environment if we are implementing a complete new function into the company? Do we really need to study outside the actual area of change?*

A. All of the following answer these questions: (1) If the functions that·the new system will perform are in an existing environment, whether automated or manual, then you certainly need to study them. You can't always expect a user (customer) to tell you all the requirements of the system. (2) Studying the current environment familiarizes you with the system. (3) You must make sure that any new system is compatible with the existing environment. You may find that you can reduce costs and increase benefits by including a function previously thought to be outside the area of change. Also, by studying the current environment, you may discover that some of the current input or output is not required in the assumed format, or is not required at all.

Q. *Should we produce one design chart or data flow diagram for the physical environment?*

A. Not really. In a medium-to-large system, you will often have many separate data flow diagrams joined by automated processes. In the automated area, many design charts may be connected by manual processes. On the other hand, when you derive a logical view for the whole system, the interface data flows should connect. If they don't, it's a sign of missed data flows or old, out-of-use data flows that are still in the system. When you derive a logical view for the whole system, you can represent it by one leveled set of data flow diagrams.

Q. *Do we have to develop mini-specifications for areas that we know will not change, that is, ones that bound the system?*

A. In most cases, no. You should develop mini-specifications to understand what happens to the data before it comes into the system and what will happen to it when it leaves the system. However, if you are sure of the area of change for your system, and a process is in your buffer zones, then you do not need the mini-spec because you can use the process notes. A deciding factor would be that you want good documentation of these areas; therefore, you may want to prepare mini-specifications if time permits.

Q. *Judging by the product we want from the preliminary study for our system, we think it would take too long to gather the needed information completely. Does this mean we will have to allow a lot more money for the study?*

A. No, not if you need to stay within budget and still give a feasibility report to management. Remember that this methodology is not prescriptive but rather that it provides a guideline. Provisions for customizing it for your particular project are included in Activity 1. If the political pressure is strong to produce a feasibility study within budget, you may want to identify only major streams of data and the types of major documents and transactions without identifying their contents. However, you should state this degree of accuracy in the feasibility study.

Q. *Why should we include a large area in preliminary study and develop test cases, conceptual design, conversion, training, and so on for this area, just to have the area made smaller after the feasibility study because it is too large?*

A. This is a Catch-22 situation. The preliminary study — including test cases, conceptual design, conversion, and training — identifies whether the system is too large for one release. Remember that in the preliminary study you are only "sizing" the project. Not much actual development effort is achieved at this level. Nevertheless, no work effort is wasted; the next release can validate the excess documentation and build on it.

Q. *Your methodology's data flow diagrams show hardware and software selection after identifying the system's man/machine boundary. However, our project must use existing company hardware and software. Will this be a problem in the development process?*

A. No. Remember that the data flow diagrams are not flowcharts. The development effort of a project is a process of iteration. Although I have shown an explicit three-level iteration in this methodology, you should also iterate through processes within these three levels of documentation. In your particular case, you may iterate through the selection of the man/machine boundary and through use of the hardware and software on this boundary to facilitate entry and distribution of data until you are satisfied with the man/machine option(s). You may also customize the methodology to show the hardware and software selections before the man/machine boundary selection.

Q. *Can you really complete all the implementation specifications without knowing how you are actually going to accomplish the implementation activities, that is, without implementation plans?*

A. Not really. This question again raises the problem of looking at data flow diagrams as flowcharts. You will iterate through the specifications and plans, but you also have to acknowledge releases if they are necessary, because releases will have a strong effect on the implementation plans. Therefore, you must iterate through the processes that produce specifications, releases, and plans.

Q. *Why do you identify releases as well as man/machine options?*

A. The releases are not necessitated by analysis, the stage at which you identify man/machine options. Instead, the releases are based on the analysis, design, and implementation activities. Releases may be based on which hardware can be installed or on the number of people or divisions that can be trained within a reasonable time period. Releases can be perceived as a further installation partitioning of the man/machine option(s). Another kind of partitioning, implementation partitioning, or versions, can be identified within a release.

Q. *You identify a monitored production period. When do we stop monitoring?*

A. You should always monitor systems. However, intense monitoring should be done to track the problems and usage patterns to produce the initial production report after most system conditions have been experienced, that is, after end-of-month processing, exceptional peak periods, and a sufficient amount of processing to identify any increase or decrease in usage. Therefore, the period of time for intense monitoring of new systems will vary depending on how long it takes to experience all the system conditions.

APPENDIX E
Rules for Reviews

Let me summarize the rules and procedures for a standard review. A review is a quality control procedure: Its purpose is to find errors early in the development of a product, to insure that company standards are observed in a product, and to insure the readability and understandability of a product. The reviews referred to in this methodology are both internal project reviews in which the developers of the product participate, and independent reviews in which the developers of the product do not participate. The procedures are basically the same for these two types of reviews. Guidelines for walkthroughs, which are informal, more flexible reviews, can be extracted from these procedures. For example, depending on the product, you may want less lead time, a less formal representation procedure, no report, and so on.

The makeup of review participants will depend on the material being reviewed but should include the developers of the material under review and their peers, such as other designers in a design review. A user representative can be helpful, especially in the analysis, design, and implementation reviews, as these will, in various degrees, affect the user. The project manager may attend if he or she is involved in the technical side of the product, but no upper-level management should attend. When upper-level management is present, developers of material under review tend to get defensive, and reviewers may try to show off their abilities by concentrating on how *they* would have developed the material or solutions to problems. For the same reason — that the product, not the developer, is being reviewed — a review or review report should never be used for personnel evaluation or salary review.

Other reviewers may be a database administration representative, a standards representative, an audit representative, a maintenance representative, a designer and coder in an analysis review, an analyst and coder in a design review, or an analyst and designer in a code review.

A review must be cost effective; therefore, the time, number of reviewers, and degree of formality will depend on the amount and importance of the material being reviewed; for example, a preliminary-level review will demand fewer resources than a detailed-level review.

The review procedures are as follows:

1. Identify the amount of material to be reviewed at one time and, if necessary, partition the material and schedule multiple reviews. The amount of material to be reviewed at one time will be based on the duration of the review, the time for which will probably be allocated by the project manager. (The optimal duration for a review is twenty to thirty minutes; the maximum time should be one hour.) The project plan will act as a guide for this process.

2. Identify the location for the review, and assure that it is free from interruptions.

3. Identify the review participants if they are not already identified in the project plan, and obtain commitment and approval from the appropriate managers for those outside the project team.

4. Assign participants to review roles. The main roles are "moderator"* (someone to keep the review in order), "scribe" (someone other than the developer to take minutes), and "presenter." The last role is optional, since the material normally does not have to be presented: It should stand alone at the review stage. However, if necessary, a developer or someone who is familiar with the material, but more objective than the developer, can present the material.

    Other roles can be a standards authority, maintenance expert, computer language authority, and so on. People who are assigned roles may, of course, also participate in the actual review. The number of people in a review is just as critical as its duration: The minimum number is three; the absolute maximum is seven.

5. Distribute the schedule and materials far enough in advance to give the reviewers time to look them over and to formulate review questions. Do this at least two days in advance, but give more lead time if the material is complex or if the reviewers' own work schedules are busy.

6. Have the reviewers raise questions and comments as the material is presented or as the moderator requests them. The best review presentations are those that require minimum verbal backup. After all, one of the aims of any documentation, from specification to code, is that it can stand alone to aid maintenance. On the other hand, if the material is presented, reviewers should beware of the presenter's adding extra details that should already be in the product (especially if the developer is doing the presenting). The scribe documents all serious questions and comments, as well as any issues that are not resolved during the review. (This is not the time to resolve them.) The moderator watches for any style arguments, never-ending issues, and discussions or questions that veer away from the material being reviewed, and focuses attentions on the subject at hand. At the end of the review or each block during the review, identify the recommendations for the material. Based on any problems found, decide whether to accept the material, accept it with minor problems to be solved outside of the review process, or reject it and schedule another review after the material has been corrected.[†]

---

*The best source of information about this role is any work on transactional analysis, such as E. Berne, *Games People Play* (New York: Ballantine Books, 1964); or C.M. Steiner, *Scripts People Live* (New York: Bantam Books, 1974).
[†]To emphasize the seriousness of this decision, I usually remind reviewers in my seminars that they *each* are responsible for the material under review.

7.   After the review, the minutes are summarized and combined with the recommendations to form the review report, which can be distributed to the reviewers and management.

Solutions to minor problems can be incorporated into the materials with verification — done outside of the review process — by the person who discovers the problem. For major problems, cycling back to previous affected processes in the methodology and reworking them will probably be necessary.

The review minutes are a good source for statistical data, which should be documented and used in future reviews.

A by-product of reviews and walkthroughs is that they serve as a training ground and communication tool for different development styles and as insurance that someone other than the developer is familiar with and can use a product if the developer leaves.

GLOSSARY

agent

a person or group that performs a process

backout processing

upon finding an error in an input transaction, returning the system to its original state by undoing processing performed prior to the error on this transaction

blitz

identifying a functional area that is reasonably complex and allocating extra resources for studying this defined area to a detailed level

bottom-up

a qualifier indicating that the product is developed or the process is conducted from a specific level of detail to a gross level of detail

cohesion

the measure of how closely related — that is, how strong — is the association of different functions that are packaged together; there are various levels of strength of cohesion

complex store

a store of data that requires accessing in more than one order

coordinating module

module that calls upon other modules to do its job; pure coordinating module disappears in logicalization

cycling

performing similar activities at different levels of detail (see *iteration*)

data capture

gathering and storing information needed for the system

data coupling

data that is communicated to and/or from a function; usually related to a design solution in which data coupling represents the parameters passed between modules, indicating the dependence of one module on another

data dictionary

a set of definitions for all data items (data flow, data element, data store, data originator/terminator) declared on a data flow diagram; the data dictionary will also contain definitions for control items and data on a structure chart and in application code

data flow	a pipeline of information between processes, data stores, or data terminators; a piece of information is no longer available in the pipeline once it reaches its destination
data flow diagram	a modeling tool used to represent a system that is automated, manual, or both; it has four components — data flow, process, data store, and data originator/terminator — which are represented graphically to model the system and to show its partitioning
data integrity	an attribute indicating that an item of data is independent of other items of data
data model	a graphic modeling tool used to represent· stored data as individual data objects and their relationships to each other; also known as a data structure/access diagram or data structure/access schema
data parameter	an item of information that is passed between processes
data primitive	a data item that does not require any further breakdown in order to be defined
data transformation	a change of status or content of a piece of data
data transporter	a process that, when acting on an item of data, does not change its status or content, and that should be represented in a logical model as a data flow
decision table	a graphic tool used to specify decision logic by showing all combinations of conditions that can appear in the decision logic and their results
decision tree	a graphic tool used to specify decision logic by showing a hierarchy of combinations of conditions that can apply in the decision logic and their results
deliverable	a product that has been rigorously defined and that meets the goal of an activity
driver	a term used for code that simulates a controller function on a design chart to aid the incremental building and testing of a system
executable	a qualifier for a process or data, indicating that it can be executed directly by a person or a machine
formal data structure diagram	a data model that declares the detailed data requirements for objects and their relationships in the system being studied; also known as a data access diagram or data schema
functional primitive	a detailed-level, specific task that does not require further breakdown in order to be specified because it is small enough and simple enough to be understood and verified by any reader

implementation	the process of building and testing a product prior to installing it; usually related to the writing and testing of code for an automated system
incremental commitment	an approach to system development that avoids giving a single inflexible estimate at the start of a project, but that instead encourages an estimate that is refined based on the level of knowledge of the system as system development progresses
informal data structure diagram	a data model that declares the non-detailed data requirements for the system being studied; also an intermediate product that may require further refinement of its contents; also known as a data access diagram or data schema
installation	the process of installing a product (system) into a production/operational (user) area
iteration	the repetition of activities to develop and refine a product, as opposed to the creation of a deliverable in one linear effort; also known as explicit iteration (see *cycling*)
Jackson data structure diagram	a design modeling tool that represents program structure hierarchically in the form of the data that it needs to process
level of detail	a range of specific information gathered during a given iteration of system development; the number of levels of detail will vary from system to system
logical	a qualifier for data or processes indicating that only those physical characteristics that are required for business reasons and that are implementation independent are shown; for data, the composition is specified in the data dictionary, but its media or representation is not; for processes, what is being accomplished is specified but not who accomplishes it or how it is accomplished
logical data model	a data model that does not indicate the implementation structure
methodology	a guideline identifying how to develop a system; as an object, a methodology is a product that shows managerial and technical activities needed to produce a working system; as a process, a methodology is the practical set of procedures that facilitates development of a system
mini-specification	the specification of a functional primitive, which describes the process necessary to transform incoming data flows into outgoing data flows
model	a representation to be used as a pattern or guide for conceptualizing, planning, and executing a system

module	a cohesive set of statements that accomplishes a specific function and that has known inputs and outputs
Nassi-Shneiderman diagram	a graphic tool used to specify logic; usually used as a form of pseudocode in design
negative test	a type of test that is expected to fail; also known as an exception test, consisting of data and/or procedures that are invalid
physical	a qualifier for data or processes, indicating that they are implementation dependent; for data, the definition/composition includes the media used for transmission and/or storage and its representation; for processes, the specifications include the agents performing them and how the processes are accomplished
physical data model	a data model that identifies how the data structure will be implemented
physicalized specification or model	a hybrid of a physical and logical specification, consisting of a relatively logical specification with as many physical characteristics included as necessary for user validation of the specification
physical-logical spectrum	a range that measures how logically or physically a model is oriented
plan	a type of deliverable that identifies how the development of a project is managed
policy	a formal statement that defines what business procedure is necessary to accomplish an objective, that is, identifies the actual use/transformation of data
positive test	a test that is expected to work correctly; also known as a normal test, consisting of data and/or procedures that are expected to be valid in the system being tested
project	the total activity of developing a system, beginning with a formal acknowledgment of business objectives and related problems, and ending with a formal acknowledgment that the solution to these objectives and problems has been implemented
pseudocode	a spatially arranged tool that is used to specify logic and that forms a stepping stone between specification and code; also a design tool identifying how a process is accomplished without the restrictions or syntax of a computer language

regression test	a test that can be used to validate a portion of the production system after a modification has been made; also used to insure that portions of the system unaffected by a change still perform correctly
resources	available or allocated time, money, people, and optional materials for accomplishing an objective
review	a formal quality control inspection of a product in which the participants may include data processing management, user management, auditors, and other objective reviewers in addition to the developers of a product; an independent review does not include the developers of a product
structure chart	a graphic tool used to hierarchically model the design solution of a system; used to show the partitioning of a system into modules (functions) and the data and control interfaces between these modules
structured English	a spatially arranged tool used for specifying business policy in analysis, consisting of a subset of the English language and the basic constructs of structured programming
structured specification	a formal description of a manual or automated system, which is the product (deliverable) of structured analysis; the specification is partitioned into a leveled set of data flow diagrams, a data dictionary, and process descriptions
stub	code that simulates a function on a design chart; used to aid the incremental building/testing of a system
system	a set of manual and/or automated activities that produce a desired result
top-down	a qualifier indicating that a product is developed or a process is conducted from a gross level of detail to a specific level of detail
transaction analysis	a design strategy in which the initial design solution is developed by identifying a number of individual transactions in the system or portion of the system, thus forming a transaction-centered design
transform analysis	a design strategy in which the initial design solution is developed by identifying a major data transformation point in the system or portion of the system, thus forming a transform-centered design

walkthrough

an informal quality control inspection of a product in which reviewers may be the creators of the product as well as objective parties; procedures for a walkthrough are similar to those used in reviews but are more flexible

Warnier-Orr diagram

a design modeling tool that represents program structure hierarchically in the form of the data it is required to process

worker module

a subordinate module that processes or acts upon data; it does not direct or coordinate other modules

BIBLIOGRAPHY

Alexander, C. *Notes on the Synthesis of Form.* Cambridge, Mass.: Harvard University Press, 1964.

Brooks, F.P., Jr. *The Mythical Man-Month.* Reading, Mass.: Addison-Wesley, 1975.

Date, C.J. *An Introduction to Database Systems.* Reading, Mass.: Addison-Wesley, 1977.

DeMarco, T. *Concise Notes on Software Engineering.* New York: YOURDON Press, 1979.

————. *Structured Analysis and System Specification.* New York: YOURDON Press, 1979.

Gane, C., and T. Sarson. *Structured Systems Analysis: Tools and Techniques.* New York: Improved System Technologies, Inc., 1977.

Jackson, M.A. *Principles of Program Design.* New York: Academic Press, 1975.

Martin, J. *Computer Data-Base Organization.* Englewood Cliffs, N.J.: Prentice-Hall, 1977.

Myers, G.J. *Composite/Structured Design.* New York: Van Nostrand Reinhold, 1978.

————. *The Art of Software Testing.* New York: John Wiley & Sons, 1979.

Orr, K.T. *Structured Systems Development.* New York: YOURDON Press, 1977.

Page-Jones, M. *The Practical Guide to Structured Systems Design.* New York: YOURDON Press, 1980.

Thomsett, R. *People & Project Management.* New York: YOURDON Press, 1980.

Warnier, J.D. *Logical Construction of Programs,* 3rd ed. New York: Van Nostrand Reinhold, 1974.

Weinberg, G.M. *The Psychology of Computer Programming.* New York: Van Nostrand Reinhold, 1971.

Yourdon, E. *Managing the Structured Techniques,* 2nd ed. New York: YOURDON Press, 1979.

————. *Structured Walkthroughs,* 2nd ed. New York: YOURDON Press, 1978.

_____, and L.L. Constantine. *Structured Design: Fundamentals of a Discipline of Computer Program and Systems Design,* 2nd ed. New York: YOURDON Press, 1978.

Additional Reading

To alleviate "people" problems in data processing such as personal or political game playing and poor communications, techniques like Transactional Analysis (TA) have been introduced to foster awareness and sensitivity in interpersonal relationships. Because I feel this is such an important area, I recommend three additional books. The first and third are popular treatments of TA; the second is most important because it stresses the idea of quality, which applies to systems (and to life).

Berne, E. *Games People Play.* New York: Ballantine Books, 1964.

Persig, R.M. *Zen and the Art of Motorcycle Maintenance.* New York: Bantam Books, 1974.

Steiner, C.M. *Scripts People Live.* New York: Bantam Books, 1974.